# LETTERS TO IAIN

## A JOURNEY OF COMMUNICATION THAT BREATHES LIFE AND TRANSCENDS DEATH

BY

# EDWARD WILSON

2023

# LETTERS TO IAIN

by
Edward Wilson

Published by Bookaholics
19, Carters Garth Close, Grainthorpe, Louth,
Lincolnshire, LN11 7HT


ISBN: 978-1-8382882-6-6

Page design: Pageset Ltd, High Wycombe, Buckinghamshire
Printed by P2D-Books Ltd, Westoning, Bedfordshire

Prepared by Bernard Bale.

# Foreword

Yes, '*Letters to Iain*' is a most unusual book – there's no doubt about that. Ed Wilson's heart and soul has been poured into writing this and it is all the more remarkable that his original intention was to keep a dear friend going and interested in life even as that life was steadily seeping away.

Ed wanted to bring some light into the darkness of his friend's dwindling life, something upon which he could focus, think about and, quite often, laugh about. This was no intrusion on Iain's end-of-journey but a vitamin of energy and a reason to go on with positivity right to the very end.

When Iain died Ed could not extinguish his dedication and continued to write letters to Iain, visiting his burial place regularly to tell him all the latest news. The scriptures tell us that we 'fall asleep in death' which surely means that there is an awakening to come perhaps as in a coma during which the world continues to turn but in this case, without the input of the deceased.

It is quite acceptable that anyone should still 'talk' to a friend or relative after they have departed – not through some kind of so-called medium but simply by thinking of them, remembering and hoping that perhaps, just perhaps, we will meet again some sunny day.

Letters to Iain reflects all of that – the laughter, the opinions, the memories even the gossip that goes on between two close friends enjoying each other's company.

The gift to the reader is being able to sit on Anna's bench in the cemetery with Ed and Iain and 'listen' to Ed's words of love and kindness to his friend, enjoy the wit and the banter, think about about what is being said, agree, disagree or just have a smile spread across your face, motivated by this experience.

At times you may wonder, "What is he going on about?"

The reality is that 'what he is going on about' is giving a gift to a friend, indeed a very special gift – Ed gives his innermost self to Iain and Iain's family – and also to you, the reader.

*Bernard R. Bale*

# Introduction and Commentary

Letters to Iain actually started out as 'Letters to Helen'.
Our wives had met at the local keep fit classes and found they enjoyed each others' company; ladies who keep fit together progressed to ladies who meet for coffee and blossomed into 'Ladies who Lunch'. Iain and I had not yet met, this was in 2010, and we were very much background figures in this newly formed Wives Club. Gradually we were drawn into the developing social side of this liaison, but very sparingly as supporting cast.

I knew nothing of Iain beyond the fact that he must be about the same age as me, 74ish, and was very easy to talk to. He appeared to me as Mr Fit, always moving rapidly on a bicycle or at a fast trot in his shorts and trainers; played golf and badminton, apparently to a standard that could give younger generations a run for their money and drove like he intended to give Lewis Hamilton a lesson in competitiveness.

I knew nothing of Iain's medical history; I simply saw this fit, energetic, comfortably-pensioned elder statesman (who didn't look all that elderly), well integrated and established in Kirriemuir with his family – children and grandchildren conveniently located locally – and Iain the proud patriarch of a happy family. I both admired and slightly envied this example of a successful and happy life.

As our wives' friendship and socialising developed, Iain and I were drawn in to complete the foursome or six-some when Sandy and Isabel, close friends from Forfar, were included. Golf club functions, Burns suppers, music nights at Glamis Castle and eating out or enjoying home hospitality became regular events and provided an opportunity for us to find we had much in common – or, in fact, that our likes and dislikes found a complementary balance in each others' preferences.

Iain liked reading – anything; but he particularly liked history and loved poetry. I am blessed with a retentive memory and could occasionally drop in an historical fact, a little snatch of Latin or a line of poetry which convinced Iain that I was almost as well read as himself. We found that we shared a healthy scepticism for politics and religion but held a fairly similar interpretation of faith, which we had each arrived at through our individual reasoning, and which was quite at odds with the conventional Gospel truth version. There was a lot that we did not agree on but we found that we could disagree agreeably!

The letters to Helen started fairly early in this 'life-long' friendship that started only when we were well beyond our allotted three score years and ten. Helen needed a little medical attention for a heart problem and I wrote what I hoped would be comic pieces to entertain and encourage her during convalescence – but also, on occasion, to try to cajole her gently into taking care of herself enough to allow the miracle of modern medicine to perform its magic.

Iain appeared to enjoy some of this humour in verse and this flattered me and encouraged me to communicate through the written word when any occasion presented itself.

It became such a part of my life that even after Iain passed away I still felt that he was not truly gone and that the letters to him should continue. Who knows? Perhaps he is looking over my shoulder?

So, here are letters and other created for Iain. I hope you might find them thought-provoking at the very least and maybe, just maybe – helpful.

*Best Wishes to You*

*Edward Wilson*

# What's In A Name?

Helen said to Iain, "That's Eddie There,
that guy across the street "
You know! The one you've still to meet!"
"Sheila's man – can you see him?
"He owns the Pub across the road
"From Gateway to the Glens museum!"

Now, Iain didn't want to sit and stare, Confusion reigned,
"How, Eddie There?"
That's not the name, as I recall
I don't remember 'There' at all!
When Sheila phoned, I'm pretty clear,
She told me "This is Sheila Here!"

(Perhaps the couple aren't wed)
"Does Sheila simply live with Ed?"
Helen, aghast, – good Catholic lass,
She could not let this stigma pass,
"NO!!! They're wed, near thirty year!"
('So why is she called Sheila Here?')

"She's Sheila!!!" Helen sounded slightly frantic
('God, why is Iain so pedantic?')
"She's Sheila, and that's her husband Eddie there!"
Poor Iain began to feel despair!
"I see him, Eddie There, who's wed to Sheila…I get that, Dear!.
But" He baulked at saying "It's not quite clear!"
He knew, for sure, he wasn't havering,
But Helen, quick to pounce on any wavering
Lest Alzheimer's might be hov'ring near!

He sat, quite quiet – he had to ponder
On Eddie There – just over yonder;
Married to Sheila, this 'Sheila Here'
Helen, annoyed! It wasn't clear
To Iain, who didn't know whence came this mess
Eddie There, or Sheila Here? Iain really couldn't care much less!

But, giving Helen this excuse
To challenge him for being obtuse
What's in a name? – 'twas neither Here nor There
Iain really could not care, except
The issue was 'quite messed'
"How do they want to be addressed?"

"What do you mean?" said Helen, suspicious
"Well what I write after Mister and Missus?"
"It's neither Here nor There to me
"But Accuracy in the addressee
"Would make me feel much better
"Were I, to say, write them a letter."

"Are they the 'Theres' or called the 'Heres'
"Mr and Mrs What? After all those years
Helen fumed, "You're rather slow
"Or trying to take the bungalow!
"Here's a paper and here's a pen
"It's Wilson! W-I-L-S-O-N!"

# Helen

## 3rd October 2012

I thought I would drop you a wee line to let you know I was thinking about you. I said a wee prayer for you last night – for a quick recovery. Don't get too excited… Remember this is a Proddy prayer: sometimes they work and sometimes they don't (I have a thousand torn up lottery tickets that will attest to that!)

Anyway, I had considered popping into the hospital to see you yesterday. Sheila was in Edinburgh on one of her jaunts and, well you know, 'when the Cat's away……'

But I bottled it; I decided that if I suddenly appeared at your bed that might be just a tad too exciting for you!!! I didn't want you thinking that a miracle had occurred.

I don't go too much on miracles, but I thought about when I saw you last week at Ninewells, that was a near miracle remember; when I congratulated you for looking so elegant in your Rangers' Blue. You were momentarily struck dumb! I thought that was pretty miraculous – it was the first time since I met you that your mouth was open and no words were forthcoming.

I considered sending you a 'Get Well' card, but cards are expensive and, well, they contain somebody else's words. I really do want you to get well, and wanted to tell you in my own words!

You see, you are included in my life story now – the part has been written exclusively for you; nobody else can fill it! And there is only the one performance of my life story. No dress rehearsals or second performances! You don't appear until pretty late in the play – but you have an essential, albeit small part to perform. So I cannot afford for you to be off sick when your cue comes up. So GET WELL!

I decided to take out a wee bit of medical insurance on you – through a couple of fairly local 'miracle' workers that I am acquainted with. There is the Blessed John Ogilvie – he got his promotion fairly recently, I think. And then, one of my favourites… St Mary Magdalene – she's the saint of feisty women. Should look after you just fine.

Then I realised that you had your own health insurance… St Anthony of Padua – a miracle worker extraordinaire. and a doctor! Right here in Kirrie! Boy, have you Holy Romans got all the angles (should that be angels?) covered.

Anyway, take care of yourself. Use shorter sentences and longer breath pauses-your heart needs the oxygen. It is only a small part you have in my play – but you can pad it out by slowing your delivery and allowing time for the applause. Your audience loves your performance and wants to keep you on stage as long as possible.

Hope to see you soon

*With fond love*

# THE GLASGOW HIGHLANDER

The ageing Scotsman seldom wears the kilt
Too many knobbles gather on his knee,
His shoulders frailer-where he'd looked well built;
This 'gettin auld' is not his cup of tea!

The garters that once stretched to firmly grip,
His hose well placed to just below each knee;
An 'eightsome' or a 'sergeant' and they slip
Exposing 'spindle' where his calves should be.

His brogues, laced up, become a burden too,
As empty stockings sag from knee to ankle:
And laces start to gather on each shoe
To settle in a most unsightly fankle!

This Prince of Glasgow feels his spirit wilt,
The nation'l dress no longer seems so cute;
He fears he's not doing justice to the kilt
And wishes be had simply worn a suit!

A lifetime he has waited for the sign;
The Saltire, in the sky, that says 'We're Free!'
Hadrian was the one who drew the line;
Two thousand years, it's there, for all to see!

But, two wee goldies seem to change the game,
An inner glow – he's feeling fit and trim;
A couple more – well that relights the flame
And Glasgow, once again, belongs to him.

Flower of Scotland' We can see yer like again,
Pull up your socks, get ready for the chorus,
A Nation of proud independent men;
I'll toast that with a double doch and doris!

*Ed @ Three Bellies*

**15th May 2013**

*Dear Helen co Iain,*

I so enjoyed our dinner date last night that I felt I should share the thought with you. Maybe that seems a little OTT – after all, it was a Dutch treat; but it was a treat!

It is so nice, at three score years and ten – plus ten per cent – to still find two people who are something more than simply 'new pals'.

It is also quite gratifying at this late stage in life to meet a couple who can be considered 'friends'. If nothing more it means that we can be lifetime friends, for the remaining years, without having enough time left to totally bore the bahoochey off each other.

As to 'boring bahoocheys' and Helen's suggestion to write a book my daughter says that my letters are long enough to have book and bahoochey boring proportions. Nice compliment, Helen, (that I could write a book) but I think I'll leave the fairy stories to Dan Brown and J.M. Barrie.

Me – I'm Joe Friday – "Just the facts, Ma'am, all I need is the facts!"

Thanks again for being such good companions, Love from

*Ed    Sheila*

# ~ ED ~

"Where are you off to" – Helen said.
"To see my friend, the venerable Ed
He's wise, he's sane, he isn't daft
And besides he always makes me laugh.

He dresses smart, but he's not so trim
Like me, old Father Time has caught up with him.
He's mellow and like a good vintage Red
He's improving with age, that's my Ed.

His writing skills are truly a sensation,
He can pen a letter to suit any occasion,
Officialdom has often felt his wit,
Particularly when he accuses them of talking S---

As mine host he has no peer
He's famous for his ability to lend an ear
A sympathetic word he will always offer
And good advice he is sure to proffer.

So to Ed my friend I pen these lines
Grateful for his ability to read the signs
When I am low or feeling poor
He's the man who provides the cure!

*Keep up the good work!*

# Commentary –
# Saving Caledonia

During the run up to the Scottish independence referendum of September 2014 I had the idea for a book – which I was convinced, obsessively convinced, might make a difference to Scotland and the World in general.

My concept was that every occurrence, throughout history, whether personal, national, or world event, possibly even Universal had a basic structure and consequence; like ripples in a quiet pool after a splash of something has disturbed the calm, and concentric circles of waves radiate outwards from this central point of disturbance.

Each circle of ripple is a bigger, potentially more powerful or destructive development; the original splash has consequences that recur through time until the wave dissipates or breaks up as it comes into contact with other conflicting wave circles created by other disturbance factors elsewhere.

Effectively history repeats itself with each developing ripple, each expanding and developing concentric circle being a replicated event in world history and we should learn from the behaviour of the first ripple how to deal with the effects of the developing circles of wave power and anticipate the next big splash and, if possible prevent it occurring. At the same time we should re-examine the events which led to the original splash and be sure we understand why it occurred and what we can learn from it.

By a similar token each of the World's or Humanity's journeys through history is like a ship's voyages broken down into sections, each passage with a precise start and finishing position with accurate start and finish times and a means of measuring distance run – a log line (or modern equivalent) – so that the course can be plotted; frequent position checks are made using star sights and sun sights or by terrestrial land bearing by compass to confirm that the ship is progressing safely and steadily towards the planned destination – the next port of call, which may not be the final destination of the total voyage. The world should be managed similarly.

The overall contention (my humble opinion) that in this passage of life, the Christian Era, the World is sadly out of position, not holding to course, and on the basis of repeated ripples of consequence, the concentric circles of replicated disturbance the World's progress through the Universe is adversely affected and we are on a course to destruction.

The start time of this particular passage is variable – not a precise time; Easter could be any time during the month between early March to late April. The original position was not accurately logged at the time, being added some years later when the log was written up and an estimated start position inserted to satisfy requirement. The only navigational aid available is a very old sounding machine, called a Gospel which reassures you that you are where you should be, in safe waters; the Gospel sounding machine by tradition is considered infallible.

On the big ripple-small ripple identity replication I also believed that my nation, my beloved Scotland was also sadly off course.

Trying to tie all this together in a book was somewhat cumbersome, and a tad too ambitious for a rank amateur to present and convince qualified theologians, scientists and historians. A Dan Brown or a Kate Mosse could probably have constructed a convincing fiction to incorporate these challenges to the authorised version, but such creativity was beyond my scope.

However, one very small ripple of concentric circle which I knew to be true, and nobody can dispute it, was my own experience on a real ship, Caledonia, which was included as a component chapter of my non-best seller.

Allow me to share it with you.

# R.M.S. Caledonia

## Crossover

**RMS Caledonia (leaving Bombay1948)**

The Anchor Line of Glasgow operated a fleet of eleven ships during the 1950s. Two vessels, Empire Halladale and Empire Clyde were managed on behalf of Her Majesty's Government. Halladale was a troopship ferrying, mainly, national service personnel to postings anywhere between Gibraltar and Japan: but the bulk of the traffic was to Korea. Ed served on HMT Empire Halladale for three months only, in 1953, just as the ceasefire was negotiated between North and South Korea.

The Empire Clyde – the former Glasgow to New York fast passenger liner, Cameronia – ferried Scots, assisted passage migrants to a new life in Australia, for £10 per person. The other nine vessels operated as a conventional Merchant Navy fleet. The three 'T' boats – Tyria, Tarantia and Tahsinia were purpose-built cargo ships operating mainly between the UK and the Far East. They were slightly more regular routed than tramp steamers – but prepared to divert from a regular schedule for a worthwhile cargo.

Three 'E' boats – not the German variety – were larger, faster cargo passenger ships built with the costs subsidised by Second World War compensation for lost ships, but to a Government specification so that they might convert easily to be able to transport tanks, and the impedimenta of warfare should it ever again be necessary. Egidia, Elysia and Eucadia ran a regular service between Glasgow, New York and the Chesapeake Bay carrying. Scotch whisky and a few passengers both outbound and returning, sometimes with Bethlehem steel ingots of immense weight, but mostly with grain from Baltimore, and tobacco loaded in Norfolk and Newport News, Virginia.

Ed served as cadet officer – not as grand as it sounds – on Egidia for two years, undergoing the classic "start from the bottom apprenticeship". Along with three cadet colleagues he learned all the shittiest jobs a seaman might encounter, or have to undertake.

Ed sometimes wondered if the real seamen were ever actually called to perform any of those crappy jobs as every bilge-cleaning task, every freezing lookout duty in the windswept, rain-soaked monkey island seemed to be allocated to the four "officer-cadets". But the voyages were short, six weeks round-trip with a lot of shore time in Glasgow, New York and Baltimore, while cargo was being loaded or discharged. Life was not all that bad and, certainly, not bad all the time.

The three 'C' boats were little masterpieces of Naval Architecture. Built to convey three hundred first class passengers, they could also accommodate six thousand tons of cargo on a fast, regular passage between Liverpool and all of the old colonial ports in the Mediterranean, through the canal and on to Karachi and Bombay – as Mumbai was then.

Circassia and Cilicia had been built as sister ships in 1936, and served in the Second World War as armed Merchant Cruisers and troop carriers. Caledonia's construction had been delayed by the War, but her keel was laid ten years later than her sister's and she completed her maiden voyage in 1948. During the 1950s these three Anchor liners were in much demand by ex-patriate passengers travelling between their posts on the Indian sub-continent – tea and rubber planters, sales and management executives of multi-national organisations and Government officials and their families – luxuriating in a three week, first class cruise, just to get to and from their place of work.

Passenger comfort was paramount. Cadet officers were part of the hospitality image to cosset passengers, and were now totally immune from the chore of menial tasks that was their lot on 'E' boats and 'T' boats. There were "other people" to scrub decks and clean bilges on the C' boats – crisp white uniforms, navigation and proper table manners were much more the order of the day.

Circassia, Cilicia and Caledonia were not ocean greyhounds, like the big passenger liners on the North Atlantic run, but they carried the gracious living standards of the 'thirties' into and through the 1950s at a reliable and stately pace.

Life on the Anchor line's 'C' boats was good – even for a young cadet officer. Ed Joined RMS Cilicia in Liverpool in late 1955 and fell in love with her as he climbed the gangway. For him Cilicia exuded luxury and class and power. This was *his* ship. Between 1955 and 1960 he served Cilicia, happily, moving from cadet to Fourth Mate and, in his final two years, as Third Mate – full Watch-keeping officer of the 8–12 watch.

Towards the end of February 1960, he was on the funded-leave that allowed study for his First Mate Certificate at the old School of Navigation in Glasgow, within the, then, Royal College of Science and Technology. He had married in November 1959 and was in no hurry to complete his studies and rush back to sea duty. Robert Bums' observations on the "Best laid plans of mice and men" proved to be a fateful prediction for Ed's hopes of prolonging his shore-based domestic harmony until Easter. The Marine Superintendent called him in to ask for a special favour. Under normal circumstances 'special favours' would not have been a consideration: the Marine Super would simply have issued revised orders – but due to the financial implications of the study-leave, a further period of study-leave would be arranged if Ed would help resolve an embarrassing situation.

Caledonia was loading at Yorkhill Quay, preparing to sail for Liverpool then onto Bombay, within two weeks, when her third officer had taken ill. Captain Blair, of Caledonia. was reluctant to promote his existing Fourth Mate to full watch keeper status, and there was no other certificated officer readily available to cover this emergency.

Captain Sinclair, the Super, did not explain Captain Blair's problem with the existing Fourth Mate and Ed did not ask. He had sailed with him for two voyages on Cilicia, and recalled a couple of instances when he had wondered about this officer's diligence and efficiency: also, although he was certificated as a Second Mate, he had been transferred from Cilicia to

Caledonia without promotion, which in itself was unusual, and now his captain lacked the confidence in this young officer to entrust him with full watch-keeping responsibility.

George Sinclair was a good man, and Ed had respected him for much longer than his own seven years' service with the company. As a youngster visiting his father on Circassia and Empire Halladale he had met captain Sinclair and liked him. He did not enjoy seeing this powerful executive having to negotiate favours from his junior staff. But Joyce had just told him he was going to be a dad in the autumn, and announcing that he was going off to sea in another week was not in the plan, or the prospect they had anticipated for the next few weeks. Ed agreed to join Caledonia for this one voyage only.

Captain Blair he knew only by reputation; a by-the-book professional seaman, sixty three years of age and close to retirement. Caledonia had been his ship, his life, for a long time. Being Captain of an Anchor liner was not an insignificant achievement but Blair, in addition to his Merchant Navy Master status held not only the exalted Extra Master qualification but also a commission as captain, Royal Naval Reserve. He had loved the celebrity of his unique achievement, at the end of the war, of being the only Anchor Line captain to hold the dual authority of Extra Master Mariner and Captain RNR. Merchant ships under the command of a captain and with a proportion of Deck officers holding commissions as Royal Naval, or reserve officers were entitled to fly the coveted Blue Ensign – only a step away from the exclusive White Ensign of the Royal Navy, either of which Captain Blair would have loved to be sailing under.

He compensated for his thwarted Royal Navy ambitions by commanding Caledonia with a precise, almost military discipline but not oppressively. He was no tyrant but orders were orders and the captain's word was law. To preserve the dignity and authority of this mystique of captaincy, he maintained a protective aloofness from most of his officers, limiting any kind of social contact to executives with three or more gold rings of seniority. Anyone bearing the title 'Chief', Chief Engineer, Chief Purser, Chief Steward and Chief Officer was acceptable – except 'He' was the boss.

Ed joined Caledonia without any formal welcome from the captain – he just seemed to accept that a replacement Third Mate had arrived. Perhaps carrying one junior officer, who could not be allowed to work without supervision, deterred him from examining too closely this alternative youngster, allocated to him by the higher authority of the Marine Superintendent. and, possibly find him not particularly confidence inspiring either. Whether because of, and in spite of his remote bearing, Captain Blair was respected by his staff and, to some degree, liked by them – at least as close to liking as you could get with someone who restricted you to a solely formal, professional relationship.

Ed recalled his puzzlement in Sunday school "God is Love, God is all powerful, you must fear God". Among themselves the Deck Officers referred to Captain Blair as 'Father' – or more correctly on this Glasgow crewed ship as 'Faither' when everything seemed fairly relaxed. But when there was any tension, any hint of error or reprimand, the nickname changed from the relatively loving "Faither" and reverted to the more ominous 'God' whom one would do well to fear.

Settling in to Caledonia was relatively easy – the three 'C' boat sisters were almost identical in construction so there was no need to become acquainted with a new ship layout. The three navigating officers, who would be his colleagues, were all known to him: John Henderson, the Chief Officer, had been the relief officer for a number of years, either covering the coastal duties when regular staff were on leave or providing cover for one voyage only – such as Ed was doing now – while regular crew were ill or on extended leave. He was a competent, professional seaman, but also easy to get along with, and he and Ed had served together previously, on both Cilicia and Egidia.

David Barclay, the Second Mate, had been on Caledonia – it seemed – forever. Unmarried, he had no particular interests away from his ship, but he was good fun – liked a joke, a beer, a cigarette and was addicted to crossword puzzles. Also, he and Ed had mutual friends, so with four matching points they got on just fine.

The Fourth Mate – young Davey Jones was easy enough to get along with although he was not in the normal mould of a sailor: non-drinking, non-smoking, never a foul word crossed his lips, he belonged to a fringe Christian movement that bound him to follow a good and disciplined path that also had lots of room for love. He loved food – although he was not fat, he could pack away a ton of food at a sitting, the light of love shining from his eyes. And he dearly loved mankind – particularly the female of the species: even more particularly if they shared his passion for things biblical. He seemed to have a sixth sense that could identify middle-aged spinster missionary ladies, heading to and from their challenging life in the East, and provide them with the comfort of another focussed, well-informed Christian spirit who understood their needs. Nobody was sure if this sharing of Christian love extended to the laying on of hands, but certainly on more than one occasion Davey had been observed slipping a loving, protective arm around a sensibly frocked waist in anticipation of the lady stumbling, should her attractive Jesus Sandals slip on the wooden deck!

Davey seemed to be all about love, and he so wanted to be loved that he seldom disagreed, even in his work, to the extent that he was totally agreeable on occasions at the expense of accuracy. Ed recalled two occasions on Cilicia when Davey's passion for being liked and agreeable had possibly motivated him to confirm an inaccurate position for the ship because it agreed with his senior officer's error, or made a nice neat cross on the chart where the ship was supposed to be. Perversely the agreeableness, and apparent precision and confidence of his chart work seemed like testimony to his accuracy rather than a need to be all things to all men, and women! By telling people what they expected, or wanted to hear, he fulfilled his radical Christian need to distribute and receive love, by way of acceptance, approval or gratitude; and he was such a nice wee guy, with the light of love, and tolerance shining from his eyes and nothing but purity issuing from his lips, that no one ever suspected that this need to tell people what they wanted to hear might not always be the Gospel Truth.

Ed shared the majority view, that Davey was a nice wee guy with some very creditable Christian beliefs and practices, that were a bit quaint or naive in the real world but, everybody was entitled to his viewpoints, and no apparent harm had come from Davey's obsession with neatness without precision, or desire to be agreeable and loved, without truth.

Except......Ed could not help the faintest gut feel that Davey's precision and sugar-coated acceptability were not entirely beyond question. He wondered if a similar gut feel had influenced at least two captains and a Marine Superintendent to recommend or authorise his promotion to a full watch keeping status. Hey, he was a nice, harmless wee guy and nobody's perfect.

The departure from Glasgow, the coastal passage to Liverpool and subsequent docking in Birkenhead gave captain Blair the opportunity to observe Ed at work. and he seemed to accept that his new watch-keeper had some credibility!

The voyage east bound from Liverpool was quite uneventful. In fact, for late March, the southbound leg to Gibraltar was very pleasant, even the much-maligned Bay of Biscay was quite benign. The stop at Gibraltar was routine and the bridge and crew worked well together. Captain Blair seemed satisfied with the apparent efficiency of the navigation team, although he maintained his formal aloofness, limiting his conversation to purely ship matters.

The passage along the Mediterranean was also pleasant with calm seas and improving temperature levels – excellent cruising weather. With no passengers or freight destined for Malta there was no demand to call in, and Caledonia pressed on to this last leg, on course for Port Said and the Suez Canal.

Air temperature had reached a steady daily level that justified uniform change from navy blues to tropical whites. Everything was pleasant, relaxed but efficient. Twice daily contact with Ed seemed to have encouraged Captain Blair to accept him as competent and dependable – able to be trusted but still not permitted any closer than the outer barrier of professional contact. Conversation was not on the agenda; communication remained formal – not stiff or awkward, but never thawing to the warmth of a chat.

Port Said, the canal and the tedious, but always slightly stressful convoy, for a hundred and twenty miles via the Bitter Lakes, led to Suez. Although a canal pilot took command for this passage the ultimate responsibilities still lay with the captain and Bridge Officers to ensure that Caledonia was in safe hands in the narrow confines of the canal, so close to other large vessels, with little room for any manoeuvre or error.

After the warm, relaxing cruise conditions of the previous week in the Mediterranean, the two days of arrival and mooring at Port Said, followed by the tight convoy experience and eventual release into the Gulf of Suez was very demanding. The normal routine was totally disrupted, with regular watch keeping hours interrupted by the additional duties of docking stations for the Bitter Lakes, or the side cut where up to forty ships had to moor, to allow the northbound convoy to pass.

At twenty four years of age Ed felt the physical and emotional demands of the Suez canal quite testing. It never really occurred to him how draining the responsibility must have been on a sixty three year-old captain who would be unable to relax for the entire forty eight hours.

The relief of the break out into the Gulf of Suez was like a formula one race starting, albeit at a more sedate pace. Forty merchant ships, of varying tonnages and speed potential, suddenly released from the constraints of a convoy before dawn, all jockeying for position southbound, confronted by a similar number and variety of vessels funnelling in the bottleneck of the Gulf to beat any cut-off time for joining into the next northbound convoy.

By the time the Gulf of Suez opened into the Red Sea any semblance of a convoy had been diluted by the different speeds of the ships, and any oncoming traffic had also thinned, now that the race to join a northbound convoy would not become urgent for another twelve hours.

Normal watch-keeping could be re-instated for the three day haul down the Red Sea to the busy corner, a left-hand turn into the Gulf of Aden. The turning point at Perim Island was a further challenge, with south and north bound shipping traffic converging on this junction, to follow the most economical route to save both time and fuel. Captain Blair had enjoyed a little breathing space after the Gulf of Suez breakout. and before he needed to take command again for the rounding of Perim Island.

Ed's eight to twelve evening watch started just as Caledonia had completed her turn from the Red Sea into the Gulf of Aden. The tense moments of navigating around a reef while avoiding other shipping had passed, and Captain Blair and Chief Officer Henderson were leaning on the port wing of the bridge seemingly engaged in a relaxed chat.

Ed thought that Perim Island seemed to stand out clearer, or closer than he recalled from previous voyages, but Davey Jones had just taken a positional fix at eight o'clock, indicating Caledonia's position with a nice neat cross intersecting precisely with the planned course line.

Captain Blair spoke briefly to Ed to ensure he understood the written standing orders – maintain a course of 077% and sound for the 30 fathom bank at thirty minute intervals. Call the Captain at 11.30 to prepare for docking stations at Aden. Simple enough.

This was normally an uneventful run – the thirty fathom bank was a very precise underwater rock shelf, which ran like a course line from Perim to Aden. The fathometer was considered to be the most sophisticated and dependable piece of electronic equipment on the ship. Radar – even in the late 1950's was still viewed with considerable scepticism by elderly captains. Merchant ships could not afford the sophisticated radar equipment of Naval ships, nor carry the technicians to operate and maintain optimum service, consequently this valuable navigational aid was frequently dismissed as an unreliable contraption.

Captain Blair subscribed totally to this suspicious viewpoint, despite the fact radar worked on a not dissimilar principal to the fathometer sounding machine, which he considered almost infallible. Ed signed the standing orders and confirmed he understood. The Captain and the four to eight watch officers left the bridge. They also left Ed with the slightly nagging feeling about his impression of the closeness of Perim Island.

He took a compass bearing on Perim lighthouse, now fairly well astern, crossed with the bearing of a prominent rocky outcrop, shown on the chart. The position confirmed his suspicion that Caledonia was inside the course line – closer to the shore than she should be. The fathometer read the hoped-for thirty fathoms, but the chart position indicated twenty fathoms. Just as a precaution he ordered the helmsman to steer five degrees right of the course to allow for correction; too far to the right of the course was deep water and correctable – too far to the left was a sharply shelving rocky seabed and potential disaster. Either the compass bearing was wrong or the compass had an error – even Ed was partially seduced by the historical infallibility of the fathometer. He switched on radar and while it fired up took an azimuth, a compass bearing of a known star, which allowed him to confirm that the gyro compass was reading true. He checked his bearing on Perim Lighthouse, which was almost hidden, blocked by the ship's funnel. Also, the quickly falling darkness was making other landmarks difficult to determine. The fathometer still recorded the hoped for thirty fathoms. The ship's position he plotted was even further to the left of the line. There were no other ships in the vicinity – this should have been a busy shipping lane – he could see the lights of four ships miles to the south.

He ordered a further 10 degrees to the right correction – the ship was now running along a line of reef shown on the Chart as seventeen fathoms – thirteen shallower than the desired depth. Radar confirmed this position: the South Yemen shoreline of sharp volcanic rock reflected on screen an identical outline to that which the chart presented. The fathometer still recorded thirty fathoms. Ed was not in any way superstitious or subject to fantasy, but there was something weird, sinister even, about the events of the past two hours. There was no wind to speak of, and no precedent of strong onshore currents driving any twelve thousand ton liners into dangerous shallows. In any event, the evidence of other ships in the main shipping lane, ten miles to the south, seemed to indicate that Caledonia was the only vessel being pushed towards the reef, while the reliable, infallible old fathometer had uncharacteristically failed. Even if the initial position at Perim Island had been more 'perfect' than accurate it did not account for the unprecedented current, the unprecedented machine failure and the seeming strength of the current that was counteracting the power of Caledonia's two big Doxford diesel engines, and the helmsman's diligent steering, by pushing her fifteen degrees off course.

The coincidence of three unprecedented influences occurring at the one moment, was difficult to believe, or explain. He had followed his standing orders, and it was not his prerogative to change the captain's written instructions without first gaining his approval. And he really had to be sure of his situation, before he called 'Faither' to alert him to the problem.

Ed had stationed his cadet to keep a sharp look-out for Arab dhows, or small craft that might be pottering about without navigation lights this close in-shore. He also had him keep a record of all the time movements, the course adjustments and soundings, during this strange episode as a precaution, and evidence of his actions.

Caledonia was now holding course, but not improving her position and was too close to shallow water for comfort. Faither had to be informed, and the young cadet was despatched to ask Captain Blair to come to the bridge. Ed watched the captain heave himself up the companionway, from his cabin on the boat deck below the bridge. His movements suggested that his tired old legs were still aching, from the heavy demands put on them by his extended attendances on the bridge, since arrival at Port Said through the Canal and round the ninety minute shift at Perim Island. He did not look. at all enthusiastic at this unplanned summons to duty, one and a half hours before he had asked to be called.

"What's the problem, Mister?", he queried, with barely disguised irritability. Ed felt that Father had possibly levitated to just short of the "God who must be feared" level. "There is something wrong with the ship, Captain, and I can't explain it," Ed showed the series of positions he had plotted on the chart; the last four making good the course heading, but miles inside the planned course line – steady along a seventeen fathom ridge.

"What does the fathometer read?"

"Thirty fathoms – never changed up or down – but it must be faulty."

"Faulty?" incredulous 'How did you plot these positions?" This, a heavy challenge!

Ed had been quite pleased with his own navigational ingenuity in utilising radar for an accurate positioning, and moonlit mountain tops to provide accurate bearings of ridges clearly identified on the chart. His explanation was rebuffed.

"Mountain tops and radar? Psshaw!"

Ed had not anticipated that his competence would be subject to so much resistance. Inside his head was voicing – 'for Christ's sake captain, I am trying to tell you that the ship is standing into danger' but, even in 1960, a couple of hundred years after Captain Bligh, junior officers did not argue, disagree or intimate that a captain might be wrong or uncomprehending, on the bridge of his own ship.

He searched his mind for some other credible and tactful evidence, to support his concerns and convince the captain that he had to take control and alter course.

The captain looking tired, slightly confused, was on the port side of the chartroom half turned so that he could address Ed, while looking incredulously at the row of little crosses plotted on the chart in a dangerous line that he refused to believe.

Ed had positioned himself at the chartroom door, so that he could keep an eye on the wheelhouse in case any other developments should arise to add further complications to this already confused situation.

The course from Perim Island to Aden was a main shipping lane, like a motorway, and should have been, at least, busy with shipping traffic, heading to and from Aden. Ed thought that this point would be obvious, and significant to the captain

"Well, all the other ships are a good ten miles south of us."

He hardly managed to finish the sentence when God became almost wrathful. Captain Blair's back snapped to ramrod attention and his head turned sharply, eyes blazing in reprimand......

"This is the Anchor Line, Mister! We don't take our positions from 'other' ships!

Ed was suddenly quite calm, the tension had gone. He imagined himself saying "Oh for fuck's sake – get off your high horse!" but he gave diplomacy one last shot.

"Well captain, I have followed your standing orders, and I find the ship out of position. I don't know what else to tell you. I want to be relieved of the watch – I have been steering fifteen degrees to the right of my course for an hour, and that is the line that we are only just making good on the chart.

Captain Blair stood for a second staring across the chartroom, blankly, disbelieving – when suddenly, enlightenment! He lunged towards the door, his right arm describing a large clockwise movement and yelled "Hard a starboard!"

Ed dashed quickly to the side of the Quartermaster, to make sure he did not go too hard to starboard, and plough into some unseen, or unlit dhow pottering about in the dark.

The Caledonia swung round and headed for Aden, somewhere in the centre of the loom of Ras Fartak Island Lighthouse, at the threshold to Aden Harbour, which was just beginning to show in the darkness to the east.

Ed thought about Kipling's two imposters – Triumph and Disaster. He had managed to avert a disaster he was sure might have occurred, had he not been the watch-keeper, but there was no significant Triumph.

John Henderson told him the following morning that Captain Blair had said, "The young Third Mate did well, last night."

Ed still wasn't permitted inside God's aloof perimeter, but at least Faither had sent him a message of approval.

## January 2009

The events of that warm March evening, the vernal equinox of 1960, had remained as an unsolved puzzle – an incomplete crossword, in Ed's semi-conscious memory for the next fifty years. The hint of a sinister influence intrigued him, and the enormity of what might have happened – the foundering of Caledonia – and the actual non-event of merely altering course to get back on track, masked the tension and drama that had been enacted to prevent a crisis from becoming a disaster.

He realised, that since his first experience of the Middle East in mid June 1953, he had found the area exciting, slightly unsettling, as if the events of seven thousand years of unresolved history and conflict were simmering away in a big broth pot of ingredients that still had to come through the boil, to produce a flavour with the right balance to suit all tastes. He always felt, somehow, that the so called Holy Land was some kind of 'work in progress' – unfinished business.

He had never glorified the experience, or the recurring memory as sinister or haunting. But the mystery of that spring evening continued to resurface, every so often, like a crossword clue that he could not quite solve, or an anagram he could not decipher. There would be no solution printed in tomorrow's Glasgow Herald; if he really wanted the answer he had to crack the clue.

He eventually came to realise that he had never really felt comfortable in the region between Port Said and Aden. He could not help the gut feel that the events of March 21st 1960 had as much to do with some local, spiritual turbulence that his ship had been drawn into, rather than any human error, or mechanical failure that had infected the bridge of Caledonia. It never even remotely occurred to him that he might be part of something bigger than a voyage from Glasgow to Bombay, and his skill as a navigator, and resolve as a watch-keeper, were being put to the test.

He had enjoyed sailing from Glasgow south to Liverpool then down the French and Spanish coasts. And the Mediterranean was pleasant but he felt a very slight growing tension – he subsequently likened the feeling to claustrophobia – building from Gibraltar, then Malta, and heaviest through the Biblical lands between Egypt and Arabia. He recalled the freedom and satisfaction he could anticipate when they streamed the log in the Arabian sea for the long haul across the Indian Ocean to Karachi and Bombay. He definitely had a suspicious unease about the lands of the Old Testament. On that March evening of 1960 he had no benefit of hindsight to evaluate the 'mysteries' or contemplate the consequences of any normal course of action. The standing orders were quite specific 'steer 077 degrees', sound for the thirty fathom bank – adjust course to follow the line of the thirty fathom bank. Under normal circumstances he would have done just that – occasionally altering course to make room for approaching ships, except there were no other ships in the vicinity. Neither was there any wind, no known currents and yet eighteen thousand tonnes of ship and cargo – not to mention five hundred trusting passengers and crew – was being driven fifteen degrees off course at twenty miles per hour.

Without the gut feel and subsequent combination of primitive navigation and 'untrusted' modern technology, and recognising the fallibility of the old, dependable fathometer, Caledonia would have smacked into the volcanic rock that was the southern crust of the Arabian Peninsula, in only forty-five minutes.

The human error of an inaccurate start point to this passage, coupled with a captain's blind faith in the biblical infallibility of a man-made machine, compounded by an anomalous current that had never been experienced before, was a recipe for disaster.

Without the enlightenment, provided by the new kid on the block, Captain Blair's world would have come to grief on the barren rocks of Aden.

There was no triumph; only the acknowledgement the faint praise that a watch-keeper had been effective in managing a crisis – with a little drama. There was no disaster.

But disaster did strike!

# Commentary – Iain's Consultation

Iain had a challenge to address before he embarked on his 'writer's agent role – a review meeting with an oncology consultant. This was the first I knew of his remission in an ongoing burden; mentally and physically he appeared to be in such good condition that it seemed the review would simply be confirmation that all was well.

The results were very discouraging – the prognosis bleak and the disclosure of this devastating information had been in Helen's presence, which added greatly to the burden of distress which Iain had to shoulder. He had no opportunity to break this bad news tactfully or gently to his wife. The information had been, apparently, delivered with shocking clarity that disaster was both inevitable and imminent.

Iain's first priority was to try to comfort and reassure his shocked wife.

**22nd September 2014**

## Dear Iain

I thought I would drop you a wee letter-knowing knowing how much you enjoy reading quality material.

Seriously, though, I decided to write to you – a letter seems to elevate the sentiment to the 'written in blood' status – to breakthrough the conspiracy of silence that seems to be prevalent at the moment.

After the recent weeks of anticipating your hospital appointment, suddenly it, the event and the results – are no longer conversation pieces. Even my wife, who likes to analyse everything down to its DNA, is strangely mute on the subject, I suspect that she has interpreted reactions, or been made party to a confidence, which she is not prepared to discuss with, even, her closest companion (I shy away from the word confidante as she finds confidences shared with me subject to a scrutiny which she finds too analytical or, in some cases, de-dramatising)

Anyway, as your new friend-again, avoid any 'best' presumption, that slot already occupied, with a queue of eager contenders in waiting, and I am not an 'old friend' or life companion – those slots also being satisfactorily filled. But, here we are, two old guys, seventy seven years into a journey, who are suddenly sharing a path with no idea how long, or how far, we still have to go.

As President Roosevelt said, after Pearl Harbour "All we have to conquer, is fear itself."

How is your faith Iain? I know you are adamant that you are a Christian – not a Catholic and not a Protestant, but a Christian. I know you lead a good Christian life and practice a good Christian ethos towards your fellow beings, (what you would do to cats that shit on your flower beds is a little intolerant), but any exception to that particular rule only serves to emphasise and endorse your strong Christian practices.

But, how is your faith? Are you sitting in this tunnel wondering if there really is a light at the end of it? Are you a passenger, wondering when this bloody tunnel might end so you will feel more comfortable, or less fearful, in the daylight?

Or, are you the engine driver, confident of the track and the knowledge that there is light just ahead? Or, perhaps, the Guard who switches on the internal lights to comfort the other passengers while reassuring them that we will soon be out of the darkness.

I don't know if you remember the old children's hymn 'Jesus bids us shine with a pure clear light'

Well, who exactly is 'shining a pure clear light'? Not the Pope. The last one thought God might be asleep!

(Maybe God is just a bit knackered from doing it all alone, without much help from the head bummers of the Faiths.) Justin Welby recently confessed to having occasional doubts about the existence of God.

You know, Iain, I love films – certain films, anyway? I often find in them, like I find in literature, some profound, or prophetic lines, which I like personally —as a message. Like, in Zulu, when the 180 Welsh Borderers are confronted with 5,000 hostile warriors. The young squaddie wails, "Why us?" and the old RSM says quietly and resolutely "Cos we're 'ere, lad!"

Well, Iain, I believe that is a message to a wee Glasgow man and his new best pal – a wee West Lothian man; "Cos we're 'ere, lad!" We were not put 'ere simply to live out a three score and ten or, even, a four score!

I believe, that before we go, we are meant to make a difference. We have each done our duty, to some extent, by our families – probably more than most in the 'being there' sense. So what are you going to do for the next few years? You are unlikely to improve your golf handicap at this stage; and the old lady next door, if she can afford a new BMW, can afford to pay a painter to do her side of the fence, next time! And you can't just sit around waiting for God – he may be asleep, or not available at all, according to two of His closest associates. I think you should join me and we go looking for Him and, if necessary, wake Him up!

So, the proposition is that you and I work together to put our combined knowledge and ability and faith 'out there' in the darkness, like a little candle throwing a little light about—you from your small corner, and I from mine.

Of course, I would have to be the Captain, but you, the chief Engineer keep the screws turning and put in the caution, or the veto when I presume too much power and try to move too fast!

You see, Crossover, 'The Tree That Never Grew' – good, bad or indifferent —is to be followed by 'The Bird That Never Flew', 'The Bell That Never Rang' and the 'Fish That Never Swam'. The idea for 'The Bird…' is there, but I have no idea yet what the next two are – but they will come!

Anyway, I need an editor – a Devil's Advocate – and nobody I know fills that role better than you.

(Sheila, I thought, might have been the one, but she is too sceptical and always wants to know the end of the story – which, in this case hasn't been written – and the whole thing would get bogged down) The first bit was pushed out prematurely, but, at least, it got rid of some of the 'early years' foundations and doubts and reasoning.

So, as I said, "How is your Faith, Iain?" Are you going to sit around waiting for God or, are you prepared to join me in looking for Him? You know, the Via, Veritas Vita bit!

What have we gotta lose? The Captain has already been told he is a fruitcake, and the Chief Engineer has been told his engines won't last forever. What's new about any of that?

You know, Sheila keeps telling me 'Nothing will ever change' and I have to agree with her, nothing will ever change, – if nobody does anything about starting to change things.

Well Iain, I want things to change! And, before I pop my clogs, or reach the end of the tunnel, I am determined to start that change – at least alert people to the Via and the Veritas bits. And I am inviting you to help me do it.

Back to my films – I also love the Magnificent Seven; particularly the bit where Steve McQueen and Yul Brynner ride the hearse up to Boot Hill, drop off the box, and ride back down from Boot Hill.

That's you and me! Me, the Driver and You the Shotgun Guard – we'll drop off this particular box and live to fight another day!

How is your Faith, Iain?

Are you up for it? What have you got to lose?

This 'odd couple' have a lot of good damage to inflict on the unenlightened. I believe we will both be around for a good bit longer, yet.

With fond love, and great respect

*Your friend*

*Ed*

## 4th October 2014

Hi, it's me again.

I did not mean to write to you again – or, so soon. I promise I do not intend to become your best pen-pal, any more than I intended to become your, lately arrived, best pal. But these are quickly moving times and, at my age, I see little point in waiting until my spirit is ascending (or, perhaps, descending) to say 'I meant to do that, and now it is too late!'.

What I am about to say may inspire the reaction in you, "How arrogant!" or, "How pompous!" But, as you once told me, "You get no shite, here!" And, I would ask you to remember the (paraphrased) quotation 'Greater love hath no man than that he risk his credibility to arrogance and pomposity in the service of his friend!'

Anyway, I have been thinking about you and, for what it is worth, I want you to know that you are not alone in this slit trench: a wee fat Glasgow man has squeezed in beside you, if only to pass the ammunition.

You know, Iain, throughout my life I have experienced lots of different relationships; ladies I have loved, and ladies I could have loved, given the opportunity. Family I love deeply and, extended family I love almost as deeply. Friends I have known all my life, and love for their loyalty and durability. And friends, known only briefly and whose names I never knew, or cannot remember, but whose positive impact and credibility resonate somewhere deep within my memory banks.

And then there are the friends, whether long standing or only recently met. whose contribution to my life is significant and not easily dispensable.

Iain Melrose, you are the most recent 'Johnny come Lately' and, possibly the most important and least dispensable of my friends, at this time. I will not give up on you easily.

OK – now that we have got the emotional, romantic pish out of the way (I hope you brushed away a wee tear!) let's get down to the bit that stretches my arrogance and pomposity to its limits.

Cancer is not the end!

You may think to yourself "Well, that is fine for you to say Wilson, you have not been told that cancer is on the move within your system!" And, of course, this is true. But then, neither have I experienced rape – but I can visualise the terror, the impotence and the anger at the degrading intrusion of this malignant assault on a being, and the total despair that all decency has left the world that I live in. I can understand the victim's mental paralysis and inability to act, and mount a defence against the enormity of this evil that has suddenly attacked.

Sheila's great ethos is, "When the going gets tough, that is when the tough get going!"

Well, Melrose, cancer is going to know it has been in a fight, because, this is where the tough get going! There are two of us in this slit trench now, and we are not about to surrender Fortress Melrose easily.

You have done everything you can to make life without you, easy and comfortable for your entire family; funeral arranged and paid for, grand-kids taken care of, son and daughter set on a secure path for life. You have even left instructions for 'family' to wash the car and cut the grass for Helen.

Can I let you into a little secret? – Helen could not give a shit if the car is dirty or the grass needs cutting, for an extra day or two! She wants to enjoy a few more years with her dearest friend and her life's companion. Despite the ongoing battle of the sexes, that we both experience, it may surprise you to realise, that this desirable, not dispensable being is you. Don't make, or consider yourself redundant just because you have arranged a funeral and committed Fraser to a weekly grass-cut.

At this moment in time, the only person who is totally prepared for you to go, is you! But you don't have to actually go, or let go, to know that you are a manager of some impressive ability whose arrangements work when he is on holiday. You don't have to, actually, resign to know that the company can survive, somehow, without you. Enjoy your seat on the board for a little while.

So, Melrose, turn that infallible management expertise and altruism through 180 degrees. You have done all that you can for the world. Now is the time to do all that you can for the one person that your world does not want to do without.

From your longest-loving life's companion to your newest, wee fat best pal, understand that we need you to hang around for a bit longer, not for ever – that would be insufferable but with your expertise you can surely negotiate a few more years. The tattie magnate who brokered deals for the benefit of the anticipated blight or wet harvests can turn the big C into a wee c and hold on for a few more years.

You know Iain, I told you I loved films – especially the old ones. Like when you and I were wee boys and went to the Gaumont club (or whatever) "We come along, on Saturday morning, greeting everybody with a smile!" And we would watch Big John Wayne and his beleaguered unit fight off the hostiles to the last bullet, and just as the last overwhelming charge was about to annihilate them, off in the distance would be the sound of the bugles. The US Cavalry were on the way, the hostiles fled and the good guys were saved.

And we all stamped our feet and cheered, because the good guys were saved – and we went home happy, on Saturday morning, greeting everybody with a smile; maybe, occasionally slapping our own bums to make our horses go faster! The good guys won!

Well Iain, there is no US Cavalry coming in answer to the distant bugles; just this wee fat Glasgow man in the slit trench beside you. And his arrogance and pomposity of jumping in beside you has just screwed up your redundancy plans – you now have two of us to save. So you better get on with it

However. I do have plenty of ammunition! With fond love

*Ed*

PS You screwed up my opportunity for independence by voting for 'Better Together. So, I can live with it, let's make this 'Better Together' work, while we are still better together!

**30ᵗʰ October 2014**

Hi – I know, it's me – again!
Well, your faith seems to be holding up pretty well – and your determination ( remember "I am determined that this thing is not going to beat me!") Maybe it is time to rethink the plan!

Not all of it, you understand – just the timing. Nobody will be too disappointed that you have to extend the harvesting period: look on it as a bonus to you and all your shareholders.

Just like when you were a tattie expert (before your son took over!!!) and you budgeted on a good, average or bad crop, based on a good, average or bad harvesting season. You can't control the weather, but, your plan seems to be justified by a bad harvest season because the slightly reduced profit is, almost, offset by the slightly reduced labour costs (providing that the weather is not too disastrous) and, wow!, are you not proud of your planning and budgeting which has anticipated, and allowed for this disaster and ensured that your shareholders are protected from the worst effects of this bad luck. Your brilliant planning and preparation has provided for them in the event of the disaster that they all refuse to anticipate.

In fact, your good planning will only really be apparent (to you, anyway) if the disaster occurs.

Now, it seems, that an improvement in the weather forecast promises a better crop than expected and you have to rework your budgets to allow for this longer than expected harvesting period.

Don't be too disappointed that the brilliant strategy of your disaster planning has to be put on hold for another year. And don't be frustrated by the need to rethink and adjust your timing and financial budgets to accommodate a better than anticipated harvest period The extra benefits generated will justify any time and effort adjustments you have to make to your plan – and your shareholders will be delighted by the extra bonus they receive from this better than expected Melrose harvest season.

Your exit plan is good, Excellent! but the plan will keep. Your partner and shareholders know that you have made generous provision for them – you don't have to execute the plan to convince them of your ingenuity, concern and generosity. You have to believe that they would rather have you continue to return an annual bonus for a few years yet, rather than the lump sum, one-off arrangement you were putting in place following the poor communication that had you believe you only had a limited time to put your 'perfect' plan into action.

So, now that you know that your faith is, at least, paying off – start to believe it!

And, start to believe that you have devised such a good plan for your shareholders that it will keep for a few years yet.

And start to believe that your shareholders are delighted that you are still the Chairman delivering the returns that they are happy with.

And start to believe that your plan for a 'bad' harvest is also sound for a good harvest – and the fact that it will take you longer than you planned, to reap the good harvest, is your reward for the faith that you, somehow, had come to take for granted.

As a recently exposed stakeholder to the Melrose plan, I am delighted with the early returns.

We have a bit of positive business still to do, you and I and if you have faith that you will be here longer than the recent, recklessly communicated, forecast suggested, maybe we can get on with exposing this faith in investment and planning to a few more people.

There has to be some reason why two old guys are still operating in 'neverland' with little but faith in common.

Keep believing!

With fond love

*Ed*

PS Yours is not the only encouraging news in Kirrie this week – Mary Rennie has been told that her lung tumours have shrunk to pin heads, and she does not need to return for evaluation for some months. Maybe treatment has improved in the past fifty, or even ten years and the light at the end of the tunnel is becoming a wee bit brighter! And my friend, George Orchiston has been given an all-clear.

**15th May2015**

I am not sure why I am writing to you at this moment…maybe I am (uncharacteristically) so well organised for this holiday that I can afford to invest a little time in my friend, Iain.

I think, also, that there are little words of encouragement I would like to share with you, but our opportunities for 'confidentiality' are limited, so the words remain unspoken. I fear that the omni-presence of one, or both of our respective 'thought hackers' might result in a negative interpretation from our communication, beyond our 'mutually understood' moral support for a friend

("Why did you feel the need to remind Iain that you say a wee prayer for him? Has he told you something???)

I have no heavy premonitions or negative vibes about your ability to win yet another skirmish, and keep your affliction controlled for another few years yet. But, I fear an unspecific intimation of positive concern – a 'coded message' of continuing support – might be misinterpreted and generate a third degree of Inquisition proportions by the two Loyolas that we are married to.

Anyway, I wanted to let you know that I don't simply turn up to scoff Helen's excellent scran and I don't simply take our friendship for granted. I firmly believe that a wee word of faith, to whomever may be listening, really does make a difference. And. for what it is worth, I continue to make a serious effort on behalf of my friend. Iain.

In a beleaguered garrison, I am sure it must help to know that there is somebody in the next slit trench still on your side, and still firing. Well, I'm communicating, man…maybe it is up to you to make sure somebody is listening; after all, like two heads, two faiths must be better than one.

See you in another week, or ten days, the time lag will probably qualify us as 'must comes' once again.

In terms of celestial navigation a wee prayer from 'closer to the Equator' probably reaches its destination quicker than from the flatter latitudes of Angus.

With fond love, Your friend

*Ed*

# REVEILLE

Five-thirty, and I hear the baying mob
assembling on the rooftops;
This morning reveille seems to be the responsibility
Of the strident choir of crows:
Not the gentle birdsong that I associate
With the euphemistically described dawn chorus,
More an urgent call to arms,
Like NCO's barking out orders
To rouse the regiment!
Stand to! Check your equipment!
Prepare for the battle of a new day!
And, suddenly, the alert is over!
The cawing and the urgency
Has moved to another set of dwellings;
Distant, barely audible; no longer intrusive.
Only an occasional caw as a solitary bird flies over
To check that preparation for the day is well in hand;
Be it battle order, review or a route match to address a new challenge!
There is a peaceful silence while the days orders are finalised.
We are not disturbed, more reassured, by the distant cawing
As the crows rouse other combatants to prepare for 'something'!
And, now the dawn chorus;
The small sparrows and finches that nest in the ivy
Start appearing: little chirrups and tweets
Like the regimental band tuning up.
And the heavier sound of movement traffic;
Vehicles on their way to 'somewhere'
Passing along the road by the front of the house.
Monday, fourth of June, start of a new day;
Start of a new week: maybe start of a new life!

The crows have done their job well!
We are wide awake, alert, ready;
Some units are already on the move!

# HADRIAN'S WALL

Latin the language, some say, is long dead; it's relevance absent today:
Why teach it or preach it, or keep it around? Why bother what men used to say?
Well Latin, the language. screens much that's profound,
Holds the key to what ails us, since man's been around;
Sometimes in a word, sometimes in the sound,
Precise in its day, its mortar, well bound:
Its structure is solid, math'matic'ly pure.
Perhaps that's the reason some words still endure.
Though vague and obscure, they still hold a clue
To the ill that afflicts us, just the key; not a cure.
Diagnosis? Theoretical – a bit bard to follow;
Like that old bitter pill, maybe too hard to swallow!
Like medical science, locating one gene,
Going back through the tangle, to where we'd once been.

To that one word or phrase that gives us the key:
For example, in Latin, there is no soft 'C'!
Kissing 'K' is the sound, it isn't debated,
Each letter distinct, each enunciated.
'E' and 'I' the same treatment; sound 'e' as in bet,
And 'i' as in give – then the closer you get
To unfankling the corruption, that's hiding the source
Of the sinister current, pulling the world off its course!
Though each word was precise it was easily corrupted
From the days when Rome's legions went uninterrupted,
In their march, East and Westward; grab imperial control
Of the hearts and the minds of every free soul
'Til they reached an imag'nary 'Hadrian's Wall'
Defended by those who rejected Rome's call.

The Celi Dei people 'Companions of God'
Refused to submit to the Imperial rod!
The Celi Dei people, from each occupied land,
Took refuge in Scotland, to make freedom's stand!
There were Celi Dei from Biscay and from old Carcassone
From Judea and Persia, and far Kurdistan,
Caballah and Coptics; not one ethnic 'whole'
But 'peoples' united, independence their goal!
The Empire persisted, for two hundred years,
But could not overcome its suspicion and fears
Of this land, Celi Deinia, which kept legions at length,
With a mystical, spiritual, unbeatable strength.
Rome could contest any fight on the ground
But, one dimensional, feared fight, 'til an answer was found

To harness this God, this inspirational force
Which inspired Celtic people to fight back. Of course,
Devious Rome had a plan, a spiritual deception,
But a century more was required for inception.
Rome had to buy time, suppress any hint
Of successful resistance; not even a glint
That the Empire which ruled, from Equator to Pole
Could be stalled: repulsed by the spirit man held in his soul!
The Press Corps reported, with spin and suggestion,
Of 'conquest and progress' a free press might question,
Where the State had invested great time and resources,
Yet failed to subdue 'much inferior forces'.
The people? Barbarians! Land? Hostile and bleak!
Not worth the conquering; this double speak
Kept the whole truth suppressed; the disappeared legion of five thousand men,
Was just not reported, hardly mentioned again!
Four great campaigns, over two hundred years,
Could not overcome the Empire's own fears
That discouraged enslavement of unworthy hosts;
They feared Caledonia was protected by ghosts.
The corruption of truth. this political spin,

Said the Wall was a means to lock sub-humans in;
How history repeats, with wall after wall,
Put up, by great states, to reject freedom's call

The World is bi polar – that's easy to see;
A north pole, a south pole, the Earth should spin free
On its axis, there in lies the trouble:
The North pole is loose – has an eight degree wobble!
"Been there for ever", you say, "Really, who's caring?"
An axle should fit neatly, secure in its bearing;
If it doesn't there's friction, which can cause overheating,
And the axle might seize, get locked in its seating!
We'll grind to a halt, the Earth will stop turning,
We'll lose out either freezing or burning.
You scoff, yet again "Prophet of doom – who let this chap in?"
"Be millions of years before that's likely to happen!"
Well actually no! And time moves quite fast,
But, no point looking forward, the truth's in the past!
Bi polar is fine, it's the normal condition,
Disconnecting one pole is a whole new position!
Corporate – spiritual must always be linked,
It's this bi-polar state that stops man being extinct.

The founders of Rome, these identical twins
Are the point where this polar disorder begins.
Romulus aggressive, and ruthless from birth,
Drew his power and his strength from the bowels of the earth.
Remus complemented his twin's ruthless streak;
When Romulus sought war, his twin'd rather speak.
Remus the thinker, and calm as a rule,
Was the steadying hand when his twin lost his cool.
Together, in balance they formed a good team,
But Romulus ended this bi-polar dream.
After working so hard to build Rome a stout wall
His humour was lost; Remus used the word 'small'!
In fact, quite provoked, he reacted with rage
Like a man-eating tiger released from a cage;

His animal instincts – kill or be killed –
With one fatal blow. mild Remus was felled!
So, balance was lost and polar disorder
Set Rome on a quest to control every border!
And, history records this, not the only occasion
A brother usurped by his twin, at the birth of a nation!,
The spiritual deception the Empire had planned?
On a scale modern marketing men would think 'Grand'!
The 'market' had tired of the old 'full strength' Rome;
A mild variant required to replace it, at home.
A new logo designed, the Brand name adjusted;
Both inferred this Brand variant was one to be trusted!
The sales force retrained, to hold distribution
Of markets in Europe. A pioneer force gave full execution
To markets abroad, in the new world, emerging.
A millennium to go and Rome was recharging!
And a new 'press release', expertly produced,
Was churned out, multi-lingual, so the world stayed seduced!
And Latin, the language? Just keep it, it links
All the knots on your time line, and takes out the kinks!

# Melrose at Murrayfield

Scotland scored!
The guy stood up –
You'd think we'd won the World Cup
He cheered the score
As did some fifty thousand more;
But, fifty thousand bums soon relocated.
On fifty thousand seats ••• except 'Elated'

This guy stayed stood, still celebrating
His 'Scottishness' getting irritating;
Too much, for Iain! "Sit down! And quick!"
"Laidlaw's going to take the kick".

The guy span round – his eyes looked 'Fight'
But Iain – laid back – "Sit down, you shite"
"Show some consideration"
For these behind, from this Home Nation"
'Who cannot see the ongoing action"
'While you indulge your satisfaction."

Lost for words – the crowd still cheering
The guy 'mimed' that he'd lost his hearing.
"Well., if your hearing's not so good,"
"Get it fixed! Deafness makes you very rude."

"Perhaps, when you have curbed your exultation"
"Your Mother, there, could fix a consultation"
Then Iain chose to twist the knife!
"Oh sorry, is that wee fat bird your wife?"
"Not just your hearing's gone to hell"
"I fear you may need specs, as well!"

**21st January 2016**

*Dear Iain,*

Here we are in January 2016.

I thought a wee New Year message might be appropriate; you know, like Liz's Christmas Broadcast to the Nation and Commonwealth, or Il Papa's address to the World in general. Nothing so grand or ambitious, of course, just a wee personal note from me to you to celebrate our joint arrival in January 2016. (I pondered if, like me, you had wondered whether your view of 2016 might have been obstructed by an old guy, jangling a forbidding looking bunch of keys, on the wrong side of pearl encrusted gates!)

Anyway, here we are, two elective Saints who have managed to avoid Paradise for another year!

It is in this context that I wanted to have a wee chat with you. Sometimes I fear that those of us who have been successful, (or relatively so) in business, are not credited with the same appreciation for applying the same practices in our personal lives as were applauded and acknowledged when we served a board of directors, or successfully satisfied, or avoided, the destructive scrutiny of Her Majesty's Revenue and Customs.

Our previous records, respectively, are some testimony to our individual success in applying the old business maxim 'plan your work and work your plan'; but that business acumen is regarded by our current 'assessors' as historical information to be filed and stored away in the archives.

That we have the bottle to apply these same disciplines and practices to something as emotional – even unmentionable – as preserving and extending one's own life is a connection few make, and we are denied the acknowledgement and appreciative feedback that recognises our brilliance in 'managing' something as mundane as our own survival for another year and for having a 3–5 year plan in place to secure a stable foreseeable future.

(We have either been 'lucky' – our brilliance overlooked – or taken for granted; the only 'remarkable' instances, nowadays, are our occasional mistakes which highlight that increasingly impending dotteriness that seems to be the special preserve of elderly husbands who have managed to survive, successfully, without any dependence on computers or mobile phones. Any suggestion of retained or current brilliance is totally eclipsed by the last passing committed stupidity, and hailed as significant evidence of our ageing, and decreasing effectiveness, by our closest observers.)

Funny the effect and impact an occasional eclipse has, once in a while, seemingly more significant than the predictability and dependability of the Sun, rising and falling each day, to provide the benefits that these same observers/critics take for granted. Oh, for a board of directors to appreciate and applaud the dividend.

At this stage my wife would be urging me to 'get on with it – get to the point!' And the point would not be got, because it was already lost, somewhere in the detail which was too intricate or boring to be worth absorbing!

The point is – that as a fellow traveller – I am impressed by the planning (and implementation) you have adopted to beat your current challenge – and the contingency planning you have put in place to cater for the unforeseen future challenges.

I reminded you once of F D Roosevelt's maxim 'all we have to overcome is fear itself!'

Well, my friend, I am again impressed; you have confronted fear, looked it in the eye, and faced it down! At around eighty years of age none of us is going to face down fear and achieve eternal life – but a successful five year plan for extended life, at this stage, is pretty impressive.

I am also impressed by the contingency plan you have put in place! I can understand that it might prove a bit morbid for you to 'share' that plan with the eventual beneficiaries. Consequently it is impossible for you to receive 'board approval' and appreciation for the excellence of your planning; it is, after all, a contingency plan and, maybe, only the really aware – or forward looking, perhaps – can understand the thoroughness of a contingency plan.

'Well Iain, maybe it takes a 'johnny come lately' to give you a bit of objective feedback. I am impressed with the five-year plan you are working your way through! It seems to be going well – just don't push too hard – remember the objective is extended life, not eternal life.

And I am impressed with your contingency planning; just remember it is, after all, only a contingency plan – you do not need to see it in action to be impressed, it is a sound plan. You can review it and adjust it for changing needs when you are rewriting your plan A – life plan – in another five years.

Anyway, have I missed the point, lost the point, or did you possibly drop off somewhere in the middle?

Maybe your deep conversations with Malcolm Rooney are all you need to put your spiritual needs into a reassuring perspective. Or maybe, since your early challenges in Bangour Hospital you have become used to, or felt obliged to fight your big battles on your own!

Well, I did not choose to fall into this slit trench beside you but I am here now; and we have a common objective! I am greatly inspired by your determined example. Let's charge towards eighty-five together! Reviewing our plans with December 20/20 vision sounds like a good target to me.

And, of course, there is faith! Proddy prayers are just as good as any others, and you feature in mine all the time.

Yours sincerely – and with love, Your friend

*Ed*

**April 2016**

Hello again Iain,
   You really are an inspiration! Even delivering a bag of tatties you manage to add a helping of uplifting news.

I am so pleased for you – you deserve a wee miracle. Of course, as you are probably aware, I am a wee bit sceptical of putting too much faith in miracles: God needs all the help He can get (from us mere mortals) to make sure that everything turns out right.

When I think of your determination and survival instincts, I am reminded of one of my favourite films – Zulu – there is so much that is profound in that story. There was no Good or Evil – no really good guys or bad guys. In fact, a lot of it was about respect for the other guy, but particularly about respect for one's own determination and disciplines that produced 'the miracle' of survival.

Like when Lieutenant Chard said, "Well, if it was a miracle it was a Martini Henry 4.5 calibre miracle!"

And the big dependable CSM said quietly, "And the bayonet with a bit of determination and guts behind It…begging your pardon, Sir."

Give credit to your 'Martini Henry 4.5 calibre' treatment. by all means, but don't underestimate the value of the determination and guts of Wee Melrose with the bayonet!

As the old song says 'Each victory will help you some other to win!'

Yes, my friend, you are an inspiration – keep up the good work. With love

*Ed*

PS Oh, and thanks for the tatties.

**22nd July 2016**

*Dear Helen*

What an inspiration you are! I watched you on Tuesday evening hirpling about, stoically dispensing hospitality and comfort like there was no tomorrow!

Well, there was nearly no tomorrow for me – when you rushed to recharge the Empire Biscuit plate and stumbled on the kitchen doorstep. My heart missed a beat; thought I was about to meet my maker a good ten years before I have planned. And I thought, 'somebody really has to tell Helen to slow down. for all our sakes!'

You see Helen, you are such an inspiration to so many of us that we do not want you to damage yourself by heaping more good examples of your dedication to hospitality and generosity, on top of the surfeit you have already dispensed; rushing off to find the other plate of Empire Biscuits, which you have hidden for just such a presumed emergency, is superfluous to requirements: our cups already runneth over!

There was a time when we would just think "Oh. let her get on with it, she's happy – and what's the harm?"

Well, the harm is that you have a 76 year-old knee that has already been repaired, and is about to be repaired again. Don't make the surgeon's job harder by compounding the problem through chipping the bone, or damaging the tissue that he depends on to anchor and secure the new knee.

You have proved your hospitality – and your Christianity; to the mournful and the hungry, '—taking Communion, with shortie and Prosecco, around your table, felt well blessed on that occasion. The hostess tripping bahoochie over bosom would not have made the Christian message any more convincing – but a 'John Wayne' catapult onto the patio would have dispatched an innocent Weegie to Paradise somewhat prematurely.

In any event, another Empire Biscuit would have been inappropriate, an anachronism – as Iain pointed out; they should be called 'Commonwealth Biscuits' now: you really should adapt to the times we live in!

And that is the whole point. You, and particularly you, have to adapt to the body that you live in; not for ever, just at this time.

How many cliches do you need? spirit is willing but the flesh is 'I am reluctant to say 'weak' as you will just see that as another challenge to prove that you are as fit and capable as ever. Well, just at the moment, you aren't but you will be (almost as good as new), if you treat your damaged knee with the respect for its age, and the service it has provided – don't make the next Empire Biscuit the one that breaks the camel's knee!

Iain has asked you, family have told you, friends have advised you, and pals have hinted that you should not aggravate the knee before the surgeon chappie gets a chance to fix it.

Helen the Martyr of the Knee may have a nice old-fashioned Catholic resonance of stoicism and commendable suffering, but Helen the Resurrected on two Good Knees would be a Hallelujah moment, a cause for celebration that might give us all a lift! We are all looking for a resurrection – why not set the precedent!

Perhaps the combined concerns and opinions of all who love you is not convincing enough, as a divine instruction from a higher authority, or perhaps you need something in writing, that appears to be the word of God, to convince you to slow down and protect that knee for the next few weeks (remember, even the most resilient among us needed forty days and forty nights rest and relaxation in the wilderness to prepare for big challenges).

Anyway, I have enclosed a little known testament to give you guidance, inspiration and faith for the miracle which is about to befall you in the coming weeks.

Meantime, if the urge to make more Empire Biscuits is upon you, for God's sake, sit down! With much love

*Ed*

PS The date of this letter is no accident – this is Mary Magdalene day: there is a lass who knew how to survive and keep doing the good work!

# Ave Saint Eddie
# (The Steddie Wan)

And Lo, as I travelled in the area where Wilkie's Land joins with Barrie's Land a great turbulence rent the air, the sky darkened, and I fell to my knees in anticipation of some dreadful fate, some fearful inferno of doom to be visited upon me.

I could feel an ominous presence, and was so filled with foreboding that I kept my eyes tight shut that I would not witness the Gates of Hell open up beneath my feet. And mine ears closed and covered lest I should hear the wrath of God directed at me, as so often predicted in the Good Book, laden with Doom and Destruction, to be the lot of sinners. "0 me miserum" I wailed.

But the turbulence and rumbling ceased, and a gentle touch drew my hands from across mine ears. A calm reassuring voice spake unto me in mine own tongue "Hullo there, Wee Fat Weegie Wan, open yer eyes, dinna keech yersel, Ahm no gonny hurt ye!"

I managed to open one eye and take a wee peek to behold a wondrous sight. The whole scene, Wilkie's Land, Barrie's Land and all the territories from The Bellies to Orchard Brae, was bathed in a warm reassuring light. My fear subsided, and I opened my other eye and turned my gaze Heavenward; the clouds had parted and there, in the very centre of this divine light hovered a mighty angel, with golden hair framing his beautiful face, clad in a long white dress which reached down to his perfectly manicured feet encased in golden hand-stitched, open-toed Lacoste sandals.

The beautiful voice spake again – not only in my own tongue of Weegie, but in the blessed and exclusive dialect of Upper Knightswood "Aye, The Big Yin sent me doon tae talk tae ye; stoap cowerin' like a wean – ah tell't ye ah wisnae gonny hurt ye. The Big Yin waants ye tae dae Him a wee favour – He thinks yer OK. by the way, cheer up! He thinks ye hiv the gift o the gab an kin dae a wee bit convincin' fur Him".

Oh God, I thought, He wants me to negotiate the SNP back into Europe, or worse, try to unite the Labour Party to recreate a credible opposition to Tory capitalism. It was as if this amazing Angel had read my mind "Naw, naw" be said, "Nuthin as easy as that, ye know!"

There, in the wilderness between Wilkie's Land and Barrie's Land I trembled in anticipation; the Labours of Hercules or the Quest of Jason and the Argonauts to find the Golden Fleece – my mind raced around all the incredible challenges that had been set to the heroes of Mythology – but nothing prepared me for the enormity of the task that the Big Yin had called a Wee favour'

The Angel of The Big Yin watched my puzzlement with some amusement "Ho ho, ye'll no gerrit!" He was enjoying my discomfort but, at the same time,"Yon purgatory wid be a doddle compared tae this!" He seemed reluctant to follow through and deliver the message that was the 'wee favour' concealing a fate worse than death. He cleared His throat three times, and the incandescence surrounding Him flickered as if all His power was being drained for Him to even utter the words of The Big Yin's challenging request.

He looked down on me, sympathetically, almost apologetically, cleared his throat for a fourth time and delivered the fateful words "Ken yon Wee Helen that bides up at Stiven?…Weel, The Big Yin depends a loat oan her tae gie succour tae a' they Blesseds, an' tha', ken the meek, thaim that's poor in spirit, ye know, the wans that ur mournin'. Aw eight o' The Blesseds!"

I was transfixed gazing heavenwards. The Angel hadn't told me the 'challenge' yet. but if it involved Wee Helen of Stiven and The Big Yin had already opted out, I knew I was on my own on this one. I pondered if I had misjudged this beautiful angel bathed in a golden aura, and considered whether the Angel of Death might buy his sandals from Lacoste.

The Angel had, again, read my thoughts. "Dinnae jump the gun, pal – ye've goat me wrang! The Big Yin really needs yer help an' tha', ye know! It's jist that wi Twitter 'n Facebook we Angels dinnae get much social contact noo adays – ah wis jus hivven a wee laugh wi' ye.

"Trouble is, wi Wee Helen, her Spiritual motivation hus goat aw oot o' proportion tae hur boadie's ability tae cope wi' the demands she's makin' oan it just noo!" He paused, presumably to check that I was following I was!

"I get it, I get it……get on with it!" Then I remembered about the 'wrath of God' and other admonitions of the Good Book, and added more meekly, and deferentially "I'm with You. Angel of the Big Yin".

He responded, obviously understanding my mixed and fluctuating emotions "Aye, yer aw right therr, Wee Glesca Wan, we huv mellowed a wee bit since thon big Book wis wrote; wur a bit less o' the wrath o' Goad stuff an a bit mair friendly persuasion noo, ye knaw! Too many whistleblowers aroon fur us tae try too much o' thon mystical stuff-fowk just think its Paul Daniels in a dog collar!" He paused, seemingly waiting for the spirit of The Big Yin to permeate my being and lift my soul with this new enlightenment.

The Angel of The Big Yin pressed on "Onywey, thon Wee Helen is essential tae The Big Yin's plans fur aboot the next ten year, ye know, but wan o' her knees is knackered an' she'll no gie it a brek! The problem is, The Big Yin huz arranged a wee miracle tae fix the gammy knee – so that she kin cairry oan His guid work, ye know. Therr's a loat goin' oan the noo-famines n' wars, an Armageddon jist roon the comer, so He's no goat time tae come doon Hissel; Wee Helens no egzacly indispensible, but The Big Yin feels He cannae dae wi-oot her at the mo!.,

He again paused to check I was comprehending; we were on the same wavelength now!

"Trouble is, Wee Helen still expecks miracles tae be like, weel, like when thon Book wis wrote – ye ken, magic!......instant, like. She kin be awfy gullible sometimes when ye tell her a wee story in Latin.

But miracles, they're no as instant noo adays. Nae mair 'pick up thy bed an walk' stuff noo!'" The Angel of The Big yin reflected on the passing of the instant miracle – the quick fix; but He balanced the questionability of the magic miracle against the permanence of the modern surgical miracle, "The Big Yin's problem is that He needs Wee Helen tae keep daein the work that she's guid at, He's goat a basketful o' martyrs that ur no' worth a curdy an' Wee Helen cannae even genuflect proaperly wi' a gammy knee. So, that's wherr you come in, Wee Glesca Wan!"

I realised that there was a fate worse than death – nobody had 'told' Wee Helen of Stiven anything and survived the purgatory that ensued. Oh Limbo where is thy sting?

The Angel of The Big Yin half turned but I was totally on His wavelength now; He was ready to deliver the final directive from The Big Yin – and then make a quick dash for the parting in the clouds through which the divine light shone down on me: like a rabbit transfixed in the headlights of the oncoming car. "The Big Yin wants Wee Helen's surgical miracle to be a success an He waants you to tell her tae 'Keep aff her bluidy knees – till they're mended like, an' the glue's haudin the knee cap thegither".

And with that He was gone, the divine light went out, and the heavens closed over.

So, there you have it Helen, a message from God to His 'not dispensable' servant to help Him perform a twenty-first century miracle:

"KEEP OFF YOUR BLOODY KNEES!"

Gloria in excelsis Magnus Unum

# Commentary on the year between September 2016–17, which contained our respective 80th Birthdays

During September 2016 my son Scott, working and living in Denver, phoned with the devastating news that he had been diagnosed with colon cancer, and it was already Stage 4 – the worst it could be!

However, he was to be operated on to remove part of his colon and investigate any possible options for survival and recovery. He had his operation, which was successful, and the prognosis that his condition was worth fighting was, at least, encouraging. In a family that preached 'hope' the words, 'worth fighting', were a challenge to be addressed.

My birthday month is October and a party was arranged for Saturday 15th, attended by Sheila's family – after 30 years marriage, my family – and my daughter Lindsey, and Helen and Ian.

Lindsey and I left the next day, my birthday, for Denver to spend time with Scott, for all the reasons that do not need to be spelled out. As birthdays go the date of 16th October was not proving to be a particularly happy occasion – one son who died, born on this same day, and a second son requiring a visit because he might have a terminal illness, memorable as the same date.

Birthdays and Easter, I do not enjoy!

In the event, Scott was at the start of a welcome 'miracle' recovery, although he still had major surgery to endure later, as a precaution that the cancer had been fully identified and removed.

During his convalescence he pursued his hobby of photography, but with limitations imposed by the chemotherapy which made his skin sensitive and vulnerable to sunlight; there is a lot of strong sunlight in Denver. He adapted his photography to suit his condition and in the next months he produced a book of wildlife photographs which was published and the proceeds donated to colon cancer research. Iain wrote to Scott applauding his bravery.

# Email note to Scott

Just a note to thank you for a truly wonderful book. The photography is superb, but the sentiment you express concerning your attitude to your condition even more so.

I have written you a letter as I am, according to my family, an IT dinosaur. So much so, I have dictated this and my long suffering wife has sent it,

Best wishes, keep up the fight,

Yours

*Iain M*

# Iain's letter to Scott

*Dear Scott.*

I felt I had to write to you as I am so impressed by your attitude to your condition and your determination to beat it, and by doing something to encourage others to do likewise.

I can only imagine how you must have felt when you received the news. In my case my first question to the consultant was "Where is it?" The reply was, "Everywhere – here's a leaflet!" My second question, "How long have I got?" No reply.

Unlike you, however, I have exceeded my three score years and ten so I could be philosophical. You, with a great career, a wife and young family to consider, must have been devastated! So, to pick yourself up and do what you have done is truly remarkable.

I feel that one's mental attitude to the condition is of paramount importance in keeping it at bay. Keeping physically fit is also vitally important. I keep telling my family that my ambition is to be the fittest corpse in the cemetery. So I still play badminton, circuit train, cycle and walk the dog – all slowly and badly, but I do them.

I feel that we have a long way to go in our attitude towards cancer. We should no longer whisper about it, but discuss it openly to support each other. I have been involved with McMillan, appearing in two of their videos. I stress you can live with the condition – my attitude is, "I have prostate cancer, but I am not ill. I may be some time, but my ambition is to die with it and not of it", because we must support each other.

All of this is much easier for me, but I am full of admiration for how you have coped – that strength must be in the Wilson genes!

Please give your wife and family my best wishes. Their support is vital.

Have a wonderful, joyous Christmas. I can only imagine it must be Heaven on Earth where you are; – three hundred days of sunshine a year, snow and skiing guaranteed, mountains on your doorstep – what more do you need?

You have beaten the dreaded C. Now enjoy life to the full!
Best wishes

*Iain*

Iain's 80th birthday was due in August 2017 and Helen arranged a secret getaway at their favourite hotel, the Open Arms at Dirleton, for the Friday night, two days before the Birthday; with Isabel, Sandy, Sheila and I to be secret surprise guests. Helen asked me to produce a few lines of verse as entertainment on the evening.

However, Iain had arranged a grander lunch for the Sunday, his actual Birthday, and asked me to produce and present the main eulogy of this birthday lunch in verse, to the assembled thirty, or so, friends and family who had all known him considerably longer than I had

It was both an honour and a challenge to produce two separate 'poems' for the same celebration at different venues; particularly as one had to be kept secret for Helen's surprise dinner party, and the main production, ideally, quite separate with no overlapping or duplicated sentiments in the two individual productions.

# FOURSCORE

When He was born – before some war –
The first wee Melrose through the door;
His mother looked on that wee face,
In those days, Innocence and Grace,
Still shone from out those infant eyes –
He seemed a blessing from the skies.
'We'll call Him Iain', said mother, Rose,
While George, His dad said 'What you've chose'
'Is, maybe just a bit audacious,'
'Ken, Iain – the word – means "God is Gracious!"
And Rosie, God fearing, but courage – not faint
Said,"Iain it is, He's our wee saint!"

But sainthood had to go on hold,
As three more babies joined the fold –
George followed Iain, then Pat and Norman;
They took no time at all in formin'
A hit squad, fit, alert, alive, the Famous Four –
Preceding any Famous Five – and Western Films or
Hibbee names; Ormonde, Reilly, Jesse James were heroes
As were The Youngers and the Daltons
(No softie pacifistic Waltons)
They'd ride out to triumph – or from disaster,
Skelping their bums to make horses go faster,
Then, into battle to confront any strangers,
Jambos from Broxburn, for them, Texas Rangers.

But Iain, (saint Iain?), took no part in the fray;
He aye had a book, to pass fight time away.
"The twins do the fighting – I'm management Aloof!"

61

"But no swearing or slang words, or I'll hit the roof!"
"George, Norman and Patrick, get on with the fight"
"No, 'take that you arsehole', or, 'hold that you shite'!"
"Next time you knock Jambos or Weegies to pieces"
"It's Take that you Rectum, or, Hold that you Faeces!"
Then into the fight – immune to the dangers,
Engaging in battle with mock Texas Rangers;
As Pat aimed a blow – an exposed solar plexus
Iain caught an accent – not Broxburn or Texas:
He'd just told his team, "Lads, don't be egregious!"
Then,"Get in there, my sons – these Rangers are Weegies!"

And Sainthood could wait, even longer, it seems;
While Iain fell in love with the girl of his dreams!
Wee Helen, of Blackburn, was better by far,
'Than Grable, or Hayworth, or Hedy Lamarr!
Graduation, a job, followed quickly thereafter.
Then marriage, and children – a life full of laughter!
With Iain, as a Dad, lots of kidding for sure;
But one of those kids could land in the manure,
If He ever discovers – sure as eggs are called eggs –
Who disclosed that His nickname is 'Little Short Legs'!
Or, the critic, still family, who thought 'Eighteen holes'
'Just a little ambitious; it's time to try bowls!'

But, sticking with short legs, so one story goes
He prefers to wear boots, to look after His toes,
And to make them last longer on His fast moving legs
He armours His heels with thick, heavy steel segs.
You can hear Him for miles, as He marches from home;
His tick tock is perfect: Kirriemuir's metronome.
But, Malcolm the vicar once feared for his kirk,
He thought death watch beetle was doing its work;
The tick tock getting louder – he imagined them chewin'
After two hundred years his braw church to a ruin.
But the tick tock was Iain, getting close to a run,
To check if there was any good work needing done!

Good work is His passion, He's always polite,
He stands back to help people board or alight
From any conveyance – a bus or a train,
Or put up His umbrella to protect folk from rain.
But one time, in Paris, His chivalry backfired
(The French don't think manners are always required!)
As Iain stood back to let all board the coaches,
The driver, getting twitchy, as departure approaches,
Thought Iain not coming aboard for this ride
Closed the door trapping Iain's outstretched arm inside!
The Metro took off with the Melrose wee legs
Digging into the platform – trying to brake with His segs.
But, embryo saints, even Rosie's wee wean
Are no match for the power of a sixty ton train!
Sparks flying from the segs, and thick smoke from the leather
Caught Helen's attention – interrupted her blether;
"What's your Dad playing at?" – a quick burst of tuttin',
Then she jumped up and pressed the emergency button.
No mention was made of the life-saving segs,
Or the magical power of Iain's wee legs.
The metronome sound was briefly suspected
As a terrorist attack – bullets fired and ejected;
When Le Monde got the truth 'just some boots that are retro',
They reported 'Scots tourist saves Gnome on the Metro!'

A total abstainer – He never took drink;
Didn't disapprove, He just didn't think
It was worth it: it didn't seem smart
To go out to get legless when you're there from the start!
An inveterate winner, He can't stand to lose
'A second best Papa' is not what He'd choose,
But they've already lost before any game starts,
He's poisoned their minds or programmed their hearts;
The mind games He plays are a treat to observe
You're already doomed well before the first serve.
But children or grand-kids, whoever He beats
Don't know how they lost "Do you think Papa cheats?"

Other skills? Well, for instance, there's Do It Yourself,
The suggestion was 'Dad, leave the tools on the shelf!'
Example, one Christmas Wee Helen, poor soul,
Planned the tree should be set in her fine China bowl.
Our Iain, determined a steady tree mattered,
Packed in wedge after wedge, till the final wedge shattered
This fine China bowl, that Helen held dear;
The tree was abandoned – they had FIREWORKS that year!
Sartorial elegance, of course, is His passion;
Though, sometimes, His favourites outlive the fashion!
A bri-nylon shirt, once, became His obsession,
All attempts to replace it – repulsed with aggression,
As bri-nylon does, it looked aged and done,
His persistence in sporting it – no longer fun.
For the family, embarrassed; while guests pursed their lips!
The shirt suddenly, mysteriously got cut into strips –
But replaced in his wardrobe to say, "This is the end!",
Iain thought bri-nylon shredded must be a new trend!
He wore it at dinner, in silence, for fun,
Then "OK, it's going. I give up, you've won!"
But what do His kids really think of their Dad?
Everything good – not one thing that's bad;
Dependable – someone you know will be there,
Always around when you're burdened with care!
Indestructible, solid – an anchor, their rock,
(Though a pain in the bum when he's spinning the talk!)
They love His resilience; support that won't bend:
If they had a choice, they'd choose Him as a friend!
They think He's a hero – John Wayne, six foot four!
John Wayne? Despite a bahoochy, quite close to the floor!

So, sainthood eludes Him – despite His credentials
To my mind He practices all the essentials
Son, brother and husband, all magically played.
(Seems you can't be a saint until after you're dead)
He's a pretty free spirit – not bound by constraints
(Not sure if such freedom's accorded to saints)

The Samaritan; good guy – a true friend to all:
Lift's you up! Even better, makes sure you don't fall!
So, sainthood evades Him, this man without sin;
Well, the guy on the gate might not let Him in!
He's not sure about Peter, the saint with the keys,
And He wonders who Paul wrote his letters to please!
His favourite Saint is the gentle Saint Francis,
"Well, he's just like myself, it's the birds that he fancies!"
And He must have paid heed to yon John, who revealed.
We had to keep Nick in a box that was sealed!
For Iain has shown that His Faith has an answer;
He's faced down. contained. the Great Satan that's Cancer!

Suffer the Children to come unto me
Is the maxim He lives by, and nurtures all three
Of His grand-kids – but still has regrets
That He could not save four, and He never forgets;
A day doesn't pass, but He sheds a wee tear
For the wee lass He misses-who is no longer here!
He shares in their interests – gives time and affection
To each – equal measure: no pets, no rejection.
Just as Lesley and Alistair thought Dad was great,
Grant, Kirsty and Fraser think Papa, their Mate!
Three more star parts, He can add to His score,
Good Dad, Good Samaritan, Papa – what more
Could anyone ask of this very fine man?
Yet, beatification has slipped down the pan!
But, God is still gracious to Rosie's wee son,
He'll keep Him around, till more good work gets done!
Bill Shakespeare's 'Seven Stages', well He's only at six,
Ere sainthood's considered He's got a few tricks
Up his sleeve; now at four score, He'll take stock, and then
He'll set a new course to reach four score and ten!
Oor Rabbie's mair like it – tho' his words may be quaint,
"Ye dinnae need bishops tae cry ye a saint"
"For a' that, an a' that a Man can be seen"
"As a 'Saints Alive' man" Is that just not Iain?

He's guided His family, He's shown them 'The Way'
He's honest, determined 'The Truth' must not stray,
He leads a good 'Life', you'll wait ages to meet a
Better follower of J C's 'VIA VERITAS VITA'.

# Saint. Andrew's Day 2017

This day, in late November, we're here to celebrate
The Patron Saint of Scotland, whose brother guards the gate
Yet, Andrew was the 'first called', our man the first Apostle –
But Simon pulled 'big brother' rank, and gave our man a jostle
Claimed Simon means "He hears God", but Simon didn't really listen,
He couldn't stand being second best – the runner up position.
"I'll be the boss's right hand man, not second to a Jock"
So he changed his name to Peter, for Peter means 'The Rock'!
"I'll build from this foundation – give loyalty a trial"
But his patience reached its limit when he made that third denial!
Then Pilate launched his hostile bid – things couldn't be much neater;
Removed the chairman from the board – and gave the chair to Peter!

The destiny of Scotsmen – 'Avoid this glory game',
Don't grab the keys to take control, don't seek the Gateman's fame
Andrew, the word means 'manly, brave'…a modest man, but caring,
He wouldn't lock up Paradise, his passion is for sharing.
This Patron Saint of Scotland, in Fife – but not elusive,
He's shared with others round the world, not ours alone – exclusive!
Russia, Georgia, Sicily, Greece, Ukraine and many more
See Andrew as their Patron Saint; and, when your throat is sore,
Like Strepsils, he can cure it, and fever – ward it off!
Extremely efficacious if you suffer whooping cough!
Fishermen and mongers, working folk of every nation
Enjoy 'The Man's' protection; he's their guide and inspiration.

East Neuk of Fife his resting place, that's where we laid him down,
Well, the three wee bits of bone we got are in St Andrews town.
A gracious man – did not resent Pete sitting near the
In fact Pete's lust for glory didn't make St Andrew cross!

But, like 'Nemo Me Impune' closely followed by 'Lacessit'
He'd respond just like the Thistle, he-liked it's style; God Bless It!
He'd keep his eye on Peter when they all sat down to eat,
For Peter always jumped the queue and grabbed the closest seat
To where was placed the trifle, the thing he liked the best;
For Peter thought it was his right to scoff more than the rest!
Our Fifer, now reposing, beneath St Andrew's toon,
He'd target Peter's pudding with his long Apostle spoon.


This Patron Saint of Scotland, he set a grand example,
Don't seek control, or shut folk out, or empire build. or trample
Your way above the hoi polloi (a Greek word, just like Andrew);
Treat all with Andrew's tolerance, though some won't understand you.
Just bide your time, no violence, no need for execution;
The world is slowly learning, we'll soon have retribution.
But take your lead from Andrew, don't bully or provoke
Or argue with the stupid man who thinks the Scots a joke.
Patience is a virtue, when you know that you're the best,
For we've survived oppression much longer than rest!
No need to turn the other cheek, or boast that you're a winner;
Just use your big long Fifer's spoon and steal the bugger's dinner!

The toast is

Saint Andrew of Scotland – The First Called

# TO A MELROSE

*(on the occasion of a Crichton turning over his supper with a fork)*

Poor wee sober, abst'nent Iain
How'd we never see ye fleein?
That's a sight that's off-times missed
The chance to see Wee Melrose pissed!
From boyhood when ye turned fae drink
An' pushed yer brain taie a'ways think.
O' thoughts profound; like clawin' tatties fae the ground
An' mak them ready, clean fur sellin'
Or, how tae woo yer Darlin' Helen!
Those Irish eyes, those ruby lips!
(Could she turn tatties into chips?)
Of course she could! For Melrose was her chosen man,
An' pittin tatties in a pan was child's play
For Helen; dependin oan her mood
Could magic ony kind of food
Like turnin' watter intae wine
She'd outdae any maid or quine preparin' spuds;
With haste; to tempt the maist discerning buds of taste!
She coined the classic 'double dip'
Creatin' the maist perfect chip!

She blanched them first – this wee lass Flannigan
Then popped them back, intae the pan again.
Producing chips, so crisp and dry!
A tear dreeped frae the Melrose eye;
'Tae hell wi' Troy and Grecian ships
Wee Helen launched a thoosand chips
Perfect! Not a hint of blunder!

Pink, or Rooster – Golden Wonder!
An Iain – Dry! Nae drink tae celebrate!
But loved his chips, an' couldnae wait,
Tae mark this dish. Commemorate!
"Ah ken! We'll dae a Burns
An' tak it each, in turns – tae laud this feast, prepared uniquely.
No wance a year, we'll haud a supper weekly!
'Nae champit neeps, nae tatties bashed
Nae sonsy face – a' stabbed an' slashed
Nae poems reverin' Rabbie's dish
'We'll grace oor chips we' tasty fish!'
We'll keep oor suppers, nice an' tidy
An' haud them weekly, oan a Friday!
The suppers? Kirrie's best – from Oot 'The Steeple'
Tae share wi' friends, our 'Chosen People.'

A Loon, a Buddy will be just Dandy! Our Quorum.
Helen, Issy, Iain an' Sandy!

# The Handover

*Dave gave a wave*
*Said, "Theresa, be brave!"*
*"I'm leaving, and wish you no malice"*
*"Don't think me a knob"*
*"For this goes with the job!"*
*As he passed her a big poisoned chalice!*

70

# The World of the News

Brexit? Low key! And millions still flee,
From oppression and famine. Unholy!
In the lands of 'The Saviour' There's shocking behaviour!
Trump and Kim? Both away with the goalie!
What once held 'Front Page', But now, at this stage,
(When Capetown has run out of water) Worldwide, hocus pocus! But now
    all the focus,
A recovering spy, and his daughter!

We do wish them well,
(While the World's going to Hell!)
And, we're glad that they're not going to die!
But, when you deceive two masters, believe,
Being paid twice. things might go awry!
I've no time for Putin – he's sticking the boot in!
Doing it here and not there? Clear – so abundant!
But, sooner or later, the fate of a 'traitor'
Superfluous to requirement; redundant!

Summary execution; eye for eye retribution.
What a mess! Now the whole World's involved.
So. get over there, Boris, Sort this incident for us,
Don't come home 'til you get it resolved!
Though Putin's just wee. he could start World War three,
And this one could be Armageddon.
So, yes, be emphatic; but be diplomatic:
Make sure you've your sensible head on!

71

# The Russian Agent

Russia, now, is in the dock, They made the deadly 'novochoc'!
Now that, itself, is not the scandal,
But, spread it on a spy door handle
In Russia, maybe, just the ticket!
But England! WeII, its just not cricket!

# Putin, Boris and Sergei

**7ᵗʰ April 2018**

Putin said to Boris
"Come over for a chat,"
"We can talk about nerve agents,"
"And sanctions; this and that!"
"Sergei's getting better, so" "Come over, for a blether,"
"Before I send you lots of snow – More debilitating weather!"

# Strategy, Tactics;
# Brilliant!

**24<sup>th</sup> April 2018**

Oh Kim, I'm impressed!
Who on Earth would have guessed,
You would prove such a shrewd operator?
You had our attention,
Stirred up World tension;
'A war would come, sooner or later!'
Some neighbours were scared
As Donald prepared
His rockets for annihilation!
Then you changed your song,
Said "You've got me all wrong!"
"I just want to have conversation!"

Big Don will claim,
That he ran the game,
And bluffed you to throw in your hand.
But, that would be poker,
There isn't a joker –
Gin Rummy? Too obvious, bland!
Your strategy, chess? Your tactics? Impress!
In fact, reading your game was quite hard!
But, brilliantly you
Delivered the coup,
By producing that hidden Trump card!

# America First

**April 2018**

America first, the leader said,
He really had it in his head
To prioritise the USA
When sending missiles on their way.

America first, the leader spoke,
"Wee Rocket man is just a joke!"
"I'll show him that I'm different class"
"I'll stick a rocket up his ass!"

# Dirleton Hogmanay

Dirleton Arms was the venue this year
For the Melroses and Crichtons to dress in guid gear,
And hie to East Lothian, "before Hogmanay,
To dance out the 'auld year' and greet New Year Day.
The men, both in kilts – tweed jackets from Harris –
The ladies in gowns, sent from T.K.Maxx, Paris!

The dinner was sumptuous, the guest list eclectic;
Then, ready for dancing, the air was electric.
Smart, Iain decided, perhaps for the best,
He'd have a wee seat-let his dinner digest.
But Sandy was up, for the wildest of dances;
His 'eightsome' and 'sergeant' drew appreciative glances.
The piper, impressed, upped the tempo of skirling,
And Sandy responded, his birling and twirling
Becoming more 'frantic as he timed with the skirl,
His kilt twirling higher with each frantic birl!
'Til Iain, engrossed, as the action got quicker,
Thought he detected – a wee flash of knicker!
He slumped in his seat (so better to view)
     Sandy's claim of 'true Scotsman', as the kilt upwards flew.
     Had this been 'Come Dancing' – Sandy's score, breaching nine
     With his kilt in full flight. there was clear panty line!
This rev'lation came at the end of the dance,
Opportunity sought; gave Iain the chance:
To score one, on Sandy, denouncing the 'fraud;
He cried "You're a phoney! You swore, "before God"
"That nothing was worn 'neath your kilt or your sporran!"
The response, cool, assured, "No, nothing is worn!"
"The condition as good as the day I was born!"

Ere further exchange, there was help, on her feet
With alacrity, Isabel rose out her seat
Her attack. from defence. took Iain by surprise,
He was further confused, as the speed of her rise
Sometimes preceded a withering look,
To bring Sandy to heel with a short, sharp rebuke!
But, no rebuke here – support to the hilt,
She insisted her man checked the length of his kilt;
But, the hem on the knee – the appropriate height –
Meant that not just his skien dhu was clearly in sight.
"My Sandys all man, but what can a man do?"
"One cant do a reel, in a kilt, dressed Commando!"
"I'm proud of my Sandy – and right to be proud"
"But, I insisted, discretion, 'Wrap your bits in a shroud!'"
"So, when he declared that 'Nothing is worn'"
"He didn't mean scuddy clad under his sporran"
"As any true Scotsman, Cape Wrath to the Border,"
"He meant all his bits are in good working order!"

# Happy New Year (2019)

**19<sup>th</sup> February 2019**

*Hi Iain,*

It is three o'clock in the morning and I can't sleep!
I've had a cup of tea and a biscuit, tried to do a crossword, but nothing is working; I've tried to concentrate on what it is that I am not specifically 'concentrating' on......my kids?, cash flow?, my health?...the mess the World is in? Nothing clicks, particularly!

Three o'clock.................I know – the witching hour! Somebody once told me "Your head's full of wee doors, and they are all banging!" Well, they are all banging tonight.

I want to sleep, to rest – but I can't. I am in the middle of a battlefield; my kids, and other units of the Pals' Battalion are somewhere off to the right. They are giving a good account of themselves! They are OK! But, you and me in our wee slit trench have taken a bit of a pounding from a mortar that almost had us totally pinpointed. Not pleasant, but we are still here!

And, through the dust and the smoke and the fear I hear wee snatches of poetry – not my McGonagalese verse – other people's classic, established poetry; just snatches, like 'fill each minute with sixty seconds of distance run! Or the one you Surprised me with by saying you had never heard of it......Vitai Lampada, by Sir Henry Newbolt..."There's a breathless hush in the close tonight, ten to make and a match to win!" Can't remember it all off-hand, and the accuracy isn't urgent enough for me to go and Google it, but the next verse goes;

> "The sand of the desert is sodden red,"
> "Red with the wreck of a square that broke!"
> "The Gatling's jammed, and the Colonel dead,"

"The Regiment blind, with dust and smoke!"
"The river of death bas brimmed its banks,"
"And England far, and Honour a name."
"But the voice of a schoolboy rallies the ranks,"
"Play up! play up! And play the game!"…

And I think about you and me in our slit trench; two old soldiers, wondering what it is all about, and wondering if it is worthwhile reloading and fixing bayonets to go another sixty seconds of distance run.

Then I think, "Yes it is!" Nobody told us to be tired or dispirited, and nobody told us it was all going to be a cakewalk! Just the mortar frightened the crap out of us for a wee while!

Now, at this stage I should be trying to produce a little sermon about running the sixty second distance at the more sedate pace our age deserves, instead of trying to compete and outrun everyone else who is the age that we were when we were justifiably and successfully competitive! Then I thought you might be entertained by the account (nearly 40 years ago!) in the Sunday Times, by one of the Royal Marines who garrisoned the Port Stanley residency at the time of the Argentine invasion.

"There were just the ten of us; we spread out in the ditch behind the perimeter hedge, facing up the road, and watched as an armoured car with a heavy machine gun led, what seemed like five hundred infantrymen towards us. The armoured car stopped about one hundred and fifty yards from us with the infantrymen bunched close behind, but spread across the road and into the fields on either side. Our whole line of vision seemed filled with Argentinian soldiers spoiling for a fight!

Despite the size of this 'army' confronting us there was no noise beyond the low rumbling idle of the armoured vehicle; this seemed only to accentuate the background silence and elevate the oppressive tension to screaming pitch!"

"I was scared shitless!"

"A captain moved forward from the massed ranks, accompanied by a corporal carrying a white truce flag tied to his assault rifle. They approached to just fifty yards ahead of us, and stopped. The captain placed his hands on his hips and started to address the general direction of the hedge."

"British soldiers, we intend you no harm. Lay down your weapons and surrender! You will be well treated!"

"There was an interminable silence – the Argentinian captain staring intently at the hedge, obviously desperate to see a white flag acknowledging his surrender offer. Not a sound from the warlike five hundred, and the armoured vehicle idling, with the low, patient rumble emphasising the silence and exaggerating, to massacre level, the feeling of hostility that seemed to be pressing on the hedge. The captain shifted his feet, returned his hands to his hips and cleared his throat"

"British soldiers"

"Fuck off, ya Argie bastard!" Jock Macdonald's Glasgow accent rang out!

"Just us ten against five hundred and an armoured vehicle – and Jock Macdonald picks a fight!"

'1 had a fit of the giggles!"

…Talk to you soon

Your loving pal

*Ed*

**4ᵗʰ April 2019**

# Dear Iain

I have no idea where this is going; but to paraphrase Magnus Magnusson, 'I have started, so I will continue!'

We are in Aberdeen, in late February, for this week's Thursday jaunt and I thought of you. Actually I thought of you before we left, and during the journey – and felt an urge to communicate. In fact, the urge was so vivid and insistent that I dashed off a letter, in my mind, with that kind of mental shorthand that might produce a best seller, if only one could translate the fluency and clarity of the mental vision, endowed on the self-believing 'enlightened', into the credible and convincing narrative that would be, at least, acceptable to an informed or questioning reader.

Well. true to precedent, now that I am comfortably ensconced and "private' in the Union Square Costa Coffee, the fluency and clarity have deserted me and I am left with that little bit of self doubt that the narrative might end up as a couple of pages of shite! (Sort of reminds me of the verse one could often read scribbled on the inside of the W.C. door in Glasgow public loos…'Here sit I broken hearted, paid a penny and only farted!')

My only consolation is that, at an early stage in your life, you must have been obliged to listen to some incredible shite and, for a time, found it convincing without any opportunity to question the concept or evaluate the philosophy of the 'teaching'.

I know, from previous submissions, that you find 'my shite', at least, tolerable because the spelling and punctuation meet a reasonable standard; enough to sustain your attention long enough to stimulate interest or provoke argument. At worst, unlike the Glasgow crapper, you won't be disappointed with the anti-climax of no more than a discharge of hot air!

Anyway, I have been thinking about you and your situation, and I thought 'where do we go from here?'

Sitting about waiting for somebody else to make your decisions is far too passive for Iain Melrose. And sitting about waiting for God is far too inactive for a determined guy who has competed and won against T.B., or Sandy Crichton at golf, Angela Smith at badminton, Grant Farquharson at ping pong………and held the Big C at bay for the past fifteen, or so, years!

And you may say,"Fine for you to say! What gives you the right and authority to consider where, or how, I should go from here?"

And, for sure, I have to reply, "Nothing, my Dear Friend gives me the right to tell you anything! But, authority is different......it's my letter, and I can commit to paper whatever shite comes into my mind!"

(The following is added in the same venue at a subsequent Aberdeen visit during March; shows you how compelling and persistent are my thoughts on Melrose!)

I have often thought that you and I were, pretty much, on a similar wavelength as far as belief is concerned. I say 'pretty much' because each of us, to some extent, is conditioned by our 'taught' interpretation of Christianity indoctrinated into both of us at an early age, by one supposed faith viewed and believed from two, possibly opposite, perspectives.

I am not convinced that this faith evolved naturally from an inner feeling, or bottom up foundation and was created, or manufactured, to suit somebody's lust for power and 'we', the target faithful, simply accepted and trusted that we were being honestly guided; indoctrinated in the 'rules' and 'theology' of the first people who had the foresight to write down the view and rules of 'God' which best suited their need to exercise power!

In other words, the victors, as such, didn't write history; the first people who had the vision and the communication skills to create a (sort of) contract which bound the world to their view of God became the effective 'long term' victors......"in the beginning was the word", and the word was – whatever they wanted it to be! And whoever invented, or controlled the word...communication...created their God who provided the power to control the World. (Not to be confused with dominated: unnoticed, behind the scenes the controllers are more powerful than the dominators).

## April 2019

Like, fast forward to 2019 – whoever controls the internet controls the 'word' by which the dominators try to influence and manipulate world events. In other words, Trump and Kim Jong Un can eyeball each other and threaten nuclear strikes – but a good hacker could disable their nuclear power and the flick of a communication switch could neutralise their combined propaganda.

(Or paradoxically, and newsworthy, a bad 'program' could render 300 brand new jetliners useless!)

As it also could with the propaganda of Islam, The General Assembly of the Church of Scotland, Rome and Henry VIII's convenient subsidary.

And, of course, there is Judaism... Brilliant! The mouse that roared! Before and during the thousands of years when Roman and Greek religious history was sidelined and dismissed as mythology, or archived as pre-history, the Old Testament is presented as the 'believed' history with one true God (Moses' secret pal up the hill) who was communicated into our programmable young minds before we really knew how to think!

...And then, the tenuous link to a real person – the late J.C. – who was effecting real change, and whose message of hope was travelling more quickly than the existing spiritual controllers could cope with. So, J C had to be not silenced not imprisoned...miraculously set free through death and resurrection, and kept alive by the dominators and controllers who exercise their power through the Word.

Except the message of hope has stayed alive, and persisted somehow, even though the Word, as dispensed by the controllers and dominators, has become corrupted.

Hope is why Father Neil, Angela Smith, Monica from Columbia, me and You went to the Old Parish Church to help Diarmid Whatsisname try to find God.

We are still looking – and we can come back to that

Anyway, how are you today? Still breathing in and out, still with the firm handshake, still with the jokes? Still with the Hope? Good!

You know, we are still within our five year plan – remember?

I think the notional target was that we review our progress with 20/20 vision at the end of five years, and that would be, I think, next April.

So, maybe the plan needs a wee late term review to take account of the change of weather; a wee course adjustment to overcome the adverse current, and keep us on track! We can do it.

You know Iain we have been in our wee slit trench for a while now – maybe getting too used to it. And any way, it is not big enough to accommodate all the reinforcements that are arriving to support us with fresh energy, fresh hope. I told you before, you are not alone. In fact, you are so blessed and rich in your 'not alone-ness!'

I hope you are still prepared to read my stuff – some of it is way out......
burned at the stake, stuff!

But you have encouraged me greatly in the past seven years; directing, sometimes unwittingly, my search for information to facts which I consider most significant – and wonder why these 'facts' have been disregarded, suppressed or diluted to obscurity. A negative polarity in control, perhaps? I still have an ambitious hope that we can make a difference, we are not here simply to serve our term, and go. As I said, some of my stuff is way out, but I intend to share it with you anyway over the next twelve months

Maybe next April (Easter would be a good target date) we can surprise Diarmuid O'Whatsisname with the God he can't find, and give him a souvenir of three long, rusty Roman nails!

If you are prepared to entertain a wee soupçon of enlightened heresy I will see you soon

Bear in mind, my heresy is the way, the truth and the life that clerics can't understand or cope with!

With much love

Your friend

*Ed*

# Diarmuid's Quest for Hope continued

**Sunday 7<sup>th</sup> April 2019**

Hi Iain,

Good to talk with you yesterday; it's three o'clock in the morning and, as Crystal Gale sang, 'it looks like it's gonna be another sleepless night!'

However, I was sorry to hear that you were having a 'less than good day!' It would be good if a wee miracle could just turn up at the moment.

I sometimes wonder if miracles are scheduled by the old Glasgow Corporation Transport – you wait for ages for a miracle, and just when hope is fading three turn up at the same time, and, like Milton's Paradise Regained, hope is restored. And with any luck the driver of the first miracle will be the Blessed John Ogilvy.(I know he is a saint now, but I liked him better when he was simply 'blessed' – he was still one of us then and hadn't been dehumanised by elevation to the peerage!

"– Anyway, as is my unfortunate habit, I digress; I digress a lot, then I forget where I was going in the first place. Mind you, I think the whole of civilisation has done that, sort of forgotten the route and got lost somewhere; struggling about in the dark!

You know, sometimes when I am in a pitch black situation, like walking into a blacked out room, hoping for a chink of light, I realise that I have shut my eyes and wouldn't see the light anyway; more afraid than I need to be because I am relying on touch to feel for the wall, and memory to move my hand to where I think the light switch should be. Maybe if I could have the presence of mind, or is it faith, to think rationally I could look backwards and there might be a faint glow from the doorway where I entered the darkness, and I would get some sense of position and reassurance – but I would need to have my eyes wide open for that, of course.

I know that this is a bit of a meander (is that a bit euphemistic?) –

perhaps the 'ramblings of a slightly deranged mind!'. This is why I write things down, so that both of us, communicator and communicatee, have a reference point to return to and check where the meander started and recheck the direction it might be heading. Too often my oratory or rhetoric has been deflated by a frustrated, "oh for fuck's sake Ed, you lost me somewhere back at the light switch!"

The point is, we have to be able to look back to the start point or, at least, to the position where we set this particular course, to see where we went wrong. Now, again I digress; they say that in a Pub you should avoid discussing religion, politics and football. As Bill Shankly famously put it

"Some people think football is a matter of life and death, but it is not. It is more important than that!"

So, avoiding football, and politics for the moment, let us stick with what is commonly or collectively referred to as religion. Politics and football are important, but they are obstacles or adverse winds and currents which affect the progress of the journey, but they are not the starting point. That begins with 'religion'.

Even the word 'religion' is a confusion – because that smacks of 'organisation' which is corruptible, and 'control' which suppresses freedom of thought. Faith is perhaps the word – not 'a faith' – just faith! Faith is, perhaps, the key or start point.

But, going back to the beginning isn't easy, and it doesn't matter for this particular exercise; we know that we (civilisation) have completed many stages on our journey, presumably successfully if not always comfortably; but on a world platform, things are not going well at the moment. Like disastrously not well! (A wee bit like the story I told you of my experience on 'Caledonia' when we were in danger of running aground on the Arabian Peninsula.) Funny how much of the world's problems seem to circulate around the Arabian Peninsula!

Two thousand years ago we immobilised the Captain – and then got ourselves lost! And now, having sidelined Him for so long, we really need Him to take charge and overcome what negative current or human error or instrument failure pushed us into this disastrous position.

Anyway, have I digressed too much? I have this big bag of information. Some of it just bits and pieces, but all of it potentially useful and adaptable to repair some old 'heresies' that need to be re-examined and restored. Many of those bits and pieces you helped me find or, in fact, directed me to.

I really don't know much about the Freemasons or The Knights Templar, but I like the philosophy of the twin pillars supporting the opening to some kind of enlightenment; even a pair of octogenarian pillars, like us, could create an effective opening long enough to let the light in!

'—Remember I told you that Iain, the word Iain, means 'God is Gracious'. Edward – the word – means 'Lord Protector' or 'Proud Guard'.

Neither of us is going to last forever, but I think we still have something to contribute in the midst of this terrible darkness. A Gracious God and a Lord Protector, what a pair of substantial pillars we could provide. Maybe we just need to open our eyes and locate the light switch.

You know, Iain, I don't need the celebrity of convincing the whole world. Like my experience on 'Caledonia' in 1960 I need only convince one man to turn the ship from impending disaster towards open water. At this moment in time you are that man!

Diarmuid O'Murchu.........that's his name; how about that! Memory, like Paradise and Hope is regained......'Dementia, where is thy sting?.'

I'll be in touch

With much love

Your friend

*Ed*

**12ᵗʰ April 2019**

# My Dear Iain

Here we are, me again with more outrageous thoughts.........more heresy; more similes and metaphors from our past, some current events and, of course hope: always hope!

But, it is me! 'The little plump Glasgow one; so I have to be realistic, there will be digression! In fact, so much seems to be happening or changing, or maybe just starting at the moment that trying to review it all, in the space of one letter may create digression, upon digression after digression. So much so that you may need great patience to pick your way through a great big fankle.

'D' is for digression – maybe the 'D' of my middle name is not Donald after all!

Anyway, here we are. Tonight {Wednesday) it is not even 3 o'clock in the morning – only 1 a.m. and I am wide awake with the proverbial 'head full of wee doors that are all banging!'

I thought I might compose myself with a wee cup of tea and a biscuit, an oatcake, actually; but a crumb of oatcake went down the wrong way and I have spent the last ten minutes trying to cough quietly, to avoid waking the neighbours and trying to dislodge this perfectly innocent, yet offensive crumb from my windpipe.

Funny how perfectly innocent things or events can occur, and somehow conspire to frustrate a being and divert or discourage him from the fairly innocuous, ordinary task of writing a letter to a pal. As if some underground destructive covert operation was in place to prevent, or intercept some secret coded message before its content could influence the course of some (hidden) conflict.

Oh yes, the crumb! Taken a few minutes the wee oatcake crumb has either dislodged. or dissolved, but has done its job of diversion, fairly well......I can't remember where I was going; Edward Digression Wilson, sure enough!

I'll start with Diarmuid O'Murchu – at least he is trying to find an answer, or, more significantly, he is asking the question. But whatever, I'll say his name again – Diarmuid O'Murchu – because it proves that my memory is functioning and provides a point of focus.

His quest for an answer caused me to reflect on my days as Third Navigating Officer on 'Cilicia' and 'Caledonia' – particularly when we had to take sun sights, or star sights to work out the ship's position. We always started out with a dead reckoning position, 'DR', the place where we thought the ship should be, by course and distance measured from the last known accurate position. The sun or star sight. taken at an exact time, related to the predictable and precise position, not of the ship, but of the sun/star, and gave a value in nautical miles.

This value was not 'the position' but was an error value showing how near or far your DR, estimated position, was from the accurate position of the heavenly body were it to be on the Earth's surface at that precise time.

A whole page of calculation, reference to Norrie's navigation tables, GMT by chronometer, sextant angles…and you ended up with a value like, say, '5 away' which meant your DR position was 5 miles away from the fixed point you had calculated, accurately, the sun to be at that time.

I hope I have explained that properly because the 'opposite of the obvious" is at play in Diarmuid's search. In the nautical example we know the exact position of the sun or star at every second of time because somebody has already worked these out and recorded these positions in Norrie's Tables. Navigation methods will have moved on, in the last sixty years, and technology – computers – will have made the calculation process quicker; but it may also have made us more 'isolated' and more dependent on improved terrestrial information – we can do it without the sun and the stars……as long as the radar and radio beams and sounding machines, technology, continue to function reliably and efficiently. We have the technology – we can function without the 'heavenly bodies'………until something fails!

In my nautical example what we were trying to determine was the exact position of the ship (that's us, the 'lost' entity) in relation to the 'heavenly body', the sun at the centre of our solar system, or a star, farther away, in the universe; the fixed reliable, in the same position every day since the beginning of time heavenly body!

What Diarmuid was trying to do was find God – elusive, presumably moving about the universe – in relation to us, the lost entity but which he, Diarmuid, presented as the 'fixed point' dependable,

'Know where we are, in control of our own destiny fixed point! See?

The opposite of the obvious! God is not some wee spaceman out there wandering the cosmos. Remember Diarmuid's little sketches that showed a wee dot, somewhere outside a square or a circle… God, the movable object, small and remote beyond the reach or boundaries of the circle or square representing the earth or the universe. Our Dead Reckoning position wasn't even credible or realistic – we appeared as the reliable fixed position with the heavenly body, seemingly 'lost', somewhere in the Universe.

The opposite of the obvious!

I don't mean to denigrate Diarmuid's efforts in any way; they were, are very useful in showing how far we are from the DR position which, at least tells us where we 'are not', and gives us a chance to work out what got us to this lost position, and plan a course to get us back to where we should be.

This little navigation analysis moved me to re-examine other 'positions' – like the start of the journey, to see what winds and currents, or unreliable equipment, bad navigation or 'arrogance' has got us, mankind, into such a lost position. As everyone keeps saying 'lessons will be learned' or we must learn from history, and not repeat or ignore the mistakes of the past!'

I chose, as a start "God made Man in His image!" Opposite of the obvious again, I'm afraid. Considering that in 2019 we are still looking for God, then clearly we don't know how to recognise Him. Instead of looking for one of Eric von Daneken's spacemen, who presumably looks like us, we should be considering the immensity, the timeless endlessness of the universe, which is rumoured to be still expanding, and realise that the God who created, and operates on that scale is not a wee punter in a Martian spacesuit waiting to be discovered on a flip-chart in the Old Parish Church tucked behind The Steeple chippy!

The ever resourceful Romans had just the word 'Ubique!'

Either open your eyes in the dark, and look back to the faint glow from the doorway………or flick the switch, and let the light in and look ubique to find the Faith that provides the Hope; God is everywhere!

That's enough of Diarmuid for one night – a lot of other interesting things have been happening.

You have had a message from the Oncology Department that they have arranged to address your kidney stone issue; that is a positive step which, at least, will reduce some of the discomfort you have been experiencing. And you had a visit from the McMillan nurse – I'm not convinced we are quite there yet, but insurance is never wasted – you can tell me about that when we next meet. Also, I believe, you had your carpets cleaned; that certainly is a preparation for a bright future! Anyway, you like a challenge and there is a subtle message of Hope lurking in there......the hope that you don't trail grass cuttings in next time you trim the lawn, or castration may be added to the list of tribulations you currently have to endure.

And me? I have news from America. My son is still pursuing his ambition to devote his time and expertise to fighting or, at least, standing up to cancer. He has interviews currently with the Colorectal Cancer Alliance for a marketing directorship in the organisation; means leaving his current job with a drop in income – but he seems to be looking on this as a vocation, and is prepared for some sacrifice. Only at the interview stage.........but even his considering the change, I felt, had a resolution of hope somewhere at its heart. I think they would be mad not to grab him. I will keep you in the loop, on this one.

In between the writing and the typing you and I have spoken – so you know my thoughts and best wishes are with you for Perth, on Monday; together, of course, with an armoury of Weegie Proddy 'prayers – they really are of quite good quality.

Real middle of the night stuff now.........well past Three O'clock in the Morning and Crystal Gayle has long since lost interest.

Just because we have been talking about God and resolving to learn from history, and me and my boy and hope and whatever digression I wandered off on, I thought I might stick in a wee true story that incorporates some of those factors.

In 1973/74, when Scott would be about six years old, we were holidaying on Great Cumbrae, in a fine holiday flat, in the centre of Millport, which we rented each July from friends in Glasgow. The flat had a tiny, rigid plastic dinghy which we were allowed to use, and we took it round to Kames Bay where Scott played happily in it, safely, at the water's edge. The little boat had no rowlocks, or crutches, and only one oar but Scott was quite happy pushing it about in the shallow water.

It was a lovely warm day, sun shining, the Firth of Clyde looking magnificent; one of those rare summer days when you could have believed that Scotland, this Scotland, was the real promised land. Everything was very relaxed; I had been keeping an eye on Scott – just watchful, nothing too overly protective, but decided to go for some ice cream, for us all, and asked my wife, Joyce, to take over the casual 'watch duties'.

Fetching the pokey hats took longer than I had expected, and when I returned the mood, somehow, had changed; Scott's sister, Lindsey was alone, by our towels building sandcastles: Joyce was down at the water's edge looking concerned and the little dinghy was thirty or forty feet out from the beach, with Scott unsuccessfully trying to manoeuvre it shore-wards with the single oar.

There was no panic, no crisis and no drama; I would simply wade out and tow the boat to safety.

However, the boat seemed to be drifting slowly seaward at about the same rate as my progress, wading through the deepening water – the boat wasn't being driven away particularly obviously, but the distance between me and the boat was not closing. It dawned on me that the tide had turned and, although the sea was calm with very little wind – light airs really, it seemed that however gentle the breeze might be, it also had changed direction and was assisting the ebb tide to ease the tiny boat further from the beach, and always just beyond my reach!

I fleetingly thought how cruel it was, how perverse God was to intrude into this peaceful family outing, in such an idyllic setting in the promised land, by allowing the normality of the tide to conspire with the lightest of winds to concern and threaten the most innocent of His followers.

I was swimming, now; but hey, if Johnnie Weissmuller could outrun a native canoe, powered and propelled by six hefty looking African heavies, I could soon overtake a tiny boat drifting gently in calm water on a windless day at Millport! I kept swimming, calling encouragement to Scott, telling him not to panic (although he wasn't) and to stay seated as not to rock or overturn the boat.

I effected my best 'racing crawl' for what seemed a sustained burst, now a quarter mile out from Kames beach, but the boat with my precious son aboard stayed frustratingly and stubbornly some ten to fifteen feet ahead of me. I had closed the gap a little, but too little!

I was tiring a bit, but noticed that Kames Bay was shaped in a tight horseshoe formation, with the sandy beach located in the wide curve, and the open ends closing somewhat to form a sort of harbour entrance' with a small reef of rock on each side of the entrance to the cove. The direction 'of drift of the dinghy, with luck, should carry it towards the rocks, hopefully preventing it carry into the Firth of Clyde with the prospect of the next stop being Largs, or even Ailsa Craig!

The little boat held a steady course and slow drift towards the rocks on the left. Scott's mother, having found somebody to keep an eye on Lindsey, was clambering over the rocks in hopeful anticipation of the boat grounding. I encouraged Scott to paddle with the single oar and assist the direction of drift towards grounding and rescue.

Joyce recovered Scott with much relief ( remember, this was her surviving son of what should have been two sons.) and hurried him across the rocks to the safety of the Promenade running around the bay.

"Jane had whisked Boy off to the safety of the Treehouse while Me Tarzan, drained of Johnnie Weissmuller's Olympian swimming power, contemplated death by drowning; I had heard it could be quite peaceful, relaxing with your past life screening through your mind at a gentle pace. Somehow I couldn't get too enthusiastic about the still water of the Firth of Clyde carrying me gently to the green pastures on the far shore. My head seemed to have dipped below the surface of these still waters twice; was that two of my three submergings in the drowning process?

Something 'restored my soul!' I found some reserve of strength to keep treading water, and look around for options. The rocks at the water's edge seemed about fifty feel away. and the Promenade a further twenty or thirty feet across the rocks. There were people strolling on the Promenade oblivious to this tragic drowning that might be happening as they headed to Farquhar's Tavern for a late afternoon pint – or aperitif, possibly – this being a yachting haven! I considered calling for assistance.

It was still an idyllic afternoon, warm, relaxing; no crisis or drama now that the 'rescued child' with his mother, had departed the scene without anyone else being involved, or even aware of this little episode of tension. If they were aware at all, what they could see was a guy out for a late afternoon swim. Perfect! – if that's what he wants to do……but I'm looking forward to this pint!

How can one intrude, and burden people relaxing on their annual holiday – they have saved all year for such calm and relaxation and, this year the bonus of such transportment to the promised land.

"Hallooo, hallooo! Yes, you on the Prom; sorry to interrupt, but I may be drowning! Do you think you could try to locate a lifebuoy or something: I hate to be a bother, but quickly!"

How embarrassing! Not my style, or yours. We'd rather die quietly, or better still have one last charge at salvation……another sixty seconds worth of distance swum!

Nothing for it but to hold my nerve for another fifty feet – take it at a nice slow, undemanding breast stroke......when suddenly I stubbed my toe on a rock, Hallelujah! The rocks weren't sheer at the water's edge, but shelved in a long downward slope to the sea bed. Was I impressed with God? Not half!

Imagine having the foresight a million or so years ago, to create an eruption that would form a reef on the edge of Kames Bay to avert a tragic drowning in July 1974. Particularly after having organised a current to drift a wee boy onto the same reef to be reunited with bis mother.

Thought, this is not some wee dot of a spaceman out on the edge of a box or a circle waiting to be stumbled upon by folk who are lost! This is something or somebody who is all around, with safety measures all in place just waiting for the human spirit to kick out for one more go and find the rock floor is a lot closer than you had feared, or even believed!

So, there was faith and there was hope. The faith that a father could save his son and the hope that he could reach him; and the faith of a wee boy that his father stayed with him till he reached safety. The faith of a man that he had enough left in him to keep going and the hope that he could reach safety and the faith rewarded by an unseen hand bringing the sea bottom up to save him.

You know Iain, my dear friend, I am all for hope. We, you and l still have a lot to talk about! And, of course every story has to have a moral; my wee story of faith and hope is no exception: "If you are a shite swimmer don't wade out of your depth in Kames Bay"

See you soon,

With much love

Your friend

*Ed*

**Sunday 14th April 2019**

My Dear Iain

I haven't even got to sleep tonight; been in bed almost three hours and, after speaking with you earlier today the wee doors in my head are banging like the clappers!

'Another five years!, Greedy bugger you know, when I said miracles were scheduled by the old Glasgow Corporation Transport, 'wait for ages and then three arrive at the same time' – I didn't mean that I was E.R.L Fitzpayne and could actually direct the scheduling. Nor can I guarantee that the first miracle driven by John Ogilvy will turn up.

'Another five years!' Well, I tell you – if I could arrange that the interest payments would be hefty, Shylock's pound of flesh would be a pittance by comparison; the next two miracles would have to be driven by first Big George Young and the other by Eric Caldow – one transporting us to Scottish Independence and the other a Scotland Rugby World Cup win!

'Five bloody years?' I'm Ed Wilson, the Weegie not Harry Potter The Wizard'. Five years, I can't believe you had the gall to ask that. Mind you, with some of the heresies that I have stored up for you to consider, I suppose anything, nay, everything is possible! Although 'eternal life' might be pushing things beyond even J. K. Rowling's creative capabilities.

I don't know if it is the new position of my bed, reversed, now sleeping west to east instead of east to west, or the thought of you driving up to Mart Lane to tell the vicar "Heh heh, I'm not going at all, for another five years!" – but sleep certainly appears not to be on the agenda.

Just occurred to me that today is Palm Sunday, start of Holy Week; sure J.K. could make a story out of that: a sort of trial arranged for Friday, and… maybe not resurrection on Monday, but a healthy redirection might be just as miraculous, and eminently more believable.

Think about it! Maybe extending life by five years for two determined 82-year-olds is less miraculous than praying for Scottish Independence or Scotland winning the Rugby World Cup.

Be nice to be able to write like J.K. Rowling, though. She could possibly convince most people of anything……I mean. a boy wizard on a flying broomstick, defeating evil with the help of a fire-breathing dragon. and it's a world class best seller......bet she could magic up a convincing God in no time!

Funny how the Occult, the semi-occult, time travel and super-heroes are so acceptable, readable and entertaining seemingly almost believable, while the concept of a caring, benign God seems a lot less marketable nowadays; if we get to the end of another five years, I am going to pop into a 'phone box, don a pair of blue tights, a cape and a red T-shirt with a big gold 'G' on it, and fly you to the promised land of Upper Knightswood!

Five bloody years, I still can't believe it! We haven't got to the end of the last five year plan yet. But I suppose we really should be reviewing it and making adjustments for the changed, and changing conditions. Just like I would have done on a ship; having to apply a set and drift course correction to allow for the effect of wind and current: or altering course to avoid hazards or accommodate other ships who might enjoy precedence, right of way, in accordance with the 'Rule of the Road' regulations that we all had to abide by.

As I said before, I like the nautical example – it provides a very complete and concise model of how I see the world But I have to clarify something – similar to what I raised in the last 'chapter' – "Did I create a world format to resemble a functioning ship, because I was acquainted with ships or, is a ship modelled on a properly functioning world format?"

A ship carries passengers to a destination; they come on at the start of a voyage, enjoy the trip and get off at the end of the journey without having contributed to the management or functioning of this little world carrying them from a beginning, through to whichever port they have contracted to reach. Effectively they 'cruise through life', enjoying, or making the best of the journey with the minimum of effort. After all, they are simply passengers. On my ship, the passengers outnumbered the crew by almost three to one.

The crew, the functioning people on board, are not necessarily united as one big happy family of 'sailors'. You can, of course have a happy ship, with a happy crew; but the crew is divided into 'catering', the biggest department on a passenger ship, and 'Engine room', the people who make the machinery work, and 'Deck', the navigators and professional seamen who maintain the fabric of the vessel, keep it afloat and ensure it completes its journey safely, and on time.

The catering department, while providing an essential service in keeping the passengers happy, contribute nothing to the speed or direction of the ship. Consequently, in this little world of a ship, they have duties to perform, but little more influence on the 'world's' performance than the fun-seeking passengers. Like the real world, a lot of people get on at the start of the voyage, work to live, or simply cruise through life on board, and disembark at the end or the voyage.

When it comes to the deck and engine crews, each see themselves as essential and important, which they are, on a ship which needs reliable power and dependable navigation to undertake the voyage. They are almost equal in importance. Power is essential, but only the navigators can see where the ship is heading and give it direction. This 'almost' equality is recognised in the status accorded the respective department heads; both wear the four rings which equate to 'captain' rank. But the Chief Engineer has responsibility only for the engine and machinery function, whereas the Captain has accountability for the entire ship. There is only one Captain.

In respect of 'our World', for some reason, we seem to have demonised the Chief Engineer, despite the essential energy that the Captain needs to keep his ship world functioning. At best we are ignoring the Chief Engineer, and for some reason not giving him his 'almost' equal status, like twin pillars supporting a functioning doorway; or pick any example throughout history or mythology where the world appeared to function less smoothly or effectively after the balancing twin, the one with 'some' essential power was disposed of by the other.

This is not some enlightened, or half baked theory of mine alone – although I did come to it through my own reasoning. Only recently did I discover that the Bishop of Alexandria, Origen, in the second or third century posed the possibility of a sort of bi-polar God who united the spiritual and the corporate to create a complete supreme power. The Pope and the Church declared this a heresy. Why are they so reluctant to consider reasonable theory, or as Donald Trump might say, an alternative truth? Or Donald Rumsfeld's "Known truths, and unknown truths".

Seemed reasonably logical to me. Then I realised that 'logos' was the Greek for 'word', and if 'The Word' is the beginning of all things biblical why do we not examine apparently logical words?

Anyway, here we are working our way through Holy Week and you have a big day on Friday; can't wait for Monday when the 'Redirection of Melrose' will be accomplished.

## Wednesday 17<sup>th</sup> April 2019

Think I bit off a bit more than was chewable. there. Wee bit of a ramble, although I think you'll get the gist of it. Could have done with a wee bit of digression just to lighten it up.

Had a funny old week – an awful lot of wee innocent, well apparently innocent, occurrences that seemed to get in the way of a smooth passage; you know? The sort of 'sod's law things', as I say, innocent things that just seem to be moving against the direction or progress you plan to make. To paraphrase Denis Wheatley "If you are going to take on the occult, watch out for the loose floorboard!"

Some things went well. of course. Interviewed two prospective bar staff; one, who sounded a good prospect. The other seems great, so offered her the job and feel I have made a good decision; starts Sunday!

Anyway, I think I'll give you a break. Like once before. I had a load of inspirational thoughts and a brilliant script all drafted out in my head, but by the time I was ready to 'create', the flow had deserted me; can still remember the key points and the general drift, but the flow is essential.

## Thursday 18ᵗʰ April 2019

Had a good night's sleep – wakened feeling more, slightly more, inspirational; not quite inspired like J.K. Rowling, or imbued with her creativity – but when you are trying to stay true to the real, 'believed' world throwing in a handful of magic dust is not in the rules.

Trouble is, much of the truth has become......anything from tarnished to downright corrupt! And, of course, cynicism. distrust or greed has caused people to contract into their corporate, physical being, shutting out the spiritual strength that once kept their physiology in balance. The positive live wire of the circuit has become disconnected which means that only the negative power flow is available to create a circuit with the Earth.

People want to believe, and go through the motions of the disciplines of religions which appear to represent what substitute for faith; but you need to reconnect the positive wire, flick the switch, or get a jump start to re-kindle the faith with hope!

You know, Iain – one of my half-baked theories is that history keeps repeating itself, with little parallel stories, repeats or remakes of the originals, which perhaps were not perfect, anyway. So, we rework it, and each director brings a new interpretation in the hope of improving and giving a fresh translation of the original work.

Now, the problem that I see with the Crucifixion story is that the author did not intend that this should have an unhappy ending; but, the director's interpretation was that it should have a miraculous ending – miracles being fashionable in writings of the time. So he modified the script to create a sense of tragedy; then, with a handful of J.K. Rowling magic dust, he arrange for the spirit to separate from the corporate and rise miraculously, triumphantly, but invisibly in resurrection!

Meanwhile, and 'seeing is believing' the corporate remained transfixed to a lump of wood, for the next two thousand years. Consequently future generations, who had never witnessed the original inspired, complete 'body and soul', and were more sceptical of miracles, were obliged to look on this sad memento of a great event, even provided little pocket copies of the crucifixion logo, and close their eyes to the truth by believing, being instructed, taught, bullied into accepting that this contrived Faith would lead to Hope!

You know, in this Holy Week, I have faffed about with words, trying to emulate J.K. Rowling, but could not make it flow.........nae magic dust!

On Palm Sunday, my wee pal Iain was buoyant and confident, and ready to take on the world ... and I was inspired. I can only tell you how my week went, with little 'conspiracy' impediments deflecting my attention – adverse currents affecting my flow, until I resolved to check my position.

Suddenly the day is Thursday – morning of the last supper. Still not too late to change the direction back to the original course, the 'happy ending' that the author intended.

So, we have the parallel working of the original story. A wee Whitbum man, who has one hundred and fifty-seven million, six hundred and eighty thousand seconds worth of distance still to run.........if he can get 'Redirected' on Easter Monday.........to complete his journey and deliver his message, or find the Holy Grail!

All he has to do is go through a form of trial, on Good Friday, that will take away the pain and allow him to focus on the challenges before him. And he only has to convince one man to have the faith that there is still a great purpose to his life that he has yet to discover.

Maybe your fascination with Western films will give a better scenario;

Butch and Sundance are sitting in the cave mouth, hiding from the 'evil' that is closing in around them. Ahead of them is the cliff edge, with a sheer drop to a raging river, sixty feet below. Sundance, who fears nothing. is terrified – he can't stand heights, is afraid of water and can't swim.

Jumping is their only hope. Butch hooks their gun belts together, shouts 'Now or never!' and drags Sundance, at a run, towards the leap of faith, into the abyss above the river that is 'raging' with renewed hope that will carry them away from the insidious evil.

May need to demote the 'Last Supper' back down to simply 'supper'. And, if you are not pleased with the casting. you can be Butch next time.

All the best.........could never totally understand "Happy Easter" – I always thought it was cruel and tragic. But hey, Wee Whitbum Man, we can change that!

See you when you are up and about!

Much love

*Ed*

# Butch and Sundance continued.

**Good Friday 19<sup>th</sup> April 2019**

As they charged towards the open space of the abyss, Sundance had no time to address, or consider his fears, Butch had no need to drag him to meet the challenge. The rush of adrenalin ensured that his entire focus was concentrated on that one moment, that one act, that one wild leap into the seeming emptiness of faith.

He was falling, or was it flying? – there was no time to consider his fear of heights, nor anticipate his fear of the water that was rushing to engulf him. His metabolism had accelerated to such a rate, fuelled by the adrenalin, that the seconds of his flight through space seemed like a lifetime; a lifetime that was over in a flash. He hit the water suddenly, almost unexpectedly despite the fact that he had prepared for this moment, through his fear, all his life and yet hadn't even thought of the impact during the 'relative' lifetime of his fall.

There were no conscious thoughts, but subliminal messages were being received and interpreted by his racing brain as he descended rapidly through time and space.........like a newborn rushing down the birth canal to experience the freedom that awaited at the end of the struggle.

Yet, this journey seemed, somehow, to be in the opposite direction to the birth journey, which carried the newly-charged life from the comfort and protection of the prenatal waters toward the new and exciting brightness that awaited. This journey, escaping the encroaching evil, seemed to be backward through a precipitous drop into the narrow gorge that channelled the rushing water through the rapids he was dropping into; as if he had to go backwards to relearn the survival skills, the instinctive fight for life that every newborn is equipped with.

He hit the water, with no time to anticipate or experience the fear he had harboured all his life. He sank – but, not like a stone; his natural buoyancy slowed the speed of his immersion in the water, there were no protruding rocks for his body to crash into; luck or, more likely, a million years of rushing water had eroded and cleared a deep channel to receive his sinking body. The shock of the water and sudden lack of air triggered the instinctive reactions from the recesses of his mind. A being's natural ability to survive in water before inspiration dictates that the being escape the water and seek air as the life giving necessity for survival.

Sundance kicked out, and flailed his arms, like awkward fins, to assist his escape from the now threatening water, which only seconds earlier had been his salvation in creating a soft landing for his flight, his desperate jump, to escape the earthly evil that had been about to engulf him.

He broke surface, out of the blackness of the water and his tightly shut eyes, trying to focus in the bright daylight and through the water blurring his vision. He was in the rapids now, rushing through the narrow rocky gorge, thrusting out his hands in an instinctive attempt to ward off the jutting rock walls which seemed to leap toward him, threatening, dangerous; rocks that hadn't moved in thousands of years were rushing towards him-yet, he was the one who was being propelled, at reckless, uncontrollable speed towards those ancient rocks.

He pushed out, as if to brush aside the first rock. It did not move; but the impact gashed his hand, and the recoil sent him spinning through the torrent towards a rock on the opposite side of the narrow gorge. He warded off this rock with his other hand, with the same negative effect; the rock did not move and he gashed the palm of this hand also. The impact of this collision sent him back across the channel and he felt a heavy blow on his feet as they dragged along the boulder strewn bed of the rapids.

He could not see Butch. He wasn't really thinking about Butch at the moment, the fight for survival had a tendency to concentrate the mind and focus totally on the priority of staying alive; he bounced off a large boulder in the centre of the rapids and felt a sharp blow on his side. just below his rib cage – it was painful, but pain and discomfort were not his major concerns as he concentrated on staying upright, and alive, in these turbulent rushing rapids.

Somehow, now, he felt no fear; no resentment of the seemingly threatening waters; after all, they were carrying him away from the Evil that had pursued him as far as the gorge: his fear of heights had proved unfounded – again, the water had been his salvation.

And the Evil that had them, Butch and him, so outnumbered that they were certain to overwhelmed had it not been for their willingness to leap into the unknown. He realised that Evil was not invincible; Evil had limitations. Evil could not, would not make the leap of faith into the limbo of emptiness to pursue a victim who had landed in the rushing rapids of hope.

The torrent was carrying him, now at breakneck speed, and somewhere ahead he could hear a low, constant roar; he couldn't quite place the sound, but it had an ominous, challenging pitch to it. He caught a glimpse of Butch, slightly ahead of him, swirling and tumbling in the racing waters. It seemed ridiculous, but Butch still had his bowler hat stuck firmly on his head.........
the roaring was sounding louder, and closer.........and suddenly Butch disappeared.

Before Sundance had a chance to think about the fate of his friend. he too was cartwheeled over a waterfall that roared into a small lake, some thirty feet below.

Again he was plunged violently below the surface. There had been no warning, and no time to gulp in a lungful of air before the water, once again, became the threat! He fought this sinister water that seemed intent on drowning him. It was as if this violent baptism had reverted him to a stage of development before evolution had refined him to humanity. He was a cornered animal fighting for survival.........he clawed and kicked at the water, fighting his way to the surface, feral and ferocious, ready to fight to the death the next threat to his life; he broke the surface of the water, and there was nothing.

He was threshing about in the placid calmness of a little lake – he could see Butch ahead of him, at the water's edge. The waterfall was behind him now, no threat, and the gentle current created by the tumbling water was carrying him gently toward the grassy bank where Butch was already lying stretched out, on his back akimbo, silently staring at the sky with a smug, but somehow grateful grin on his face. Sundance pulled himself onto the waterside grass and lay beside Butch, in a similar position, with his arms outstretched.

He looked at the sky for a full minute then turned his head to take in Butch, still wearing the smug, silent grin-but his eyes shut now. Sundance suddenly slapped the back of Butch's outstretched band and cried, almost angrily, "You're nuts! You could have got us both killed!"

Butch opened his eyes to contemplate the sky again ... and started giggling. Through the giggling he mouthed "Well it's Easter, aint it? Somebody had to get your egg rolling!"

Sundance exhaled a long, long breath and fell back on the grass again. He stared at the sky. Butch was still giggling, a satisfied, infectious sort of chuckle. Sundance started to chuckle also they both chuckled louder together, broke into loud happy laughter.

They had left Evil stranded on a rocky ledge above Faith Canyon, survived a roller-coaster ride through Hope Rapids which feeds into Stillwater Creek. Now lying on the lush green grass at the water's edge they felt the elation gently subside as their adrenalin returned to more normal levels.

Sundance felt the ache in his foot and some discomfort from the wound just below his rib cage. He looked at his hands with their gashed palms, then looked at the sky again; he could stand a bit of discomfort...... It was good to be alive. He stretched out his arm again, and felt for Butch's hand. Butch was still lying in that same position, staring at the sky. Sundance grasped Butch's hand in a firm clasp of......friendship, comradeship? Perhaps love.

And Butch responded with an answering, reassuring grip. His friend Sundance, the Bonny Fighter, had made the leap of faith into the water of hope, where Evil would not follow, and come out the other side; the Bonny Fighter restored. He continued smiling at the sky and gave a little satisfied chuckle. His friend Sundance was OK.

What's not to laugh about?

With much love

*Ed*

# Commentary

Iain had a kidney stone removed on Good Friday 19th April 2019. The relief from suffering was instantaneous, and he was restored to the active service – fighting fitness – level he had felt before the kidney stone had intruded on his fight with cancer.

Not a typical Good Friday – suffering was relieved!

Maybe, after all, our fightback is achieving some almost imperceptible change!

**28th April 2019**

# My Dear Iain

What an inspiration you are to me! I am just off the 'phone to you apologising that I haven't written any continuation of Diarmuid's search for God, and I am quite motivated – directed almost – to arm myself with my trusty Parker ballpoint pen. Not only that, but I have reached for the new pad that I told you I had invested in to write, over the next twelve months, recording my progress on Diarmuid's search, for your evaluation and approval.

Been a funny old week since Easter; you have been through a bit of physical turmoil and I have experienced a tad of emotional disturbance; nothing too heavy, in my case, but distracting nevertheless! I think, this particular Easter, we – you and I – (well, me anyway!), were subconsciously anticipating some kind of uplifting Easter. And of course, the only template we had, on which to base our expectations, was the original Easter, the movable feast that has been, sort of, force-fed to us for the past two thousand years!

Now, on the basis that history repeats itself, we should learn from history and, my latent belief that history, as it is happening. is a parallel happening, a revised version of an old production, I thought that we might review this Easter that we have acted out, and see where it compares with the original production staged by Peter and Pilate.

'Oh Iain, I have to digress! Peter and Pilate, eh? You know, I have always thought of the late JC as 'the Navigator, the Pilot'. And I know that you don't totally agree with my theory that corruption of 'the word', thus corruption of 'any word', has much to do with World corruption and, consequently, much to do with the deterioration of the state of this World, but......

Good old Peter ditched the original Pilot and took direction from a 'sounds like' Pilate.........who refused to heed the Navigator's warning "this is not the Way! This is not the Truth, this is not the Life!" We, you and I, the World – should have changed course two thousand years ago!

Anyway, Easter! On the 'all the world's a stage' and 'one man......many parts' bases, we can represent the 'play' if we stick to the rules and the general theme that the original production was trying to present. For two thousand years Easter has been celebrated as a 'happy occasion', with a miraculous resurrection as its central inspiring motivation. (I know that I have made this point before, but I am not trying to stress the 'miracle' – that has been overstressed!)

The producers of that first Easter play went a 'bridge too far' perhaps... and maybe hit us with the opposite of the obvious; the miraculous rise from the dead. Surviving crucifixion without dying would have been miraculous enough!......and, with the passage of time, and the advances in medical science, people all over the world are surviving the crucifixion of cancer; and people are standing up against that manifestation of evil, that latter day crucifixion, that holds a body impaled, immobilised and seemingly impotent. The passengers and the also-rans of the world, conditioned, programmed, by two thousand years of indoctrination and unquestioning acceptance of the inevitable...if the miraculous 'Son of God' is still pinned to the cross what hope is there for little old me? Maybe they, well all of us, have to see that this, the original version, is not the Truth, and what we are living is not 'the Life'. And what we have to do is go back to where it went wrong, to that place where we didn't change course, and rethink the 'Way' from there.

You know how I like to think of myself as a bit of a wordsmith – not a great vocabulary – but I like to play with those words that are available to me; like Pilot and Pilate.........a wee bit of spin; happens all the time through history, so why can't we do it?

How about you and me make it our challenge to spin 'crucifixion' to, say, CRUCIFICTION? How would a Latin scholar translate that? The Cross – a story? The Cross, a fiction? The cross, a made up story!

Anyway, I know this Easter a lot of sad things happened across the World; some of them to good Catholic believers, but some to non-Catholics who believed in something equally precious to them. On the basis of 'history repeating itself' it seems there could be a parallel with the medieval events, when the Pope approved the slaughter of all residents of Carcassone to guarantee that all threats of alternative faith were eliminated by murdering faithful, obedient Catholics along with the suspected heretics and non-Catholic Cathars. The Empire sacrificed many faithful adherents to the pain and ignominy of collateral damage to ensure that all resistance or opposition was eliminated.

Let us suppose (give your mind a treat) that this Easter the important happening, the biggest threat to the Empire (the original Empire!), was our little reworking of the original story. That this was, in fact the real thing; and the simple truth must not come out! (Remember we are thinking on a—universal, eternal, timeless and limitless scale); not Diarmuid's man-sized God space-hopping the World, but a Universal God waiting for an arrogant little mankind to, maybe say, "Excuse me, I am drowning, can you chuck me a lifebelt or perhaps, drift me towards a submerged rock?" It has happened before in a less 'world event' impacting situation. Although, in your world and my world important, and therefore, a World event! But let's just fantasise that we have stumbled on the truth and the Empire had to create these world shattering tragedies, this Easter, to blitz our little truth into irrelevance!

Remember, the Empire, or the authors of the testaments started all this miracle and supernatural fantasising. I'm just trying to make it sound more credible. Like I said the other day, J K Rowling did it with a wizard on a flying brush – and she could make it believable. I try to present a credible version of the truth, and it sounds fantastic and unbelievable!

You are just a wee 81-year-old guy from Whitbum and I am just a wee, fat 82-year-old Glasgow man; we both have our problems which are, maybe, deflecting us from the big issues that we should he addressing (Old quote "I could do great things if I wasn't so busy doing little things!) Maybe the world has 'immediate' problems which deflect its attention from the real solution to its problems!

The problem is, that two thousand years on, we are still fighting the same Empire. The turning point is Easter, but, two thousand years ago the Navigator failed to effect the course alteration, and the Pilot, appointed by the Empire, maintained the course to disaster.

This Easter we, you and I, have made a course correction. In our little reworking of the Easter story, there is no death, no need for a miraculous resurrection, and maybe we can still influence the prevention of pending disaster, in our own worlds and in the wider World. And one week later, the pain and discomfort has been, at least, alleviated and to some degree controlled; a breathing space, perhaps! If we can slip back into our little slit trench analogy (that was five years ago I fell in beside you!) I am encouraged by your declaration today, "I'll give the bugger a fight!"

You know, Iain, I have been 'giving the bugger a fight', in one way or

another, since Easter 1963. And my son and my daughter are in this fight
– as is your Son (bereaved like me) and your Daughter – all united and
determined to make our World a better place. I have always felt that this
improvement has to happen within my lifetime; otherwise, what is the point
of it all.

You and I are not simply on the passenger list! Even if I don't see the
eventual 'betterness' but can influence the change of course, well, that
would be something.

Well Iain. I said to you recently, that I didn't have to convince the whole
World – just start by convincing one man, the Captain of this significant
ship – don't believe the old navigation books, turn right towards the open
sea!

If Easter really is a change of course, a 'new beginning', and we have just
awarded ourselves another five years of meaningful existence, let us get on
with it, let's do the opposite of the obvious, let us use the Empire's capacity
for spin; let us turn Via, Veritas, Vita back to front!

We've awarded ourselves the Vita, let's seek out the Veritas and show the
World the Via!

You know, Iain, with your ability to inspire, and my capacity for bullshit
(we've suffered somebody else's 'truth' long enough!) we can change the
World!

With much love,

*Ed*

PS There must be a bit of syllogism in there somewhere:

'Two perspectives of the same position creating two propositions for
solution of a common problem!'

**Friday 21st June 2019**

## Dear Iain,

This is catch-up time. I haven't abandoned the quest for Diarmuid's Holy Grail. However, as I tried to indicate in my 'interim' card, a tsunami of procrastination somewhat overwhelmed my little raft of digression.........
left me floundering for a bit – anyway, getting my breath back now!

To paraphrase Omar: 'The moving finger writes and having writ moves on – but, at least we can look back to what it 'writ', and try to catch up by reading faster than it!'

*Flashback to:*

**2 May 2019**

## Dear Iain'

Thursday, and Aberdeen again. Been thinking about you since Monday and that fine book you presented me with.

I am afraid the gesture took me somewhat by surprise, and the implications of the gift did not properly occur to me until after I had left you; another of those occasions when the demands of running about, addressing 'little issues' draws one's prioritising away from the bigger picture.

I apologise if my reaction seemed less than might have been due such a significant gesture and precious gift. I had been expecting a shortlist of the customary pre-holiday reading material you supply for my education and enlightenment; a peek into Solomon's Temple, John Knox's inside leg measurement or Masonic secrets, essential but obscured from today's world

I realised, too late, that this fine book was not intended as holiday reading but is, in fact, another step in the preparations you have been making, over these last few years, for family and friends. I am touched and honoured to be included in this intimate circle.

However, although I consider that many of the more intricate arrangements you have put in place are entirely appropriate, giving me a precious memento at this time is, perhaps, just a little bit premature. But, a gift is a gift.........I shall cherish it, and keep it available should you need to refer to it.

Thank you.

In terms of your arrangements-we have had this conversation before; 'Don't hasten the implementation of your splendid contingency plan – it will be every bit as effective if implemented later rather than sooner! Don't suddenly be impatient that the moving finger isn't moving faster than it has always moved!

## Flashback to:

### Thursday 20th June

The moving finger will have to do a wee fast forward now, if I want to get Diarmuid moving again.

Some eight weeks of procrastination have walloped past in what seems like a blink.

Bon Scott has come and gone, Sheila and I have been on holiday for two weeks, my mini operation is history (well, sort of!) and you and I managed a couple of 'exclusive' dinners somewhere along the way. A visit to Restenneth maybe got us back on the Holy Grail trail.

Remember our original 5 year plan – make each day count and review the plan with 20/20 vision.

## Flashback to:

### Saturday 22nd June

Now into the second half of 2019 – thirty one million, one hundred and four thousand seconds of distance still to run before we even get to 2020 and review the plan!

May I paraphrase Omar, yet again?

"The moving finger is writing –"

".........and moving on"

"We cannot change what it has writ!"

"But we might be able to influence"

"Half a line, still to come, of it!"

Don't be impatient to see the effectiveness of the insurance plan……
the Life plan is still working just fine – and sixty seconds worth of distance
enjoyed is just a nice sedate pace to proceed at!

Diarmuid O'Murchu will be back on the menu before the finger gets too
far ahead!

Enclosed a wee bit of topical verse for your entertainment.

With love

*Ed*

# Ne'er Cast a Clout

Oh dear! Theresa has gone; No triumphal exit:
No regretful 'Dear John', Just an incomplete Brexit!

**'Til May is Out!**
A leader, unthanked, by a 'so thankless' led
Now queueing to replace This leader, now dead!
Was it Brutus? No Boris, (Who so likes a natter)
Keeping quiet in the wings' Thus avoiding the spatter!
No blood on his toga As blow after blow
From the Tory unfaithful Urge Theresa to go!
The conspirators gather To compete for the realm
Will Jeremy, Boris or Mike Grab the helm?
Will Rory's soft Brexit Still seeking a deal
Be supported in England, Have voter appeal?
Or Dominic imprudent, Unaware, perhaps rash?
For considering Bread Queues Just a 'poor flow of cash!'
The ladies went first, Leaving squabbling boys,
Pity none is called Hobson, For that seems the choice!

*Ed @ Three Bellies*

**Tuesday 28<sup>th</sup> January 2020**

# My Dear Iain

Here I go again – long-winded Louis – it is two-thirty in the morning and yes, I have been thinking about you. In fact I have been thinking about you all day since you jumped out of your car to walk me down Glengate for a bit this morning.

By the way, I am sorry this will end up as an unedited, longhand schoolboy scrawl, my trusty laptop is in for repair and I lack the copperplate handwriting skills that you possess and I wanted to respond to you more quickly than waiting for the ideal circumstances. In fact, the ideal circumstances may not be the 'perfect' circumstances but you and I have to act when the mood is on – the 'carpe diem' or even the carpe moment opportunity.

I have somehow let a whole year slip away.

I have regretted, somewhat that, as I now realise, my attention has been diverted and absorbed by my own little problems – first the polyps, then the atrial fibrillation accompanied by the mundane but ever-present cash flow crisis.

This last is a chronic condition that has persisted for almost all of the twenty years I have been in Kirriemuir; but just at the moment it is relieved with a little help from my friends and a contribution from my daughter who is doing shifts with no pay to reduce the staff costs.

Just at the moment I am prepared to believe that miracles happen! I can't quite see the light at the end of the tunnel but, at least, I feel that I am moving through the tunnel towards the light that I always believed was there. During the last twelve months I am afraid that the tunnel darkness overwhelmed me for a bit.

I don't know if that was simply selfish…or maybe a wee bit of shell-shock from a constant bombardment of 'bad luck' – evil conspiracy…O me miserum – Poor Me!

Then I remembered that we came together when I fell into the slit trench beside you…me, the reinforcement for the old soldier who had been keeping evil, of one sort or another, at bay for a long time. Like the young recruit, fit and fresh, who is going to win the war for this old guy……until he undergoes his first experience of heavy bombardment and has the shit frightened out of him and the old guy, the wounded guy who has held this front line trench for ages has to provide the encouragement to his erstwhile saviour by saying, "Get a grip, it's only noise – nothing actually hit you!"

So I have calmed down and taken stock of my situation and here we are still in our slit trench and you have reassured and helped me see that I am in better shape than I was beginning to fear.

And you? Been a taxing year for you, I am aware! In fact, on top of the responsibility you feel to protect and save everyone around you, perhaps the negative impact of 'losing' some contemporaries, that you were never meant to save in the first place, has weighed more heavily on you than you might have thought. Maybe they were not really within your gravitational sphere for you to be able to influence their destiny – they were somebody else's satellites, somebody else's responsibility.

You have done a grand job of looking after, protecting and preparing a future for your own family and providing help to people who even just fall into your gravitational pull, temporarily and somehow become your responsibility…You are really good at it!

You know Iain, maybe we could sit here in this slit trench for a good bit longer, not tire ourselves out by trying to take the fight to the enemy; just let the war wage round about us and make sure that we don't stick our heads above the parapet to get smacked by a wee bit of shrapnel. No point in being collateral damage at our age!

In a previous note I tried to estimate our future time-line in terms of 'sixty seconds worth of distance run'; a bit ambitious. Not the future or the time-line but measuring in seconds, too many millions, or was it billions of seconds, we had to keep track of? Too much calculation and demand on memory for my old brain. Maybe a new five-year plan, measured in monthly steak-night dates? That would be something to look forward to rather than watching our time-line tick away second by second.

Anyway, we have just completed our previous five-year plan – remember – so we could look back on our progress with 20/20 vision.

Well, here we are in 2020! Still breathing in and out, a little battle worn, a little less looking for a fight – but still prepared to have a go.

Another five year plan would be only sixty steak nights – that's a nice easy target figure, and we would both be 88 – a nice round number to go for! Maybe planning to reach 88, for either of us is expecting a miracle.

But, hey, don't knock miracles, you have benefited from one or two in your lifetime…and created one or two for a few folk. And, at the start of this letter I acknowledged the wee Melrose miracle when you got me to 'pick up my bed and walk!'.

No Harry Potter magic, no water into wine, just a wee bit of human determination coupled with a wee sprinkle of spiritual inspiration and sixty steak nights will be a doddle.

Do you know that at the end of Butch Cassidy and the Sundance Kid when they ran into the hail of Mexican bullets? Apparently they survived and lived to a ripe old age.

And the February steak night is your responsibility.

With much love

*Ed*

**5th March 2020**

My Dear Iain

It's a while since I dropped you a line – despite the fact that I have resolved to put pen to paper on many occasions; well intentioned of course, but the good intention in each instance soon faded to "Well maybe tomorrow, Jack!"

In fact, the good intentions seem to be fleeting spirits of thought that lack the motivation to invest the physical effort to produce a carefully crafted and interesting communication. (It occurs to me that I have devoted over a paragraph to say "The spirit is willing, but the flesh is weak!") Maybe I simply lack the urgency of the girl in the cheese advert who knocks the guy to the ground with the exhortation "Oh, get on with it!"

Anyway, here we are – long winded as usual – resolved to 'get on with it!'

# Commentary – not up to completing!

**21st March 2020**

My Dear Iain

I have kind of lost my way, a wee bit, in these recent months; I don't know whether I have already sent this letter, and my computer skills are sufficiently limited as to prevent me finding a filed typed copy within my system. However, in the course of looking I came across some of the old letters I have sent you.........My God, you haven't half had to endure some shite from me over our relatively short friendship! I bet you are relieved that we were not school pals and you had been obliged to read some of my crap for the past seventy years...I think I must have a bowel for a brain!

Anyway, it seems a while since I dropped you a line, despite the fact that I have resolved to put pen to paper on many occasions; well intentioned, of course, but the good intention quickly turns to "Well, maybe tomorrow Jack!" The good intentions seem to be fleeting spirits of thought that lack the motivation of applying the physical effort that produces the 'carefully crafted letter' you deserve. (It occurs to me that I have taken two paragraphs to say "The spirit is willing but the flesh is weak!" Maybe I lack the urgency of the girl in the cheese advert who knocks the guy to the ground, jumps on top of him and says "Oh get on with it!"

Anyway, again – here we are, long winded as usual, resolved to get on with it!

The last two months have been a bit trying for us both – albeit at significantly different levels of 'trying-ness'. I think occasionally of us, in our little slit trench coping with the same enemy, the same threats (to some degree) and how much better you seem to cope with the noise and tumult of battle than I do. Maybe you are more battle hardened – like the old soldier, watching the new recruits arriving, full of enthusiasm about how quickly their presence will change the course of the war, and thinking patiently "Just keep your head down son until the blitzkrieg is over and the smoke clears a bit." And the old soldier's benign amusement as the youthful confidence drains, somewhat, in the intensity of the bombardment.

Somehow, I feel, this last twelve months have been a wee bit of a bombardment – for both of us and your steadfast confidence continues to inspire me.

Maybe I should take some confidence in the knowledge that our little management plan was, somehow, effective; I recall that we embarked on a 5 year plan to reach 2020 and here we are, a little worse for wear, but still breathing in and out. A little stirred, and a little shaken – but still here!

You know Iain (is this something else I have told you before and don't remember?) I keep a little card on my desk; my very untidy desk; the card reads "Everything will be OK in the end; if it's not OK, it is not the end!"

Well, things aren't totally OK at the moment – but we are still breathing in and out – so it is not the end. But we have come to the end of our five year plan that had the objective of looking back on our progress with 20/20 vision.

Maybe we should look forward with that same 20/20 vision. Another forward plan perhaps; not too ambitious at eighty three-ish years of age but, say, optimistic and plan for another three years. After all, had you listened and been influenced by the experts you would not be making plans of any kind.

Maybe we should just regard these experts as the battlefield medics who have dressed our wounds and provided painkillers to keep us focussed; but it is not up to them to decide whether we simply drift away......or live to fight another day! Maybe, in the grand scheme of things we are, after all the fighters who prevail, despite our wounds, and make a difference.

If everything really will be OK in the end – you know, and I know that everything is not OK at the moment – so, if it is not OK and therefore not the end we might as well believe we have to fight on; and prepare another three-year plan: live to fight another day, or for another 1095 days in fact!

This, on the basis that no one, not the enemy, not the experts nor the God we haven't found yet, can tell us where the end is!

You know Iain, with your ability in a fight, my imagination......and maybe a wee contribution from John Ogilvy, we could achieve anything!

Thinking of you

With much love

*Ed*

# Angus in Lockdown

**April 2020**

My Dear Iain,

Been a difficult old week. I know that you have not had your sorrows or complications to seek and I, to a much less uncomfortable degree, have had a few complications of my own.

It seems ironic that the 'underlying symptoms' that we each have in our own way, and which were of the ultimate importance last month, have suddenly been relegated to a secondary position in relation to Covid 19 which we so far have managed to avoid. And yet, the threat of something we have managed to avoid has permeated and pervaded every facet of our lives – from impeding traditional treatment, restricting freedom of movement and discouraging social contact; even intruding into the accepted niceties of loving family life by discouraging physical contact and restricting one's social circle, be it casual contacts, friends or close family loved ones to encroach no closer than a circumference with a radius of two metres. We are sorely affected by Coronavirus even if we have, thus far, avoided being infected with it!

You know Iain, it's a funny old life. You and I believe in something that a lot of people can't, don't or won't understand, Even you and I reach our belief in a shared interpretation of 'faith in something', without actually agreeing exactly what that something is; without necessarily agreeing how we got to this same position yet approached it from two different directions. Both of us believed that there was more to life than following a path for, say, the statutory three score years and ten, then reaching an ending before or beyond this notional lifespan not really sure what it had all been about. Neither of us was prepared to accept the blind faith of being born, existing for 'the duration' then taking our leave, supposedly armed with the faith that we were moving on to another wonderful life on the assurances of religious practitioners, who weren't necessarily convincing us that they had any more credibility or authority to equip us for the next stage of the journey, than we ourselves had. Two wee unremarkable Scotsmen, with conflicting views on many fronts, but with a shared determination to find the truth before we inflicted an interpretation, or a creation, of faith on others. We both felt that the truth was fairly close, but somehow the directions we had been equipped with were not taking us to the truth we felt was just beyond the horizon of our knowledge.

All our lives had been dedicated to this quest, not full time of course; we had to provide for our families and attempt to do the right thing by others less fortunate; by the time we joined forces three score years and ten were somewhat behind us. I am not sure whether we were a couple of latter day Knights Templar trying to find the Truth or a pair of Don Quixotes trying to do the right thing in a world that seemed more disposed towards corruption. Whatever guise we presented to our supporters or critics there was strength in this new companionship of two people trying to find the right direction to follow – the via veritas vita – that religion seemed to hold a copyright on; like a mystery tour that some people paid heavily for without ever knowing the truth about the destination.

Oh Iain, there really seems to be little point in continuing with this letter – April is not being a good month for you.

The blitzkrieg of this Covi19 pandemic, which has been launched against the world in general, has really complicated everything. Everybody is at full stretch or immobilised by fear; nobody is allowed to move except emergency medical staff and essential services. All medical appointments are restricted and all operations cancelled – including my colonoscopy; the effects of that are not pressing although the uncertainty brings with it its own ration of fear: I do not have Corona virus, so I am not afraid – I do have a dodgy colon condition which is present with unexplained symptoms, so I am concerned!

But you, dear friend, still fighting, still with the cheeky sense of humour; you are finding it really hard going. Morphine can work miracles at a time like this...... But it is not a miraculous cure

In our allegorical slit trench we are still together. But in the 'this world' the messed up world of headless chickens and pandemics I am not supposed be here! But hey, what difference is it going to make to either of us – seems like only a 'Private Ryan' with Covid 19 is worth saving at the moment. My previously essential surgery has been relegated so the bed can be reserved until Private Ryan is located and you-well, you were not supposed to make it beyond 2014 or 2015, at best, according to informed medical opinion of that day.

I haven't been anywhere since I was obliged to close the Pub three weeks ago; so, I can't bring Covid 19 to infect you – and, even if I could, I don't think it is going to make much difference to you at this stage.

You know Iain, we pretty much agreed on what was good and what was evil in universal terms, but we never really got to locating the loose ends or unravelling the great big fankle of information about empire and the Christian era or continue with Diarmuid's quest to find God.

So, here we are in our wee slit trench. I didn't realise the significance of visiting you today – it is 9th April 2020, so what?.........See! That is what is so confusing about movable feasts!

Tomorrow is Good Friday – this is the evening of The Last Supper, and here we are having a wee clandestine get together, despite the curfew of lockdown imposed by the ruling authorities.

I have no doubt at all, considering the care you have put in to your departure plan, that you organised this down to the last detail – the final ripple, the last concentric circle a faint copy of the splash.

I recall exactly your response when I said,

"You know Iain, I waited 74 years to meet a friend like you"

And you held my hand, and with a wee twinkle in your eye you said "I've no' met him yet!"

How we both laughed!

***Iain died on Tuesday 14th April 2020 – the day after Easter.***

**4th August 2021**

# Hi Iain.

Happy Birthday,
I have just walked up Cemetery Road to sit with you for a moment.

Some incline, that Cemetery Road; I am convinced it must hae been designed by a very commercial undertaker, a century or so ago, who saw the repeat business potential in any permutation of six pallbearers succumbing to a heart attack, having carted half a ton of oak coffin and contents up that very steep hill. I thought I was pretty close to Heaven by the time I had struggled to the level that you are on.

Anyway, here I am, looking across at you, and your wee granddaughter Anna who lies next to you; I am having a well earned rest on the little memorial bench inscribed 'Anna Jane Melrose – Forever in our Hearts'. It is sad when one so young is taken so soon, but I am not overcome with sadness at this moment – there is just a lovely sense of tranquillity, peacefulness, a feeling that everything is going to be fine.

My intention is to carry on, up the hill, past Barrie's grave to the top of the cemetery, beyond the monument of the glistening white Black Watch Rifleman, in the 'on guard' position, keeping a watchful eye across the Strathmore valley for any threatening approach from the South.

I feel you are in good hands!

Me? I have to walk up the rest of the Hill, which is even steeper than Cemetery Road; I have done it before: you have no idea the sense of achievement it gives me, at eighty four, to walk up Cemetery Road, along the path between the headstones and past your wee slit trench, then climb the last challenging, near-vertical. Hill to the back and out on to Hill Rise – and still be in the land of the living. "Nearer my God to Thee" is fine – but not just yet. I have a few more letters still to write,

I'll be in touch

Still your loving friend

But I don't think I have to keep reinforcing you with loving thoughts – we both know where we are now!

*Ed*

# Letter written 7 years late – with the benefit of hind sight!

**28<sup>th</sup> August 2021**

*Oh Iain,*

What have we done?

It seem as though we have stirred up a hornets' nest of hostility and misfortune that could annihilate us. We can't see it in 2014 as we are living it, but I can see it now, in 2021, with the benefit of hindsight – from one of my imaginary historical ripples or concentric circles of history that took a long time to develop after those frightening two years that followed our decision to fight back.

I can see now that we really were in some kind or parallel existence – even multi dimensional, when you take in the real time day to day life in Kirriemuir in October 2014, our imagined life in our little slit trench – taking the fight to an unseen enemy; the real time experience of my battle to save Caledonia in 1960 and the ripples and circles of historical battles we have fought in our own lifetime: or those that have been fought throughout this so-called Christian Era, where ordinary people were obliged to fight a war they didn't know they were in, and battle or suffer from evil, in some form or other.........illness or plague, misfortune and corruption – all explained away, and therefore accepted euphemistically as bad luck.

But it seems that our decision to resist what we have been told is inevitable, and fight our 'bad luck', has released a torrent of pent-up evil upon us that we cannot really see in the real time of 2014 as we are living the experience, while we are actually living through the misfortune – along with the millions of others who can't see the problem, because it is all around them called 'normal life'.........just your luck.

But, somebody has imagined this scenario before, this pent up evil that can be released if you decide to challenge the conventional gospel truth that we have been programmed to accept, trying to separate the fact that we see from the fiction we have been taught.

Remember, in the film 'Raiders of the lost Ark', when they opened the box, and Indiana Jones had warned his companions not to look, as the released evil swept round the cavern afflicting anyone who wasn't aware or protected.........nae favourites! Well, our experience was not as instant. or dramatic as Indiana Jones's because we are not performing in a two hour film where quantum leaps of time, and information, can be compressed in order to tell the story within two entertaining hours.

I mean, who would believe our miraculous parallel story of two 78 year-olds, sitting in a slit trench holding off, fighting back – prepared to charge with fixed bayonets even, – an unseen enemy whose armoury contains all the evils of the Universe as they are presented to mankind. in today's real time, to afflict the health, wealth and well-being of any or every mortal being who might discover that there is another way.

Well lain, in October 2014, I can tell you with the benefit of hindsight we brought a whole ton of shit down on ourselves that hit everyone in our lives with some measure of threat, or impact on health, wealth and well-being.

And, with the typical tyrant's philosophy, nobody was excluded......'don't worry about collateral damage; kill or maim everybody and you are sure to immobilise your foe'.

I don't know whether it was revisiting the saving of Caledonia, which had possible historical parallels, or our decision to collaborate to examine and expose some biblical anomalies, but September 2014 was the start point of 'something'.

Your cruelly communicated prognosis of your cancer condition was the opening salvo – in, say, our little slit trench allegory – in a sustained bombardment, of health, wealth and well-being issues, – which lasted for over two years.

Just as 'the Lord works in mysterious ways His wonders to perform', so to, it seems, does the other fellow 'work in devious ways his evils to inflict!' Everything can be explained away, of course, as 'Well, that's life!'; but try to look at it from another perspective. Suppose this is not 'life' but 'purgatory' and we all just accept the normality of it, with the discomfort and the risks, because we don't see there is an alternative. So some folk learn to swim in this sea of purgatory, make the best of it, and those who try to climb out are held back by some malign hand, pinned to the cross we 'all have to bear', unable to help ourselves or see the answer because the answer is on a different historical parallel, or some future ripple that we cannot see because it isn't formed yet.

All through 2015 and 2016 the sustained bombardment continued, but we were fighting back now. You, the old soldier of long experience, had previous battle experience; only now I discover that you overcame tuberculosis as an eighteen year old in a two year fight in Bangour Hospital in Midlothian and, of course, more recently you had staved off cancer for seven or eight years until your current prognosis of, effectively, no hope and fairly imminent death.

Well, the tough got going! But our nearest and dearest were exposed to the real time, real life damage of the imaginary bombardment we were experiencing in our little slit trench. Helen was, of course, shell shocked by the same mortar bomb of your cancer review, and she still suffered residual bouts of recurrent post traumatic stress disorder from the tragic loss of your little grand daughter seven years earlier … you both did, to some extent. And she still needed some medical tinkering to keep her heart in good order. She was also slightly incapacitated by disorder in her knee.

I had an unexplained discomfort in the area of my colon, which had worried me for some time but was now labelled as Irritable Bowel Syndrome – not exactly a diagnosis, more a folder to park a problem in until a more convincing title can be found; like a pending file.

This uncertainty left me with a nagging fear which, when added to the other worries of poor trading and cash flow during George Osborne's period of austerity, caused me chronic concern which was accompanied by bouts of debilitating, pervasive fatigue which visited me from time to time; I wasn't depressed, just very tired.

Sheila, as you know, does not share our beliefs; she accepts the fact of the existence of Jesus, without any kind of magic or hero worship, but is intolerant of any religion and totally sceptical about God or eternal life. "Ibis is all you have, no promised land, no afterlife; so make the best of it!" So she made the best of it – she accepted that this sea of purgatory was real life ( like her version of our slit trench analogy) and swam about in it serenely, because there was no alternative, until something caused a splash that spattered her with the unpleasantness that was the surface of purgatory. Of course, she would retaliate by splashing you back with a backlash of this surf ace unpleasantness, sometimes to drenching proportions. Consequently, in the tight little religious circle of her 'Now' credo the people closest in her life were the ones most likely to disturb her calm.

Strangers, who meant little to her could be discouraged by a warning splash of retaliation. Family, extended family and friends were the closest swimmers in this pool of purgatory and therefore the most frequent threats to the serenity of making the best of it by splashing about and causing a disturbance, which provoked a 'justified' retaliatory response.

I recognise now that ever since we, Sheila and I, left The Temple in Joppa and settled in Kirriemuir I have splashed about emotionally, or spiritually trying to find, maybe my interpretation of 'the way' which just caused disturbance in the otherwise tranquillity of the 'life with no alternative' that she was trying to make the best of. If I tried to explain this, even today in this future existence, she would find it crackpot because it depends on some form of spiritual or god-like presence, which isn't real, or, on some version of allegorical modelling which isn't convincing fiction. I did try to explain my situation to her in real time, real terms some years ago – and she thought I was nuts. I think now she has decided that I am simply eccentric and occasionally she becomes very intolerant that this eccentricity is simply taking us round in circles and intruding on her determination to make the best of this 'once in an eternity', lifetime.

However, her acceptance of this real life, as it is, and rejection of the possible existence of any spiritual influence in a world of realism did not did not exclude her from being a victim or protect her from the real life effects of the imaginary bombardment we were experiencing in our wee slit trench. During a significant portion of 2015 she experienced a series of health problems including a need for dental surgery, an eye problem and latterly a prolonged period of discomfort, eventually diagnosed as a kidney stone.

In the real time world of 2015 all of those medical and emotional disturbances affecting, individually, a variety of people would be considered as unrelated, with no connection at all; no common factor, identifiable epidemic. What about an epidemic of bad luck? And we were the first ones to identify it! Only with the benefit of hindsight can any pattern or organisation and co-ordination be observed and provide a suggestion of intent

People who believe in God, a one true God; a loving God credited with providing 'All good things around us' have, maybe, been programmed to believe something that renders them trusting and compliant and unaware of who is creating and providing all the bad things around us? If God is the provident right hand who is the destructive left hand, the sinister one; the other fellow?

In the real time world of 2015 you were setting a great example of conquering your fear by fighting the cancer within you through keeping fit and strong, and inspiring Helen, Sheila and me with your inner strength. Which was just as well for me, because on a mid week break to Inverness as a pre birthday treat I suffered a funny turn and had to seek medical attention at Raigmore Hospital. The emergency staff were very thorough and could assure me that I had not suffered a heart attack, but I would need further tests to identify what had caused the problem.

This, of course, was good news ... except the mischief had been done, another concern had been created and added to my worry basket alongside my unresolved irritable bowel syndrome and the frustration at being unable to move my business toward success, or dispose of it. There was also the latent stress of these secret worlds I was operating in – but could share with no one.

If there really was a sinister force which, at the very least, could create an immobilising fear that rendered the human soul impotent and powerless to fight the threats of modem living, then there was no point in exposing people to the danger of having half a story which simply made them vulnerable to the kind of attack which we now appeared to be experiencing. I thought that I had once experienced a precedent of this kind of spiritual terrorism; after saving Caledonia my beautiful three year old son was taken with cancer just before Easter 1963. Not a joyous uplifting experience!

So. who is this 'other fellow' creating all this mischief and torment? Well Iain, remember this letter is back from the future. At that time in 2015, approaching 2016 we thought our lives were normal; I was trying to encourage you to stand up to cancer, which was going well and the illnesses and stresses experienced by us and our loved ones were simply the crosses we were programmed to bear. Sheila's positive attitude ensured we kept socially active and our main interests and worries were centred on world news and politics. So, the other fellow? Well that has to be a work in progress – this story cannot be told in two hours like Raiders of the Lost Ark.

Be in touch, Much love

*Ed*

# Hindsight

**31ˢᵗ August 2021**

Hi Iain

I hadn't intended to communicate so soon again from the future; but time is of the essence: we octogenarians do not have all the time in the world to complete our quest!

I feel that I have left some of my splashing about, theorising, a bit inconclusive; really only having formulated the question, although in our, yours and mine, lives identifying the question – that there even is a question – is in itself an achievement

Like, when you or I tell our wives a story about some event or encounter that, in our estimation, is complete; it has a beginning, a middle and an end! We deliver the punch line,

"So, do you know what he did? – He slammed the door in my face!" And, that is the point of the story, this guy's unacceptable behaviour of slamming the door in my face; but, instead of invoking a sympathetic, or disapproving of the guy's rudeness, reaction to the story is uncomprehending and provokes only the query,

"Why, what had you said to him?" This despite the fact that you have just delivered a blow by blow account of the entire episode. So this 'unnecessary' question seems to imply that you haven't told the whole truth and you must have provoked the guy.........or the alternative question

"So. What did you do?" Which seems to imply that you haven't produced a satisfactory ending to your story, or suggests some impotence that you did not kick the door in and beat him to a pulp! As they say in today's modem jargon "Whatever!" And the 'whatever' is that you have failed to communicate effectively.

"So, when I went for my life preserving, energetic walk this morning I

127

had been mulling over the unanswered question of 'who is the other fellow' on and off, all night.

When I started my climb up Gordon Park and Douglas Street I felt a wee bit of discomfort, like indigestion but, being very cautious, I decided not to ignore it or dismiss it; Sheila says I am just a hypochondriac.

I recalled my friendship with wee Frank Massie – he was a hairdresser who rented a chair from Lynn McGregor, in her wee salon Oslers, in the Lower Roods. I don't think you knew him Iain, and I think you may not have been empathetic to the flawed side of Frank's character.

Frank was gay and an alcoholic, so in a judgemental environment, such as Kirriemuir tended to be, he had his detractors and his supporters. I was a supporter; his love affair with alcohol caused no problems for anyone but him, and his work ethic and his generosity to family and friends were admirable qualities.

He loved crosswords and cryptic puzzles, and his depth of knowledge on a variety of subjects was quite impressive. Although we never discussed history and religion in any great depth he believed that history and, particularly history as portrayed in the Bible, contained cryptic clues to the true nature and subsequent impact and consequences of the events presented in the Scriptures.

He was also aware, more than I was, of the prophecies contained or hidden in the Testaments, particularly, in this first decade of the second millennium, of the imminence of the second coming which had been predicted to occur around two thousand years after the death of Christ.

(As Michael Caine might have said "A lot of people don't know that!")

Our shared crossword and cryptic clue enthusiasm also found fertile ground within Scottish history – particularly where Scots words and dialect, family names and place names offered great scope for word bending and 'sounds like' clues; these being often employed in the Herald and Scotsman crosswords which we favoured as a daily challenge.

Probably the most notable and relevant, in this Angus town at the threshold of ancient Pictavia was the similarity of 'sounds like' between Pict and picked. Of course we were aware of the derivation – of Pict from the Latin picti, painted people, but we couldn't helped speculating, in our crossword clue mode, that the Pict people who defended Caledonia so vigorously from Roman domination were, in fact, refugees who had 'picked', or chosen, ancient Scotland as their last frontier to resist the

Roman domination and enslavement which appeared intent on consuming the entire world.

Anyway, getting a wee bit close to serious digression there. Frank died suddenly in 2010 just before my birthday.........birthdays and Easter really do not contribute to my happiness!

Sheila and I had a drink with him in our pub, on Saturday evening – 9th October. He was popping indigestion tablets, in between pints of lager of course. However he did seem to be experiencing acute discomfort and we asked if he had seen a doctor, but he insisted it was indigestion. Jokingly (well half fun) adding that he had enjoyed his life, and really didn't fancy the challenges of old age anyway. We left sometime after six o'clock, with Frank intending to collect a Chinese take-away, which he had already ordered, and go home to watch television.

On Monday morning he failed to appear for work; this was unheard of: no matter how late or how heavy a drinking session might have been, or how heavily he might have felt cold or flu symptoms – he had never failed to attend for work. Attempts to locate family were, so far, unsuccessful and police were reluctant to initiate decisive action until a keyholder could be located. Denise, his colleague phoned the pub to see if we could check on him, as his home was located close by.

I had gone to his house but got no response; his flat was on the first floor, so I brought a ladder from the pub so I could access the living room and kitchen windows located to the front on Croft Terrace. I could see his outdoor clothes lying across a chair in his living room, but no sign of Frank despite my reasonably full view of the room. Any clear view of the kitchen was hampered by the kitchen units and shelving; but his Chinese take-away was lying unopened on a worktop and I thought I could see him lying on the floor, in the narrow floor space, between the units.

A police constable had now arrived to investigate and asked me what I could see; I suggested that she go up the ladder and check for herself, but she declined on health and safety grounds. There was still no key, so I offered to break in the door, in the hope and possibility that he might still be alive, but she forbade me as this was council property and the Police would be held liable.........unless I was prepared to accept responsibility for damaging council property.

I was a bit disappointed that any police urgency and scope for dealing with a life or death emergency was so much at odds with mine, but this initial frustration proved academic as Frank's sister arrived with a key and the doctor confirmed that Frank was indeed dead. I never heard the presumed exact time of death, which could have been anywhere between, say, 7pm on Saturday and pub opening time on Monday.

It seemed such a waste … he hadn't even managed to open his Chinese Take-away!

You know Iain – that wasn't really digression, just a few thoughts as I walked along Shielhill Road; but I had started off thinking about my search for the 'other fellow'. I have to confess that I haven't found him yet, but as always, it is amazing what you uncover when you start moving things about to try to uncover something you have lost or find the mouse hole or wasps bike. And, of course, you have to poke about carefully to avoid being stung. In fact, in terms of looking for something, I can't understand this current world obsession with investing vast sums of money, investigating space when we don't even know what's under the South Pole and meantime the 'home maintenance' of the world is going all to hell!

I catch another waft of song from my youth – I think Rosemary Clooney and Tennessee Ernie Ford '—both had hits with 'This Old House'. The verses regret all the maintenance that has been neglected and one verse observes

*This ole house is agettin' shaky*
*This ole house is agettin old*
*This ole house lets in the rain*
*This ole house lets in the cold*
*Oh my knees are agettin' chilly*
*But I feel no fear or pain*
*Cause I see an angel peekin' through*
*A broken window pain.*

And it makes me think again of all the warnings that those we trust to manage 'this ole house' of a world have ignored and just left 'blowing in the wind'; and I think that the new priority of looking for somebody to blame when the world is burning up or flooding or starving or chucking bombs about while fighting a pandemic is wasting time; we should be checking out that angel through the broken window pane to find out if he is the harbinger of doom or the advance guard of the Argylls '—with pipes and drums blitzing down Aden High Street.

And I start thinking again about the 'other fellow', and I decide that a mischief maker is not the angel that is going to help us. And, of course, our original quest was to look for God. Just shows you how the 'other fellow' can play tricks with your thought processes and draw you off the straight path you are trying to follow.

I am now at the crossroad of Shielhill Road, just before the golf course and I decide the 'other fellow' can wait; if I find God first He'll sort him out or help us do it. And, anyway, I have decided that all the clues I need are, somehow, in this circular walk that takes me out of Kirriemuir for a while and then back in along the Brechin Road, up through the cemetery and out on to Hillrise and back to the Roods. I have the feeling that Kirriemuir is another of those little concentric circles of life; the life we all accept because most of us, the workers and the drones, haven't known any other so we don't realise that we are making the best of a kind of purgatory.

So, I turn right into East Hill Road and follow it up to where West Hill Road joins it and I carry on until I pass the Kirriemuir boundary sign. As you know Iain, it's a bugger of a road to walk – no footpaths on either side and the verges are, at least, eighteen inches high and covered with long grass; not ideal if an old codger like me has to get off the road quickly. Commuter traffic is fairly busy at this time in the morning and oncoming cars edge over to give me plenty of room; I give them a wave and mouth a thank you and almost without exception the driver responds with a wave or a thumbs up. I feel a little lift of enthusiasm with this modest morsel of communication – like we really are all Jock Tamson's bairns and part of a cohesive family.

But occasionally sod's law disturbs this spirit of unity and co-operation, in fact, more often than occasionally. There is enough room for two cars to pass each other without hindrance, but if I am on the road one of the cars has to stop, or I have to jump up the high banking and hang on to the fence atop the dry stone dyke that borders the fields on the other side. Sod's Law – whatever can go wrong could go wrong when you least expect it. It is almost as if some mischievous sprite organises this inconvenient congestion on an otherwise empty road; something to watch out for.

The weather is gorgeous at the moment and the walk down East Hill Road towards the Brechin Road presents a breathtaking view of the Strathmore Valley; it seems to be quite heavenly in this stretch of road outside the Kirriemuir boundary, alone with my thoughts and a few drivers who are prepared to make room for me and acknowledge me with a friendly wave.

I could go on about the rest of this walk down Easthill Road to the Brechin Road, turning towards Kirriemuir again and back up Cemetery Road and along past your wee slit trench; recounting all the detail of my thoughts and gradual enlightenment; long windedness and digression......
Sheila would be nagging desperately "Get to the end of the story – who is the killer?"

Trouble is I don't know yet. I haven't got a Hercules Poirot denouement already prepared, ready to deliver in the final chapter. But I love that word 'denouement', the unravelling. It is the French word that seems to complement our own delightful Scot's word fankle; a tangle in a time line, without knots, that just needs to be unravelled to restore history to a straight line without kinks, to reveal the truth – the veritas that links the via to the vita.

Talk to you tomorrow.

Much love

*Ed*

**1ˢᵗ September 2021**

# Hi Iain,

Seems that I am on a roll at the moment; the weather is glorious and I am again taking my life preserving morning walk: I have the wee tight bit in my chest again – which I am not ignoring – but I don't think at this age it is any more ominous than having a body, like any old car I ever owned, that has to be driven more carefully in its later years. Gordon Park and Douglas Street and then The Roods, up to the level of Shielhill Road is particularly testing.

I suppose the significance of this, in the allegorical time travel we are involved in will be lost to a lot of people – like Burns' poetry – without a side bar of interpretation to translate the Scots words which we either take for granted or have some inherent understanding of their normality and meaning. Roods, the old Scots word for cross, and shiel being a hut or haven on high ground, where shepherds once took shelter or rest. So, I suppose, in the translated language of one of our rippling circles of another time I am struggling up the last high section of the cross towards the flat level of Hillrise for a bit of respite on Shielhill Road. Is that getting carried away with similes and metaphors and allegories – coincidences? Clutching at one of those little snatches of sound, from the past, that come out of one of the little banging doors in my head. No wonder we Weegies describe people we don't fully understand as 'Effin Headbangers!'

Like the distant bugles of the US Cavalry coming to relieve big John Wayne and his beleaguered garrison – or, better still the sound of the pipes and drums of the Argylls marching down Aden High Street, in full battle order to let the 'other fella' know that Mad Mitch and The Jocks were in town and looking for him.

There used to be a popular song, 'the answer my friend is blowin' in the wind' performed by Peter, Paul and Mary; how about that for the name of a group to engender some historical parallels? Maybe somebody really is trying to tell us something from another era – or even, from an earlier time in this era. Is that too much fanciful speculation? Maybe I am nuts, as Sheila thinks. In the one dimensional world of 'Now', that she is doing very well at making the best of, she fears that I, and my family, have excluded her from some secret and mysterious conspiracy; which is partly true! But how could I explain to her that I, and my kids and you, are all engaged in an intermediate battle in the middle of 'Saving Private Ryan' that even you and my kids are not fully conscious of because it involves time travel and moving into other worldly dimensions? How can I explain to her that there is no conspiracy because at the moment the entire scenario – this real world that I see is all in my head?

How could I invite Sheila to leave the comfort zone she has created in her one dimensional world of Now and join me in this imaginary world I appear to have created? How could you even begin to convince Helen to abandon the faith that you have both shared for around eighty years, because you discovered late in life that it was not the way, and by channelling the truth that you always knew was in your head you extended your life for seven years beyond the point where, an 'expert in your condition had tried to convince you, would be the end. And how do you convince Helen that by letting in that wee chink of light to shine some veritas on the doctrine that religious faith had programmed you to accept, you determined you were not going to die on the cross.? You beat Easter this year! OK. so you only extended it by one day, but hey, 'one small step for Man, one giant leap for Mankind'

Remember, my dear friend, 'Iain, the word means God is Gracious!'

See you tomorrow,

Love from

*Ed*

**2nd September 2021**

Hi Iain

Where did I leave you yesterday? Top of the Roods, at the start of Shielhill Road.

I did a bit of serious thinking as I covered the stretch along to the junction with Golf Road and East Hill road. By the time I got to this point I had decided that the 'other fellow' is not Satan, and Satan is not St Peter as is implied in one of the accounts in the New Testament verses. The context in which Jesus is supposed to have linked the name of Satan with the actions of St Peter is quite passing, almost casually dismissive; but its near insignificance as a reactive passing comment leaves the analytical reader with an impression that St Peter is potentially evil – which he may be – and Satan is indeed the Devil that everybody believes is responsible for all the evil and mischief in the world.

Satan is not the devil. the other fella; Satan is, in fact, a necessary contributor to the progress of the world. The 'underworld' that Satan notoriously inhabits is, in our ship allegory, the engine room where all the power is stored and generated to to keep the Earth functioning and turning.

So, in that context, the Chief Engineer – Satan – is producing power at full speed, as directed, while the Captain is nailed to the masthead unable to tell the Chief Engineer to slow down, or the helmsman to alter course; and the watch keeper is blissfully following the old standing orders which were designed for a set of circumstances that no longer exist.

If this were the miraculous world of fiction we could hope for a Superman to fly down and push the prow of the ship round until it was heading safely towards open sea; or a Harry Potter, on his broomstick, to fly to the bridge to alert the watch-keeper to the impending disaster: or better still for Harry to fly to the masthead and release the immobilised Captain so that He can take command of the situation.

But, in this real world that we inhabit we don't have Superman or Harry Potter, we only have people, and there is nothing that happens on this earth that does not happen except through the actions of the people inhabiting the World at any period or era or, by the Earth itself slowly turning within a great field of magnetism that encircles the Earth like a giant dynamo, or generator producing a power that makes our Earth unique amongst the planets because it is self generating and self evolving. The 'ancients' knew this – look at an old Celtic cross – it is a cross section of a dynamo creating power from a central core as it revolves within an encircling field of magnetism.

Iain, somehow human beings, at this period in time the inhabitants of this Christian era have broken or arrested the progress and evolution that keeps our world in balance.

There may indeed be some great Super League game or competition between Good and Evil going on within the Universe, but we are not part of that super league yet. We are still in the Little League, here on Earth, within our Solar System and we have to learn our game properly by participating fully in this Solar System little league.

You know Iain, whether it is a Super League or a Little League, or everything is just a great Universal game, the game has roles and the game has players who should play within the rules and, of course, the game bas a referee to ensure that the game rules are observed. In our Little League the players are human beings and the course of the game is dictated by the proficiency and skill of these players; no Superplayer beaming down to score the winning goal or Harry Potter sweeping up the field to make that wizard touch down.

There is only us – human beings; and making a hostage of the referee's son to force him to help your team leapfrog evolution from the Little League into the Super League is definitely a bad idea!

But, somehow in the real world of two thousand years ago God, this benign magnetic God. saw a problem in the World, that needed fixing by some hands on management. The rules of the game dictated that only human beings could participate in little league games; so God had to convert a little part of Himself into human form to convince humanity that they were on a destructive course.

The rest of that little allegory is, as they say, history or, at least, a substitute for history, Gospel history; somebody's version of history with a bit of magic dust thrown in for flavouring to disguise some of the less savoury ingredients.

While this little portion, the circuit breaker, of the great ringfield magnet we call God was removed and transformed into human form we could recognise – a Messiah called Jesus – the normal functioning of the power supply was interrupted – broken. The earth was still turning, generating power into the circuitry but because the positive pole had been temporarily disconnected all this generated energy was flowing through the negative polarity and making direct contact with the Earth which was seriously overheating from this overload of energy.

Without the little circuit breaker that we, humanity, recognise as God's son Jesus the normal power process was interrupted and the process that keeps the Earth and Humanity turning and evolving at a controlled pace, designed to last for what we call eternity, was malfunctioning and erratic.

So, at this time in our evolution we, the World, this Earth we inhabit is suffering from bi-polar disorder because somebody has hidden or kidnapped the circuit breaker. And none of the certificated and qualified theological experts, who make big bucks out of telling you they know where it is can read or interpret the coded messages that persecuted people left in the Scriptures two thousand years ago!.

And the rules of the game are still that nothing on Earth can be magicked, except by human activity. But without the God-controlled bi-polar circuit some people have enough stored battery power to operate fairly efficiently but the majority, trusting and dependent on the main supply are relying on a circuit that is powered with negative energy and overheating at its connection with Earth.

(Now a pedantic perfectionist electrician may find lots of faults with my electrical analogy – but you get the message.........so fix it, spin it so it reads as accurate!)

Oh Iain. I have to take a break here; if you think this is outrageous heresy or feasible but complicated just imagine how my wee Glasgow head with its limited education and wee banging doors feels trying to make this digestible enough to satisfy the great SMUG who have awarded themselves degrees and qualifications to record their expertise in addressing our spiritual and mental needs – or the great CORRUPT who are enthusiastically looking after their own needs while all of them fumble along in the dark trying to locate the light switch.

The fucking light switch is lying on a hill somewhere in the so called Holy Land where YOU left it two thousand years ago; and the Popes and the Archbishops and the Chief Mullahs and the Chief Rabbis of the three great religions that are supposed to be awaiting the second coming are blocking our view of the light switch. It is still there, sticking up on that bloody wooden post where one of you lot put it, the next lot keeps it and the last lot keep trying to destroy it!

The clue is spun into the Scriptures that 'informed' theologians keep trying to interpret for us "No one comes to the Father except through Me!"

Oops, sorry about that wee rant – you can take the boy out of Glasgow but you can't take Glasgow out of the boy. I get a wee bit frustrated when folk complain that they cannot see the light, and find they have their eyes tight shut; or they are keeping the light hidden for their own nefarious purposes.

Anyway Iain, it is three thirty in the morning again......the witching hour; the time that Catholic priests generally believe is the best time to exorcise Demons.

Well, that reminds me that I haven't dealt with the 'other fellow' yet; leaving him loose and unexplained gives him a presence and credibility beyond his status......a mystique!

There is no great mystique – he is part of the human condition, but he changes his form to suit the uncertainty of an occasion. I have tangled with him before and, at least contained him; he is not a nice character worthy of respect: I called him Damian Roth, on that occasion, an anagram of the real person or human form bully boy he effected in that incident.

So, for the rest of the letters I will file him in a folder marked Damian Roth because he really doesn't feature again until the next cold case that you and I go on together.

Well Iain, in the real world of Kirriemuir on this, now, 3rd September I have reached the junction where I go right along East Hill Road and leave Kirriemuir for a wee bit until I come back along Brechin Road to come back into Kirriemuir to meet you

Need to oil the hinges on the wee doors and close them for the night.

See you tomorrow

*Ed*

**3rd September 2021**

Hi Iain,

Here we are again – still on Shielhill Road, and I realise that I am procrastinating with a vengeance; I really could do with a bit of reflection and a wee bit of digression to keep me focussed. This diving about, flying from one parallel of time to another can be very confusing – not recommended for the faint-hearted or the weak-minded. and ideally not without a co-pilot to remind one of the original objectives we set ourselves.

You know, Iain, as each of the wee doors in my head opens or closes I hear little snatches of song from some period in my past real life that seem to have a current relevance; but because history is in a great big corrupt fankle the little bursts of music are not reaching me in any sort of chronological order.

In my early teens I was full of naive heavenly sunshine – saw myself as a young Christian soldier in the Boys' Brigade; 243rd Company of the Glasgow Battalion. Headquartered in St Margarets Church of Scotland at Knightswood cross: I was also a dedicated member of the Scottish Schoolboys' Club – a Bible-reading organisation that met on Sundays in big houses in Mitre Road one week and Kirklee Road the alternate Sunday......I even remember the house numbers after seventy years. I enjoyed the discipline of the Boys' Brigade and the impact of marching young, proud and strong behind our pipe band with Captain Swann at our head, and Lieutenants Lindsay and Mitchell on the flanks and Lieutenant McAlpine bringing up the rear. Staff Sergeant Big Eddie Jeffreys had a floating role. scouting ahead to ensure that traffic was aware and stopped to allow the cream of Knightswood's youth free passage to spread their faith through the streets of their little world of Glasgow W 3.

Big Eddie was the company PE instructor who organised our keep fit and athletic training at sessions in the gymnasium of Knightswood Senior Secondary-School. He was also on the entertainments committee and the pianist who accompanied me when I was selected to sing the Boys' Brigade anthem 'Sure and Steadfast' at our annual Easter concert in Whiteinch Public Halls.

Big Eddie had a younger brother, corporal Harry Jeffreys: I had a younger brother Henry, who later became popularly known as Big Harry and I was still Edward – so I didn't see any cryptic connection between a Big Eddie who had a brother Harry accompanying a wee Eddie who has a brother Big Harry to sing 'Sure and Steadfast'. Perhaps there is no connection in the names and wordplay, and the only significance was that I had to go out on the stage on my own and sing the first verse to a packed house, before the curtains opened behind me to reveal the entire company who joined me in a rousing rendition: all those young Christian soldiers belting out 'Sure and Steadfast' to an appreciative and proud audience of family and friends from all over Knightswood.

My selection had been at very short notice; I was not the first choice. Strangely the originally chosen singer, Alistair MacDonald, was the only other Jordanhill College School pupil in the 243rd at that time, all the others being mainly Knightswood School boys. However, at the dress rehearsal Alistair had some sort of meltdown – I can't remember if he was unwell. had stage fright or couldn't make the high notes comfortably; whatever, I was drafted in at short notice and had to learn the song overnight to try to be word perfect

In the event, I was not word perfect but only in two words and managed to carry it off on the first night with some quick improvisation without any apparent interruption or detriment to the performance: except that Captain Swann noticed and commented "You got a couple of words wrong tonight!" And I replied "I know sir, but I won't make any mistakes tonight!" And I didn't.

Oh dear Iain, digression again. Do you see what happens when I go back in time, along my own time log line? I get caught in a comfort zone of specific, clear memories and go off at a tangent, reminiscing, and forget the serious purpose of this imaginary time travel.

Sadly "Sure and Steadfast" was the grand finale of my singing career which ended in 1953; my acceptable 'boy soprano' did not develop into a rich marketable Elvis Presley or Frank Sinatra, although my ability to perform under pressure must have been noted by some spiritual Universal talent scout. As so must yours have been although we were oblivious as teenagers to the lifetime of preparation we would undergo to equip us for the weird challenges we have been presented with at this late stage in our lives.

I went off to the Merchant Navy to learn, just enough, about navigation and ship handling to save Caledonia and, as I suspect now, to try to prevent a faith or a church from foundering; and you, dear friend went into Bangour

Hospital to learn how to suffer and overcome affliction to prepare you for the big battle of your later years when you pushed back cancer and refused to be beaten by this malignant disease

I enjoyed ten years of an 'ignorance is bliss' sort of existence with my happy day job progressing through the ranks on a ship that I loved, Cilicia, and finding romance in Glasgow with a girl that I loved; everything was fine while I was on Cilicia. My accepting the sudden 'stand in' challenge to join Caledonia, to avert disaster, was the turning point from my 'God is good' comfortable life, in Christian isolation, to a sad, real world of crosses to bear and demons to fight and frustratingly complicated Biblical crosswords and cryptic puzzles to solve.

Saving Caledonia brought a ton of shit down on my head, just like you and I experienced when we made our big splash in this sea of purgatory and decided we were going to fight back against the scourge of cancer that was now, the now of 2014, active within you, and predicted by an expert to be likely to beat you, pretty much by the summer of 2015.

In October 1960, having saved Caledonia, I retired from the Anchor Line to spend the rest of my idyllic Christian life with the wife that I loved and our new baby. Our son, Roddy, was born on the 16th October 1960, my birthday! I absolutely doted on this wee boy – the best birthday present I ever had – or could ever receive. I was the luckiest guy in the world – we were the complete perfect family.

Just before Christmas 1962 Roddy was diagnosed with kidney cancer and despite undergoing two operations and intrusive and uncomfortable therapy, he was dead by the 8th March. The best birthday present ever was gone. I was shell shocked!

You will remember Iain, you once said to me, "I know how it feels to be a bereaved Grandfather – I can't even imagine the grief of a father." Except it came out a little bit garbled through your emotion and it sounded as though you were saying that a grandfather's grief is the worst imaginable – but I knew what you were saying.

But, in answer to your query, I can tell you about the grief of a father, "It is fucking awful! Devastating!" Your own Alistair could tell you!

But, multiply that impression of the impact of grief on a father by a few hundred times, and you might begin to understand and appreciate how a bereaved mother feels, how your daughter-in law Hazel must feel.

I cannot emphasise enough just how devastatingly awful it feels; the shock, the despair, the total impotence you experience as this most precious water of this most cherished life dribbles through your fingers and leaves emptiness that is filled with anger and resentment, and self loathing of your own failure to protect and save this most precious life despite the love and the prayers you have dedicated and the trust you had that God would 'suffer the little children' is worthless.

And shell shocked bereaved parents, particularly the suffering mothers have to maintain as normal a life as possible for the sake of their other children and family who look to them for healing and compassion.

It is funny how life keeps repeating itself in the little comparable circles – whether it be events in time or in the emotions of people. It doesn't matter whether God created Man in His image or creative man imagined God in a human form. It means that God will experience the same reactions and emotions as Mankind. So God's despair and anger and need for revenge is no different from mine or any other bereaved father. And Mary, mother of Christ, mourning her son for the rest of her life, and refusing to accept the reality of His death and carrying his living memory through eternity, hidden lovingly deep in the recesses of her soul, along with the suppressed grief and anger and self loathing, is no different from every other Earth mother who has lost a child and feels some guilt that she could not save him. My wife Joyce endured such a secret existence for the duration of her life despite endeavouring to present an untroubled demeanour to her other children who deserved a mother's love and nurturing to equip them for their own lives.

It is funny how history, also, keeps repeating itself – if you can recognise the slight changes in appearance that evolution has demanded or, like the works of Shakespeare or George Bernard Shaw, being updated to suit a modern setting and please any current audience of that time period. But hidden below Kiss Me Kate is still Taming of the Shrew and layers below My Fair Lady is still Pygmalion.

And all those little individual ripples and circles of splashes, created by the disturbance factors in the lives of human beings are exactly the same shape and nature as the concentric circles of the earth's surface as they radiate outward from their respective polar origin ever widening – north expanding southward, and parallel circles from the south pole widening in circumference until they' meet and merge as one great circle at the Equator, which keeps turning from west to east to meet the sun of each new day every twenty four hours. And any event, of any era is locked somewhere between the two poles and is precise by navigational positioning where a meridian, a great circle of time, intersects with a parallel of latitude or the equator – the great circle of time and movement.

Except, of course, Easter which is a moveable feast. You know Iain, somebody somewhere is determined to make it difficult for us to locate and interpret the truth about Easter.

And Iain, there is a relevance about my digression through the Boys' Brigade combined with the Scottish Schoolboys Club – a much diluted parallel of the disturbance factor of 1963 to reflect the preparation some prophetic power exercised in 1952 to prepare me for a later challenge. Giving a solo rendition of Sure and Steadfast was not, I now recall, my last performance. Before a packed house of relatives and friends there was another last minute singing challenge for one wee guy from Knightswood and his bereaved wife.

We were not churchgoers, we had no regular minister. Roddy's funeral was held in the Cooperative Funeral Rooms on Paisley Road; the undertaker arranged a minister to attend – I remember he was from the Erskine Rose church – and we met only on that day. I had chosen the hymn 'Just as I am, Young strong and free, to be the best that I can be…' which had been a vesper we sang at the end of each SSC Sunday meeting. However, for some reason, on the day, there was no musical accompaniment available and the minister thought it would be very touching, since I knew the hymn, if I would lead the assembled mourners with the first verse. There seemed no alternative.

I managed to start the first verse, pretty well, and, like the curtains parting ten years earlier in Whiteinch Public Hall the assembled company weighed in with a fine rendition, picking up the verse from –

'For truth and righteousness and Thee, Lord of my Life, I come!'

But I couldn't continue, and my poor bereaved wife overcame and suppressed her own grief to come forward and lead me back out of public gaze into the relative anonymity and comfort of the mourning congregation. This really was my last public performance!

I suppose that wasn't really digression; more a planned detour to give a demonstration of two parallels of latitude, ten years apart: concentric circles of repetition of events that had there origin in the same tragic disturbance factor or splash of fate that no one expected. A kind of Easter tragedy acted out by real people 1,929 years after the living God had to surrender His hold on His Earth-bound Son. And the Earth mother had to carry the burden of her own grief while she gave comfort to the distraught father. A little earthly model to help understand an original major event.

And back on Shielhill Road. as I walk on that parallel of latitude around the model World that is Kirriemuir, you know Iain, that same sort of model that the Health experts, who gave us our daily Covid 19 briefing, have created to try to understand this great evil pandemic that has engulfed and immobilised the World at this time in the Earth's history. Well Kirriemuir is my little model world to try to understand and interpret the functioning, or indeed the malfunctioning of this real world of Earth that we inhabit during this so called Christian Era.

Wow!, Bit of a soliloquy, that one!

Now, the difficulty with any ball or globe is that you can only see a portion of it at any one time. Even if you imagine you are out in space, and hold your model at arms length, you can only see from the pole to the equator, and then only about a similar half between the two great circles of time, meridians of longitude, that circle the earth connecting the north pole to the south pole.

As Tony Blair keeps saying pompously "Now look Iain!" then pockets another million or so for delivering some bullshit in a convincing and interesting manner, that covers up the fib about the weapons of mass destruction his pal George says exist!

Well look Iain, this is Ed who sends you letters that hold your attention, presumably this far, in the hope of making you think and solve your little world's problems that are a model, a replica, of the Big World's problems.

So, do look Iain; this portion of the model world, that we can see comfortably, roughly equates to the Christian era in time, between the meridians, and roughly equates in area to the geographical spread of the old Roman Empire. And, somehow, our problem – and the answer to that problem – is located within that quarter of the Earth we can see if we can view it from the right distance, and the right perspective, with an open mind. Or we can view it on our little model earth that is Kirriemuir, that somebody started to create two thousand years ago as a little time capsule of cryptic clues and anagrams and 'sounds like' answers that can be found in any Glasgow Herald or Scotsman crossword.

Just like my outcrop of rock that came up to stub my toe and save me from drowning as I tried to save my son, so Kirriemuir has been sitting here and developing across the centuries, evolving and adapting the clues, to be prepared and appropriate to whichever era the crossword fanatic who can read the clues actually appears.

You know Iain, I reflect on this Shielhill Road, this moment in time, and I realise that I can go back down the Roods, through the Cross, and over the town square, past the Three Bellie Pub and Food Hub – born in this pandemic – then down to the bottom of Bellies Brae, to the lowest point in Kirriemuir and find the statue commemorating Bon Scott, the front man of the legendary AC/DC; Bon Scott the powerhouse who had a massive impact on the world but burned himself out by producing and burning more energy than his body could cope with.

And his followers, from all around the world make an annual pilgrimage, on his birthday to pay homage to his effigy in this deep gorge of the occult lower world side of Kirriemuir where the sunlight seldom penetrates.

And, from this vantage point on Shielhill Road, above the cross of the Roods but still below the highest point of this model that is Kirriemuir, I can realise the line from Hillrise stretching down to Bon Scott's statue, almost hidden in Bellies Brae car park like the almost straight section of a great circle, meridian of time, reaching from near the top of our world – where God should be – to the bottom, the underworld below decks, where Satan the hell-raiser and chief engineer power creator is burning himself out generating power for a world that is going round in circles.

And it seems as though the quarter of the globe that is visible to us contains the overall canvas of the Christian era operating in the Godless world with all the components, the active ingredients of the Christian era strewn around like pieces of a jigsaw puzzle just waiting to be rearranged into a recognisable picture.

Over a hundred years ago J.M. Barrie, the Kirriemuir-born playwright, created the imaginary world of Neverland where Peter Pan flew about leading the Lost Boys and uniting the indigenous tribes in a fight, an ongoing fight, to defend their right to freedom from the oppression of the Eton-educated Captain James Hook and his marauding band of pirates.

Was Barrie perhaps imagining or creating a model of ancient Caledonia which provided a refuge, on the outside edge of the expanding Roman Empire, for the oppressed peoples fleeing the Roman brutality in the so-called Holy Lands, who had picked Scotland as their 'backs to the wall' last battleground in their defence of free will? Not natural allies, and retaining their individual ethnic identities and practices and beliefs; small nations, or tribes, allowed to practice their hereditary customs and who did not always agree with each other, but learned to disagree agreeably!

The Romans called them Caledonians, an apparently aggressive, argumentative people who fight amongst themselves until Caledonia, this Scotland, is threatened by a Godless empire that wants to deprive them of their freedom. Refugees from disparate nations and clans who suddenly are united by the memory that they are all Jock Tamson's bairns and their individual strengths are magnetised into a powerful Confederation of a Free People united to defend their freedom to live in harmony and religious practice as they choose without being homogenised into some servitude of Imperial domination. To ensure that the Empire understood their ethos they posted their defiance in the language of Empire.........Nemo me impune lacessit!. Wha' daur meddle wi' me!

Sorry Iain, a wee bit of Weegie emotion erupting there; like a kettle that has been on the hob too long and starts to boil over!

And, of course, there are little snatches of evidence around Kirriemuir that are throw-backs to Barrie and his creation; like the Wyvern, that serves as a weather vane atop the Old Parish Church steeple – a Wyvern which is the symbol of Mary Magdalene, who has left evidence of her passage to sanctuary and freedom along the Celtic fringes of a safe route from the so called Holy Land to this great hill fortress of Kirriemuir at the gateway to Pictavia the land of the Caledonians. – the Romans identified as Celi Dei'ans – Companions of God.

(It's all there Iain, somewhere in the big fankle of Mythology, History, the Scriptures, Google and Wikipedia in plain language or cryptic interpretation if one has the patience to untangle the bights in the line that obscure the Truth.)

And, the very creative Barrie has taken this symbol of Mary Magdalene, this Wyvern from atop the Church steeple, with the church clock that chimes every quarter hour, loud enough to reach every corner of this model of the world that Kirriemuir represents, and represented it as Captain Hook's nemesis, the crocodile with the alarm clock ticking in its belly that will pursue the evil Hook relentlessly until he falls into the open jaws of this historic reptile, trapped in the hellish belly of eternity where time has caught up with him.

And I realise, Iain, on this parallel of time at the top of the Roods I could take a short cut and skirt along Hillrise and come, pretty much, to Barrie's grave which is fairly close to the top of Kirrie Hill – but not quite at the top.

Is it too much of a 'clutching at one too many straws' coincidence, or too conveniently fanciful to reflect that Barrie died in 1937, one year after I had arrived in the real world just in time to catch hold of Peter Pan's shadow which was in danger of being trapped in the window by an unaware housekeeper? … maybe a wee bit too much magic dust in that speculation!

In the real world of just now I think about Barrie being not quite at the top of the Hill. And I think about Barrie's predicament, like all the other writers who see the Truth but cannot convince a sceptical world to open its eyes and see the light, so he presents it as an Aesop's fable, an allegory or a fairy tale that might direct a child's mind to believe in the ultimate victory of good over evil.

Iain, I am going to take another Indiana Jones quantum leap of presumption here. Barrie realised that the little model world of Kirriemuir was a microcosm of the real thing but that somebody trying to view from any real time vantage point, like me standing at Hillrise on Shielhill Road, had a restricted view of the world or model of the world that they were in.

So he built a camera obscura on top of Kirrie Hill so that future generations could look down on a wider view of this top half of the model and search for the clues and so on that lie hidden in the buildings and streets and history of this ancient hill fort guarding the entrance to the last wee bit of free 'real' world on the edge of Empire!

Then I think, who is at the top of the hill? And I remember, it is the white granite statue of the wee Black Watch rifleman with his bayonet fixed, standing in the on-guard position looking southward across the Strathmore Valley from where he expects the threat will approach.

Oh, my goodness Iain. I have just looked again at the wee Rifleman and noticed, certainly from this angle, he looks a bit like wee Frank Massie who I left standing at this spot a few days ago before I digressed off for a wee meander through the layers of time that are memory.

Wow, that's enough for tonight – or as it is now, this morning; start of a new day and I have to get up and go for my life-preserving walk,

Talk tomorrow,

*Ed*

## September 2021 between 3rd and 6th

# Hi Iain,

I have dated this vaguely as between the third and sixth September to give me breathing space to catch up. The thoughts and relived experiences are pouring out the wee doors quicker than I can write them down to send to you.

From this top of the Roods I can see back the full duration of the two thousand years from now, back to the first Easter. But, the opposite of the obvious is once again in play in this crazy world of concentric circles of time that we are operating in.

Although I am standing on top of the Roods in 2021, I am also standing on top of the empty Cross of…now, I worked it out to be sometime in March or April of 34 AD; Jesus allegedly being 33 and about 4 months when He died.

Iain, I should have guessed it would not be so simple as that; I Googled it and checked with Wikipedia……Jesus H Christ, does somebody not half want to keep the date of that first Easter vague and moveable! Not only is the date within the year moving each time, it seems as if the actual year of the Crucifixion is also uncertain and vague, being either 32AD or 34AD, but not possibly 33AD. This assertion based on a combination of mathematical calculations carried out by a US navy navigational expert; but his findings and assumptions influenced, also, by the date of some other event which occurred some 450, or so, years earlier. Cruci-fiction indeed!

It is almost like a parallel of my experience on Caledonia sixty years ago when wee Davy Jones, the good Christian fourth mate placed the position of Caledonia on the chart, exactly where the Captain wanted and expected the ship should be; except, Caledonia was too close to the land and, perhaps, caught in some anomalous inshore strong current which was driving the ship to disaster.

Iain, a different start point, which influences the position of that first Easter from 450 years earlier, isn't within our search area of the reference books of the New Testament but contained somewhere else, perhaps, in the Old Testament of Hebrew history or, even, archived as irrelevant somewhere in Roman or Greek mythology. I will just have to do what I did back in 1960, and disregard the phoney position and have confidence in my own identified position; and that is atop the cross of the Roods from whence I can see back two thousand years; which really, in the event it is the empty Cross of two thousand years ago, my view takes me forward from then to now!

But Iain, the challenge we set ourselves, Diarmuid's quest, was only to locate God and, at least to our own satisfaction, we have found an answer to God – the benign encircling field of power which had to assume human form to walk among men to show the Way!

And, to achieve this He detached a little segment of Himself to create God the Father and God the Son. for a little while, so God the Son could walk on Mother Earth, to alert mankind to the error that was pulling Earth off course and to show the Way for Humanity to bring itself back to a safer passage. With the little segment of magnetic power – a bi-polar bar magnet – removed from the great circle of magnetic field that held the Earth in balance, God the Father was also reduced temporarily to the bi-polar condition of Man, with less secure power than existed in the ring field magnet.

The Gospel truth story of Holy Week could do with a bit of analysis – some first century writer has made an Indiana Jones type of quantum leap. to magic God the Son from entering Jerusalem on a Sunday, undertaking all sorts of strenuous activities on the Monday, Tuesday and Wednesday, organising a significant farewell party for the Thursday night, attending court and being found guilty on the Friday with a long trek carrying a big cross up a hill to be crucified, hang there for, allegedly three days but, in essence, die and be buried in a cave by sometime on Sunday – then be out the cave by Monday.

What does seem in no doubt is that Jesus died on Calvary although even that identified location seems subject to a lot of highly qualified and sophisticated argument; but again, Iain, the answers or clues to that truth also lie further back in time and recorded history than we are prepared or intended to go.

The one fact that is indisputable, it seems, is that Jesus was brutally murdered by the State manipulating and contriving the vote of a subjugated people through the old Roman 'thumbs up or thumbs down' system of deciding whether a Gladiator should live or die!

Both God and Mother Earth were distraught, as any human parents, at the murder of their only beloved Son. And God. the Father, now reduced to human form with positive and negative bi-polarity suffered the same immediate shock and depression of any human father who has been rendered impotent and unable to intervene with any 'God-like magic' or miracle to save this precious Son.

But in the real or human world of 34 AD, as the bereaved father, having reminded the mourning world to respect and praise his son, succumbed to the overwhelming grief that he was suffering, his wife, the earth mother Mary isolated and contained her own grief for the sake of the love of the father of her child and, for the sake of humanity, that her son had not died in vain. So Mother Earth came forward to comfort and bring God back to the safety of the supportive congregation while she called on the companions of God, Peter and Paul, to help her make a start on her son's plan to lead the World away from destruction, while God regained His strength and restored His son, who had survived that first Easter, just as you, Iain, proved to be possible by surviving your last Easter.

Your one small step for Man but one giant leap for Mankind!

And Mary, the living earth mother and human replica of Mother Earth, suffered a parallel pain of agony and self loathing as the suppressed grief for her lost child welled up inside her soul; she felt incredible guilt for being unable to save Him and, indeed for having brought Him into this world at all, to suffer and die a painful death when all He had tried to do was bring to earth the love of God.

Iain, in our little analogy and assumption that the repeated circles of happenings are models of a past event that should be learned from, and not repeated, and God cannot communicate directly with Man – and He is not about to repeat the last abortive tragic attempt – is it possible that both God and Mother Earth are sending bigger and louder warning signals that the world of the Earth is on a self destruct course, and has been ever since the power supply was disrupted by a massive shortage in the circuit, two thousand years ago!

Now, God rendered bi-polar without the benefit and strength of the great ring field supplied by the earth's rotations harvesting human energy to create a positive charge, but receiving only a negative supply, both God and Mother Earth lapsed into a depressed state while forced to carry on the day job of keeping the Earth functioning until a positive flow of energy could be restored. There is no big mystique – God made Man in His image or man made God in man's image – either way God was now committed to behaving like any bereaved earthly father depressed by the potentially fatal attack on His son, and the devastating consequences it held for His wife.

And Mary the earth mother, or Mother Earth who is naturally bi-polar, but now suffered some bi-polar disorder with the interruption to the positive supply, would not let her son die, and held on to God's hand while still clinging to the Son of God's companion, Peter, who had been nominated as the foundation stone on which Christ's Church should be built. Thus the Church of Christ was established, in the midst of an alien Empire, and survived despite the absence of Christ's leadership, as the Watch-keeper, through this so called Christian era. Mary had Her hands full trying to keep the foundation of the church connected to God who was too distracted to observe and control the corruption of false prophets and opportunists who were placing His son's church in a vulnerable position and pushing it, off course, towards destruction.

Mary's call to the Companions of God was eventually answered a second time when a relief watch-keeper boarded the Church............lain, in our original allegory, or model, Caledonia was the church, skirting round the bottom of the Arabian Peninsula of the so called Holy Lands. Disaster was averted as God the Captain saw the light, enough to alter course towards the open sea. But the relief watch-keeper was scheduled to remain only until the end of this current voyage we now depict as the Christian Era; a new navigator, spiritual leader, would have to be appointed before any new voyage could be undertaken.

Iain, in our analogy of little circles being, either, prototypes of big circles yet to be formed through time or history or, models of those big circles from past history that can only be viewed, in part, from inside, or from too far away to see clearly if one tries to view the whole circle from a distance, to give us some indication of what might be on the dark side; somehow I suspect that you and I and our wives – in my case two wives – have been unsuspecting participants in rehearsals for some major production which has only one performance that has to be right on the night.

We, among us, have experienced living with, and overcoming most physical afflictions; and endured the frustrations of being diagnosed with conditions, physical and mental, by practitioners who had the qualifications to prove that their opinionated diagnoses might be pretty well infallible. I find this attitude a mite irritating in the arena of mental health, which is a relatively newly appreciated burden on society, and yet youthful psychiatrists and psychologists are dazzled by their flashy new diplomas, which render them oblivious to the experiences and opinions of laymen who, perhaps like me, have studied the problem for a lifetime and found some solution, albeit a temporary fix, that they cannot see or recognise. In my case somebody who had lived a shorter time than I had of working life was trying to convince me I was nuts; while, in your case, a doom laden expert tried to convince you that because he had run out of ideas you would die within months!

We prevailed, Iain, and we went looking for God, with Diarmuid's help… Oh, I have to digress here. Remember Diarmuid who is to some extent an expert in matters Theological, and, also, a thinking priest who does not accept that all the directives the church makes are justifiable or, even, based on a sound premise; his concern with the act of pro-creation, or love, being classified as the original sin: I think his scepticism and concern was well justified. A concept that programmes millions of God fearing or God respecting or God loving people, impressionable or malleable people that the foundation of their Faith is based on a sinful act between the founders of that faith has to be a misconception. Good on you Diarmuid, I like your sceptical questioning mind, while you still retain the faith and determination to seek the Truth, the positive Truth – the Veritas between the Via and the Vita that the late J.C. was trying to teach or show us!

Seems as though there is a lot of jiggery-pokery going on in the minds of the professional and qualified people who are supposed to communicate the Truth through a positive 'glass half full' to us impressionable wee guys who are looking to them for reassurance or guidance.

So there you have the result of Diarmuid's quest – our search for God. He has been suffering from depression – a bit of bi-polar disorder – which Pope Benedict reported as God sleeping. Pity the only person at that time who was allegedly permitted to communicate with God couldn't awaken Him. Particularly so, seventeen centuries after the Bishop Origen of Alexandria suggested the condition and the disorder but was severely chastised for heresy and discredited for his perspicacity.

Could have saved a perfectly good Universal Church from being infected by corrupting influences while poor Mary had her hands full holding God and Peter together until some positive magnetism could be restored to the system. What a purgatory that must have been for poor Mary who had started out as the Mother of Mankind. A wee burst of positive power and corruption can be destroyed.

Do you remember Iain, our original pact. to shine our wee lights – you from your small comer, and I from mine? Well, it is 3.20 am – ten minutes to go to the witching hour and we have already chased a few demons about the Universe!

I believe a Wee Short Legged Whitburn Catholic man and a Wee Fat Glasgow Proddy man make an unlikely but formidable bi-polar unit.

l am so glad you are my friend and companion on this journey,

See you tomorrow

*Ed*

**22nd September 2021**

# Hi Iain,

No, I haven't put the wrong date at the head of this letter, but I have to indulge in a bit of planned digression to attempt to clear or untangle and explain a couple of little kinks and bights – to use a nautical expression. that contribute to the fankle that has occurred, or been created, in our ship's log line; this allegorical ship that is our World, with its time line of history, stretching out astern, that should be towing and turning freely, but is hampered by some piece of jetsam it has become entangled with two thousand years ago.

We know that this end of the time line of world history is still moving forward, because we are living it; and we know that the little reversed propeller at the free end of our time line is still turning and recording some progress: so if both ends are operating and identifiable there can't be a knot in the time line – only kinks that can be unfankled. But we need to get on with it before this fankle accumulates more flotsam and jetsam, like some other suppressed or spun record of history, and becomes so heavy that it distorts the true reading of the history that we are supposed to learn, or breaks the time line off completely, and that is the end of everything. As they say Apocalypse now!

So Iain why don't we, in this sophisticated twenty first century, when we are so arrogant that we can invent and build a mechanical brain called a computer, and create our own spirit world called the web, why can we not see and simply identify the problems of this twenty first century and solve them, as God might have done had we not stopped listening to Him or following His original plan?

As I tried to illustrate in our little 'saving Caledonia' experience, human frailty put us in a slightly vulnerable position. Ignorance of the existence of any negative current compounded that original mistake and dependence on a man made machine, that had developed a fault, left the ship standing into danger. Had the Captain not felt the instinct to demand an experienced replacement for an inexperienced officer there would have been no one to see and believe the incongruous truth that three unconnected events, human negligence, a natural inshore current and an infallible machine failure had somehow conspired to create, what is now popularly described as, a perfect storm.

Can you see Iain, what has happened to mankind? We cannot see the Truth; that Veritas that connects the Via, the way of the continuous journey of humanity, with the Vita, the life that we have to keep moving. We are dependent on perpetual motion to keep the earth turning and the creatures of the Earth evolving to adapt to any era of this eternal journey through the Universe.

Remember Jack Nicholson in the film 'A Few Good Men' – when Tom Cruise demanded the Truth and Nicholson replied angrily "The Truth, Sonny? You couldn't handle the Truth!"

That is us, mankind in this so called Christian era – we cannot see, or handle the truth that we have stopped evolution!

The truth is, that if the dinosaurs could have developed their brains to match their body size they, like us might have arrogantly believed that they were the ultimate stage in evolution – and now the world would be full of dinosaurs and we would all be up to our armpits in Dinosaur shit, because the Dinosaur would have been the consumer society of however many millions of years ago.

We are the dinosaurs of this so called Christian era. and we are already up to our hips in our own dinosaur shit of plastic and fossil fuel waste. We are so arrogant and sophisticated that we have created machines to do our thinking and entertain us – computers and smart phones – and we ignore or cannot see or hear the subliminal message of entertainment, the protest songs of Peter, Paul and Mary or the hidden messages of films and plays like "Why us?" answer, "Because we 're 'ere lad!" Or Jack Nicholson shouting "You couldn't handle the Truth, Sonny!"

The truth, or the answer to our questions lies further back in time than we are capable of going with this cold case – Diarmuid's Quest, to find God.

God isn't some little remote dot on the edge of a box we imagine as the Universe – God is progress, evolution, the spirit that keeps humanity moving and clearing up after itself. And we cannot rely on our own super brain computers and I phones to provide the solution that prevents the shit of this era from reaching our armpits-because we haven't realised that we are in control of our own destiny; and our mechanical brains can only solve the problems that our human brains have identified and solved, to provide a template, a model, to programme into the mechanical brain's processors and memory banks.

And legions of creative thinking people have seen the problem, or part of it, and certainly the prospect that we could live 'happily ever after' if the glass slipper fitted or the seven dwarves could help Snow White find her prince.........whatever! They are all fairy stories with a magical happy ending, but without miracles!

Our fairy story for this Christian era doesn't even have the happy ending; the prince is still hanging on the Cross and Cinderella is making the best of purgatory by believing that NOW is all there is, and that programming the children to accept this as the Truth will serve them well and happily enough. No need for God, the male contributor to creation, that is essential for Mother Earth, or 'earth mother' to keep the species alive because somebody has defined the act of pro-creation as the 'original sin' and introduced guilt into the act of reproduction.

Iain, can you guess where I am going with this? We are not talking about the act between a man and a woman to create a new life – they are only the model for the more spiritual union between God and Mother Earth who have to see through the eyes and minds of Mankind that Humanity has to keep recreating itself to adapt to the finite earth world we live in – or exist as dinosaurs for a while and drown in our own shit, or suffocate in our fossil fuel consumption and become extinct!

You know, Iain, I have been impressed by your accumulated knowledge – from your good education and experiences of successful careers and family life; all stored in and neatly stacked in massive memory banks while you, even you, got on with doing the best you could for everybody – like a Good Samaritan – journeying through the World of NOW, helping people make the best of it.

But you were programmed and conditioned by the family habit to model your life on the example of a faith provided, and adopt the life disciplines programmed into you except, the thinking part of your brain, behind the McAfee or Norton security, the part you still controlled gave you doubts about the fairy story that did not have a happy ending, without the dependence on miracles or waiting for two thousand years for the Prince to show up.

And there is Helen who thought the story was beautiful and embraced the faith, because it seemed to provide her with everything she needed – a

God who surrounded her with love and provided her with a husband who dispensed goodness and a lifestyle full love and comfort and enjoyment; until her faith is rocked by the cruel death of your little grand daughter. But her original family programming and her ongoing dependence on this faith sustained her acceptance, without question, of the miraculous beginning of the Christian era and belief in a miraculous ending.

And to help her cope with the doubts created by Anna's death, she keeps the memory of Anna alive in her heart – parked in a little special place – and thus, a part of evolution is again put on hold, because a little bit of Helen stops moving on from that shock.

Sheila believes in NOW! Accept it, get on with it. enjoy it. make the best of it! Because that is how her mother programmed her to survive the realities of life. And once you have your children, programme them also in this faith – and, if you have done it well enough, you will have equipped your children, and perhaps their children, to survive and enjoy a life making the best of a NOW existence. But, after NOW. what then? Evolution has stopped; and all you have been, as in our shipboard analogy, is a paying passenger who enjoyed the voyage and got off at the end.

The problem, well as I interpret it, is that suspended evolution has occurred for Western styled Democracy – the American dream, perhaps, and the demons or parasites of Capitalism and Communism have pushed in to fill the void created by the moving finger creeping ahead of humanity's ability to follow the trail and keep abreast of evolution. And the parasites cream off the fruits of the labours of a creative mankind who cannot see the failure of a leadership that has allowed corruption to usurp control of religion, the banks and the government of nations, and blind mankind to the need to re-create his way of life to adapt to where planet Earth has evolved to.

If you suspend evolution of the species you don't keep pace with the revolutions of the Earth between the two balancing and magnetic poles, and you interrupt the process of regeneration; this regeneration of power that occurs as the positive energy of human spirit which passes through the great magnetic dynamo of the Universe to be recycled and returned through the molecule of each human birth, as positive energy to maintain evolution through re-creation to maintain and inspire humanity to keep evolving through regeneration.

There is no great mystique, Iain; the choice is between drowning in the dinosaur shit of this twenty first century or cleaning up the mess that we have made with our fossil fuels and our plastic waste, while the Eton educated Captain Hooks and their Pirate bands cream off the profits and enjoy the good life in this fairy tale era of consumerism in the NOW religious era.

The big secret that the profiteers have identified and kept from us is that the Earth is a self-sustaining entity – possibly unique in the Universe, because it is the prototype; the model on which future civilisations might be based so long as we, mankind, do not screw up this great Universal experiment.

The truth is so outrageously simple that. as Jack Nicholson said to Tom Cruise, "The truth, Sonny? You couldn't handle the Truth!"

The trouble is, that since this Christian Era, so called, is communicated as a fairy tale, this becomes the prototype, the template for gentler adaptations with happy endings to be imagined and published in the hope that humanity gets the message; remember, even the all powerful God had to assume human form and communicate through allegories. Humans throughout this era who have seen, at least, something of the light of truth have continued to use this somehow subliminal communication through song and drama, or Fairy Tales with a happy ending; like Cinderella finding her prince, despite the negative efforts of her wicked stepmother and the ugly sisters, or Snow White finding her prince with the help of the little people, the seven dwarves, who could see the difference between good and evil.

Or perhaps, here in Kirriemuir, the Wee Red Toon, J.M.Barrie's inspiration for Neverland – the domain of Peter Pan, the boy who wouldn't grow old and fought evil – was Barrie's vision of Scotland which was Caledonia, the land of the Companions of God who resisted and discouraged domination and subjugation by a Captain Hook of the Roman Empire which controlled the, then, known world.

Oh Iain, I have to stop here; time is catching up; in fact, has overtaken me.

I need to assume that we are on the same wavelength now and you accept some of the quantum leap interpretations of history and the fairy story predictions I am having to make. I see that I started this letter on 23rd September, which was a quantum leap from the previous letter of 6th September; a lot of real time, day to day, activity took place which I will tell you about sometime, perhaps in some inevitable future digression.

Meantime, in this NOW era, I have a bus to catch; we are having a wee jaunt to Aberdeen on a City Link bus: one of the compensations of old age in Scotland … my bus pass!

Talk to you tomorrow.

*Ed*

**Friday 1ˢᵗ October 2021**

# Hi Iain,

Sorry to leave you so abruptly yesterday; as I said, Sheila and I had a bus to catch. We went to Aberdeen for a day out: a wee escape from our real world of Kirriemuir – or, is that now our model world?

I am getting so used to flipping about between historical worlds, current worlds, allegorical worlds and models of future worlds that I have to check, on occasions, that you are still with me.

At this very moment on 1st October 2021, in the real world, it is 4.44 a.m., I see that on the wee digital clocks on both the kitchen range and the microwave; which is, in itself, a minor miracle because, sometimes, these displayed clock times seem not exactly synchronised. Anyway, I actually wakened around 3.35am. – a call of nature – and registered that it was just past the witching hour, and I hadn't fought with any demons, other than the demon of 'not being able to go the whole night without taking a piss!' I always remember that quote from a Sean Connery and Nicholas Cage film where they infiltrated Alcatraz to prevent a mad military commander's threat to destroy the world.

The FBI man was impressed with the elderly Connery's superman-like quality, because he had slept all night without going to the bathroom.

Time seemed to be pressing me on all sides; in the real world of my own body I am compelled to wake at the witching hour with only one demon to address. I go to make tea in the kitchen, in the real world of Kirriemuir, and the digital clocks show me a pretty good 'blind brag' poker hand, three fours, not unbeatable by any means, but worth taking a punt on. For some reason I am moved to check in The Herald and confirm the time of sunrise, around 7.20a.m., and my eye catches a reference to the Climate Conference scheduled for Glasgow, and its imminence with a start date, now, only thirty days away, and I haven't completed the letters that I started writing to you about ten years ago.

The problem is that I seem to have evolved into a reporter and can give you a reporter's interpretation of an event only after it has occurred or if it is actually happening as I observe it. I am not a creative writer who can imagine a convincing episode of serious fiction and produce a fairy story that holds the children captivated. I fear that I am somewhat pedantic and can only report the Truth or, I accept, my view or interpretation of the Truth. And the truth, as I see it, only comes to me in batches of memory; I don't suddenly Google my brain to conjure up a convincing fiction. But, having caught a snatch of Peter, Paul and Mary blowin' in the wind and connected the real characters of of the Cruci-fiction two thousand years ago, by some tenuous spiritual link, to the entertainers of fifty or years ago, I listen to what is 'Blowing in the Wind'; a bit like you and me, Iain: me on Anna's wee bench and you still in your wee slit trench, listening to me and nodding as you see the light from my small corner.

Then I think of my old marketing maxim 'always look for the opposite of the obvious', and I wonder if you, you cunning old dog, are actually the storyteller who has somehow engaged me to write down the story that you have been blowing in the wind, until I feel that wind and see the light from your small corner in time for the conference in Glasgow to see the light shining from two directions.

You know, Iain, I have to go back in time – passing time – because the events and thoughts have been occurring more quickly than I can write them down; in fact, twenty four days have elapsed in which Sheila and I have done quite a lot of normal living – the little things that have to be done, to keep 'Now' going, that interfere with the parallel big story that I would like to tell but have to store in my memory until I have time to convert the thoughts to written words.

By the way, on the 6th September, just before I put these twenty four days on hold I noticed, as I entered the Cemetery at your level, that the second bench in had an inscription which I merely glanced at previously and assumed to be maybe an Italian, because the name looked like two foreign words. However, on closer scrutiny I now see the words as Lucem Petimus, which I recognise as Latin and, alongside, the school crest of Webster's High School. My Latin is not as good as yours so I had to check it out on Wikipedia.

As usual with Latin there are alternative interpretations, from the literal translation to the accepted meanings which may be used; Lucem Petimus "All will be revealed today" or "You will see the Light."

Hey Iain, I did not magic up a memorial bench from the pupils of Webster's High School, and place it in Kirriemuir Cemetery, close to your wee slit trench, so that it could fit in with a letter I wrote to you, back in

2014, seven years ago, about your small light shining from your small comer.

Anyway, it is still before sun up; have to go for my lifesaving walk and meet the dawn of this new day – somewhere on Shielhill Road.

Talk to you again in a couple of hours

*Ed*

**Tuesday 2nd October 2021**

*Hi Iain,*

It seems as though I have opened up Indiana Jones' Ark of the Covenant, and all the stored information that previous generations didn't cope with is rushing towards me.

There really isn't time now for me to tell this story at a leisurely digestible pace. Like somebody said in the so called Good Book, "I am the Alpha and the Omega". and I could delude myself that this is me, as the apparent author of these letters we have exchanged. But, the Truth is, I am not the beginning and the end, because we, you and I, arrived somewhere past the middle, closer to the end, and tried to find, at least an explanation for the God of creation and extend your life beyond the notional life span, your Omega, so that the story can be told, and understood, in time to make a difference.

Iain, you made a difference, and got me, the wee fat Glasgow Man to try to tell the story for you.

And, with your typical determination to take care of your family, after you are gone, you built in all sorts of contingencies for your children and grandchildren to take care of Helen, the mother, the Mother Earth of your family. And you also took out some insurance by engaging a scribe to record what you have learned during this so called Christian Era so that a future generation might learn from your experience.

Like all the good people who have tried to determine the Truth of existence you find the story simple, and yet too complex to explain to children – the People, the Children of God who inhabit the Earth in any given generation; because before they can think for themselves they are programmed by the previous generation to believe in miracles and demons and bogey men, and ugly sisters. And the children are taught fear before they have learned love, and keep their eyes shut to avoid seeing the frightening evil.

And people like you, the good people who have preceded you with the wish to convince any generation that love was important, told the story as an allegory, an analogy – a fairy story with a happy ending, just so long as the Prince arrived in time; and the glass slipper didn't fit one of the ugly sisters competing to be the earth mother that the Prince of Peace would marry. And, of course, there was a time constraint; the magical happy ending had to occur before time ran out, when the clock struck midnight, and the good life that the Fairy Godmother had bestowed would turn to dust.

Well Iain, we know the end of that story; Cinderella made it home just in time to keep the magic alive and give her prince time to find her and live happily ever after.

Iain, as I procrastinate on this parallel of time that is Shielhill Road, I realise that I am on the same level of Kirrie Hill that J. M. Barrie got to and did not have the final answer; so he invented Neverland, the domain of Peter Pan, 'The Boy Who Wouldn't Grow Up' but was protected by his little guardian angel, Tinker bell.

He was also in love with Wendy, who lived in the real world – the world that would not let Peter in, and had shut the window on his shadow, his time line, that he needed to remind him of who he was and where he is at any point in time.

At the beginning of the twentieth century there wasn't enough accumulated knowledge in the, then, real world like the advances in medical science or the discovery of genetic markers and DNA to see the past more clearly, and have a stab at predicting or imagining what the future picture might look like. Those pieces of the jigsaw that now allow the human understanding to see the emerging picture before Mother Earth comes up and says "That's it, kids – lights out!"

And we, the children of God and Mother Earth, the real world – not Neverland – are fast approaching 'Lights Out', and all that is there are the emergency lights that people keep alive like our two little candles still flickering; you from your small comer, and I from mine.

And, of course, Barrie's little glimmer of hope – Tinker bell – who drank the poison to save Peter.

Iain, Barrie couldn't see it, or how to explain it convincingly a century ago; but his Tinker bell, the mother earth, the Good Fairy that protects Peter Pan (the mankind of Neverland), and has swallowed the poison of two thousand years of activity with Satan – who is really not a bad person at all! – just the chief engineer, the chief executive of earth, burning the fuel that was available and which the ship was designed to run on during that era. But Tinker bell has swallowed the toxic fumes to keep Peter alive because He is the Alpha and the Omega, and we are not ready for Omega quite yet!

Barrie could not quite see how to awaken the sleeping giant of mankind – but he knew how to stimulate and motivate an audience. He had a narrator. who made an impassioned plea to the Audience to believe that their involvement, their awareness of the danger to Tinker bell, their applause, could revive Tinker bell who would save Peter, the boy who wouldn't grow old but would continue to protect Neverland from Captain Hook, the Eton-educated Pirate who wanted to take over the World.

And the children responded first, clapping and cheering to keep Tinker bell alive and save her from the noxious fossil fuels, and the Mum and Dads caught the excitement and started clapping. and eventually the sound of belief and enlightenment spilled out of the Glasgow conference centre and broke through the arrogance of Humanity that believed it was the ultimate development because it had invented a machine to do all the thinking.

Well Iain, I've been at it again, since the witching hour and, as yesterday I have reached the part where I go for my life preserving walk. around the great circle, that takes me from Kirriemuir Fire Station up past the Episcopal Church of St Mary, that has had no vicar for a while now, and over the top of the Roods, skirting around Hill Rise via Shielhill Road and out of Kirrie, for a bit, down East Hill Road; then in again, just before Cemetery Road – that steep climb up to where the black Audi is parked opposite the gate to your level: I can look forward to a wee bit more Veritas communicated from your wee slit trench. Then I have that last steep climb up, and past Barrie, to the top of the Hill.

You know Iain, it is always an achievement, or perhaps a relief, to come out of that back gate at the top of the Cemetery and find that I am pretty much alive. And I take in the wide expanse of Kirrie Hill – great for family picnics on a good day – with the superb play area for children and the delightful Camera Obscura that Barrie built so that future generations could view the model world of Kirriemuir without any obscurity.

I complete the Great Circle back at the Fire Station and go home to clean out Satan's altar – the little coal fire that Sheila insists is the only thing that keeps her cosy in her world of Now.

And, I remember that I left Frank Massie, patiently waiting to make his entrance at the start of Shielhill Road, before I digressed or took a quantum leap of about thirty days.

Remember, in one of our parallels, we got as far as 16ᵗʰ October where my life began so there are only fourteen days to go before I reach 85 years, almost a quarter of a great circle of 360 degrees.

Be in touch

*Ed*

## Sunday 3rd October 2021

*Hi Iain,*

I was getting myself a wee bit het up yesterday; putting pressure on myself to meet some imaginary deadline to tell you the story. Maybe it is the imminence of the Climate Conference in Glasgow, at the end of October, and I have unwittingly given myself that as the target date to try to unfankle the time-line of this Christian Era. which has taken almost two thousand years to tangle.

The problem is that any little episode has only occured to me on my daily walk, and a little chat with you, in your wee slit trench. And everything has to have an air of secrecy about it, because the whole concept is so crackpot, otherwise we would be judged to be suffering from dementia; I mean, think about it............we started out wanting to make a difference: now we seem to have evolved, or regressed, into the most unlikely special forces unit. Two eighty-four-year-old SAS men, specially recruited to operate behind enemy lines to gather intelligence that the new generation can trust to fight with. Like the FBI guy in the Sean Connery, Alcatraz film might have said "Two old guys who can't even get through the night without taking a piss!"

You have to agree, particularly that we have to keep this secret – it is a very crazy notion; two octogenarian warriors, one already dead and the other wondering if he can complete the mission before time catches up with him! Mind you, I do recall writing to you once "Greater love hath no man than that he risk his credibility for his friend ... or in this case, Mankind!"

Oh Iain, I have to digress a wee bit again. You know how I keep catching little snatches of song that seem relevant, even significant as messages from the past urging us, mankind, to stop and think and learn; and get on with what we should have learned – stop procrastinating!

Well, in the episode that I am about to relate to you, Sheila, in her Now existence, gave me a Willie Nelson disc, 'Legend', and every track seemed to have a relevance, like a shout from the Now generation with the enlightenment that will restart evolution and help humanity make the quantum leap from being twenty-first century dinosaurs to realising that we are already in the Garden of Eden, which can be self-sustaining if we tidy up as we go along.

Anyway, Willie Nelson; I can remember, right off, three of the tracks, 'Crazy' and 'All the Girls I've Loved Before' which seem relevant to the story I am relating to you: but the third song, which shouts at me on this Sunday morning, before I take my circular walk around the J.M. Barrie parallel is,

"It's been rough and rocky travellin"

"I'm glad to have my feet back on the ground"

"After takin' several readings"

"I'm relieved to find my mind's still fairly sound!"

And that is how I feel on this October morning; but I can't help a little fantasising that Sheila, even in her Now existence, wants to jump to the end of the story and thinks that Willie Nelson, another octogenarian, already has the answers or, at least, the markers to the answers recorded in song – this was in 2007 – before you and I even met, when Willie Nelson sang of his tour around the 'new world' with his companion Paul.

Iain, it is 6a.m., I need to go for my walk; pick you up later, I don't have Satan's altar to clean today.

*Ed*

**Sunday 3ʳᵈ October 2021**

## Hi again, Iain

Had a good walk this morning; the weather is definitely Autumnal, but I can stand that: in fact, I find it rather pleasant. For me, more comfortably balanced – not too hot nor too cold!

I am one of those people who should listen to the old adage 'if you can't stand the heat get out of the kitchen!" In fact, in the sort of quantum leap mode that I appear to be experiencing at the moment, I leap from my wee Glasgow man head to my Universal time traveller head and see that our world, our Mother Earth can't stand the heat in the kitchen either; but she has no where else to go so, really, if we want Mother Earth to survive, somebody has to turn down the heat before it becomes unbearable for her.

I suppose, Iain, that is what this conference in Glasgow, that starts on the 31st October, is all about: trying to get universal agreement to reduce the heat before the kitchen sets the whole house ablaze. Somehow I feel it should have a good start; it already has God's endorsement – after all, He is the One who has sent all the messages and warnings of fires, floods, tempest and eruptions: you name it, whatever Biblical precedent you can remember or imagine, to jog us out of our arrogant lethargy and realise that we are this Era's dinosaurs who have to change, to adapt to this world, this Earth that is finite. But could be self sustaining for eternity so long as humanity adapts to live within the limitations of a finite Earth rather than hoping that the finite Earth might expand to accommodate our unchecked development towards Dinosaur extinction.

In a world that loves Science Fiction, does nobody see the history, from the Big Bang, that the single cell virus of human life survived and mutated over millions of years, evolving into mankind and beating off all competing viruses that were not blessed with a thinking brain, but relied only on animal instinct to survive. And mankind beat off all challenging viruses, because he could think, until arrogance infected this unique brain into believing that Mankind was omnipotent and Earth was indestructible – like some unsinkable Titanic steaming at full speed towards the iceberg. That same arrogance that believed a fifty thousand ton man-made structure would simply brush aside a million tons of ice that had taken an eternity to form.

Are we so arrogant that we do not see this other virus, already worldwide, that is mutating and developing and killing us off just as surely as man's activity killed off evolution by becoming bogged down in our own plastic and fossil fuel dinosaur shit?

Anyway, Iain, maybe the enlightened brains of the World will come up with a plan when they meet in Glasgow to discuss saving the Earth.

Funny how much Glasgow, the dear green place – that is its word meaning – has featured in these letters; you know, like a wee fat Glasgow man falling into your little slit trench when you were determined to survive until you had made a difference.

And you made a difference, because you survived beyond the time, well beyond, that an expert had predicted was your omega, and you survived beyond Easter, maybe just to make a difference to the end of a story. And, of course, your spirit lives on and encourages me to keep fit by peching up Cemetery Road every day to visit you and write a wee letter to make sure we record the truth, without making it too cryptic in an allegory or a fairy story that has to be interpreted to be understood.

-You know Iain, I tried to read and interpret Revelations, but it was too complex for me-like Sergeant Joe Friday in Dragnet. 'all I want is the facts!'

But I found some 'reasoned' facts in Wikipedia – like Sir Isaac Newton's calculations that our world would end in 2060, if it carried on operating as it had. And, also attributed to Newton, by working out the difference in time span – a year in Jewish history is different, or needs interpreting to match up with a year in our present era; the years 2008 until 2021 were the period most likely to herald the Second Coming of the Messiah.

Now, here we are, already at 4th October 2021. near the end of that Second Coming; and in the month of October with an Earth changing conference due in Glasgow at the end of the month. I know that I am clutching at straws that are 'Just Blowin' in the Wind'. but the October significance reaches down into my experiences, some of which have already been stored in our Pandora's Box of 'Letters to Iain'. Our Ark of the Covenant truths that need to be aired; the Veritas that unites the Via with the Vita We have Glasgow, and we have October; and a wee fat Glasgow man who was born on 16th October, the same date as his infant son who was a victim of cancer, the Christian Era scourge of mankind: and waiting patiently in the wings for his cue is wee Frank Massie who informed me of the prediction that 2008 was significant, and who died in October 10th, and his wake held in my pub on 15<sup>th</sup> October, the day before my birthday. Another less than 'Happy' birthday.

If you are prepared to expand 'eerie', October of that year would be about when Sheila and Helen met and became friends and created the bridge for you and I to meet and start this correspondence which, so far, is ongoing; eternal would be pushing it a bit too far. ongoing is fine for the moment.

On the basis of our theory that every happening is a parallel of a previous occurrence, or perhaps a model of a past or future event, is it possible that we are some sort of re-enactment of the Scriptures editorial squad who tried to encode and float the Truth under the noses of an oppressive Roman Empire? And in the hope that somebody would solve the crossword – oops, sorry; no pun intended – sent teasers and subliminal clues blowing in the wind for future generations to see the anomalies in the Fairy Story and seek out the Truth!

## Wednesday 6th October 2021

Oh Iain, I broke off there, and had to attend to one of those little things I have to do to keep my own little story of a life going; but which interrupts me in my urge to do great things and complete, or even continue Diarmuid's quest to find the God of a Universe that is expanding quicker than I can think and write our record of events. Sheila reminded me that I had to cut the grass, to keep our little domestic world of real time Kirriemuir tidy. It sort of reminds me that, while making green energy the priority, we still have to keep ecology in balance so that the grass and the ivy and the boundary hedge don't grow beyond the point where we can keep it in balance.

Anyway, I got the grass cut and came back to attend to these letters, and recall your prediction that my stuff would probably only achieve publication posthumously; I am rather banking on the prospect that your prediction refers to your posthumous situation and not mine. As you know, I am not one for celebrity, but it would be nice to be around to find out if our letters made a difference.

I am also banking on your suggestion, back in 2019, that we should just start another five year plan. Well, two years have already gone, but that gives me another three years until I am 88, a nice round figure; I can review then if another five, or even three year plan is feasible.

Meantime, after the grass tidy, I came back to our letter project and, kind of, got thumped by one of Denis Wheatley's occult loose floor boards.

I was trying to communicate with a publisher in the hope of giving our thoughts in these letters a wider audience – you know, so that they might see our little lights flickering and clap Tinkerbell back to life. But my computer, and my mobile 'phone both started acting funny; each seemed to have a mind of its own and I could not, with my limited IT expertise, get either to respond properly.

I know that there has to be a rational explanation – they are machines, for God's sake, but I was again reminded of the sounding machine on Caledonia, over sixty years ago, which told me I was safe, when I wasn't, and seemed to conspire with two other unrelated events to create a little crisis or disturbance situation. I wonder if these present, real world malfunctions are reminding me that I may not yet be safe, when I am preparing to rush toward the light at the end of the tunnel, Eerie indeed!

Maybe my Damian Roth is still trying to have a parting kick, as I pass him and start shining our lights in the corners where his boss may be biding his money – you know, like in the old song "Money is the root of all Evil".

Anyway Iain, I will leave you here – I am sure my 'mechanical equipment 'will have defaulted back to normality by the time I start again.

*Ed*

**Thursday 7ᵗʰ October 2021**

*Hi Iain,*

I had a quiet evening, early night and a good sleep, but here I am again at 3 am, – don't know whether it is witches or wee wee that wakened me; or perhaps one of the wee doors in my head creaking on its hinges. The wee doors aren't banging so much now – they more swing open like cupboards, that is closets in the USA, which are too full to close properly, and a piece of something that I thought I had lost falls out – like one missing piece of jigsaw that helps me complete the puzzle.

I think what fell out of this particular little door was the puzzle box lid – you know, Iain, the bit with the picture on it to remind you, or guide you to the complete scene that you are trying to reconstruct.

I keep finding the opposite of the obvious in this Diarmuid's Quest that we find ourselves on; you know, us having to start at the end, the place where we are now, and work back to find the beginning, instead of the conventional or logical start at the beginning and work forward. Wrong!

The Universe is still expanding, so the great circle of its circumference is changing – like the movable feast – or the ripples in our imaginary pool after the calm has been disturbed by the splash. So, unlike our Christian Era story, with a movable feast beginning and a, presumably, finite end – that Isaac Newton predicts will occur in 2060 – our situation is that we know where we are in the NOW, and we have to work backwards to secure the beginning to find out if this so-called Christian Era actually is the Alpha and the Omega or, perhaps overlaps or merges with the ripples of a previous era, which has not lost all its power but hitches a ride on the Christian Era's newer stronger ripples; or waves from a simultaneous splash of a separate disturbance whose ripples merge and obscure the bigger Christian Era ripple for a while until these smaller wavelets are almost totally absorbed. So don't overlook the opposite of the obvious.

And the box lid with the picture on it? Well that reminds me that we were looking for God; and the question is, really, is that God the Father, or God the Son, or God the Holy Spirit?

Well, I guess that God the Father is riding that expanding great circle that is the circumference of a Universe that is still expanding; we are unlikely to catch Him, unless fleetingly in a little model we can create out of our imagination. But, God the Father did this job for us; he created this model world, self sustaining. with its own capacity to regenerate and remain mobile – up to a point like an electric car that every so often has to recharge from the main power supply of faith, The Way, or more precisely doing things the right way to survive.

And He arranged for a Captain, a navigator, a Watch-keeper to steer this model world through eternity – a saviour who like Tinker bell would ensure that this world, this Peter Pan, the boy who wouldn't grow old, would live contentedly in this self-sufficient Garden of Eden, J. M. Barrie called Neverland.

God the Son – He is the Saviour who was appointed watch-keeper and navigator to steer mankind through this Christian Era but corruption, in the shape of Captain Hook and his pirate band kidnapped the navigator and stole the shadow of goodness and protection He was meant to cast over Neverland – the Garden of Eden, this self sustaining Earth and held the world to ransom by arresting evolution the constant motion that keeps the planet rejuvenating and adjusting to be self sustaining.

And the Holy Ghost – well, I guess that is the inbuilt spirit, in every animal, the will to survive like your determination and refusal to be defeated by cancer; or by your refusal to be programmed by a blind faith or a bad example that dictated that man, the Son of God. should endure the pain of the purgatory of the cross, and die on some indeterminate date that a previous era had selected and commemorated as the appointment with death! The Holy Ghost is perhaps the 'thinking bit' that is unique to the human animal

And me? Definitely not part of the Trinity; I am just the spare navigator who transferred from Cilicia to Caledonia to ensure she headed for open waters and avoided destruction.

Talk again tomorrow,

**Friday 8<sup>th</sup> October 2021**

*Hi Iain,*

What a walk I have had this morning; the wee doors were banging again, and I could hear the music that was 'Blowin' in the Wind'.

The tracks from the Willie Nelson 'Legend' disc are still reminding me of incidents in my lifetime, and today I keep thinking of his journey on the express train 'City of New Orleans' and the rumble and throb of the train's wheels, that the guitars and drums of the musicians manage to replicate so effectively, as the train hurtles along on its five hundred mile journey. And I think of our journey, this time travelling, and imagine us rushing through the tunnel with the light at the end, in Glasgow, where the COP 26 conference is to be held in another twenty three days.

I had posted off a batch of our letters, to a Publisher who is going to judge whether your assertion, that they are worthy of a wider readership, bears any weight. Part of that anticipation is the possibility that publication might beat your prediction of posthumous publication.

Anyway, I followed my usual route, in fact today it was my intention to collect Frank Massie who has been waiting patiently, to make his entrance, at the top of the Roods since the start of September; but, as I said, the wee doors were all open and I could hear different tracks from the Legend disc, all playing simultaneously, as if each had a message I should be addressing … 'Crazy' and 'You are always on my mind', and 'A good hearted woman' were all competing to be heard: and I gave it a lot of serious analytical thought as I followed the great circle along Shielhill Road into East Hill Road out of Kirrie, down to the Brechin Road turning back towards the Kirriemuir boundary sign just a bit before Cemetery Road.

I have to steel myself for the challenge of the climb; I can see the black Audi that is always parked across the road from the Cemetery gate on your level, but today it is partially obscured by a little red Ford Fiesta. I don't know why that seems significant but it does.

I am managing the incline of Cemetery Road more easily now; not easy, but a little more easily than a year ago. I now don't look ahead, as I climb, to see the distance to reach the black Audi … the constant reminder of the challenge still to complete; the constant reminder of the steep incline of two or three hundred yards, or so it seemed, was becoming discouraging, daunting!

I now concentrate my gaze on the road surface and the movement of my feet, taking the "One step at a Time" that Lena Martell recommended in her classic hit of, maybe, fifty years ago. As I said, the climb is easier than I had experienced at the start of this pandemic, but I am still pleased to reach the gate on your level and stroll, less demandingly along to your little slit trench. I suppose, since we are searching for truth in this quest, I should admit that I actually try to effect a casual saunter, as if the Hill meant nothing to me, in case anybody is watching and wonders if this old guy is in distress.

Anna's bench is quite damp with the early morning dew – it is only five minutes past sunrise – but I have plenty of tissues, you know to contain an old man's nose drips, and I wipe a dry patch on the bench and sit with you for a while.

The song coming clear to me is the Willie Nelson and Julio Iglesias duet 'To all the girls I've loved before'; I recall, in a previous letter, making a comment about 'ladies I have loved' and had always intended to explain that I wasn't slipping in a subtle suggestion that I had been some sort of great lover in my younger days: far from it! The ladies I was referring to were all connected or associated by some trauma. bereavement or compassionate involvement; unfortunately, these were not 'passionate involvements'.

I sat looking across at you and Anna, for a while, until I heard the town clock strike out its quarter hour, The 'ding dong ding dong, ding dong, ding dong, ding dong, ding dong of 7.45 am, real time of course.

It brought me back to Earth after a quick flight of fancy to seek out any hidden explanations for the music 'blowin' in the wind' about forgotten ladies. And, that was it! I could see the full picture of the unfinished jigsaw puzzle, and had to hurry home to find the pieces before I forgot what the full picture looked like.

The problem is, Iain, the whole picture is a bit like an historical tapestry, with little scenes of individual story lines – perhaps all the little models, or replicas of the bigger pictures, that need unravelling to allow some little kink in the timeline to stretch out and reveal another wee contribution of truth that has lain hidden, perhaps as a cryptic clue, and unexplained by all the pundits who hold certificates that convince them that they are the experts, and the only people qualified to analyse this field or subject.

Now Iain, this is not a digression – I won't get sidetracked and analyse every detail of this little detour; but Shakespeare was one of those little hidden deviations for me: I admired his writing, and understood some of his perceptions on the human condition. But I was too confused by my school assessments and reports which recorded 'could do better' or 'must try harder'; I now see that possibly those comments were intended as encouragement to stimulate an unawakened mind. I read them only as criticism, despite the effort I was making to try hard and do better!

Shakespeare was just another chore of schoolwork to burden me with, when I was already working as hard as I could, and fast coming to the conclusion that I was a bit of a thickhead, and that other people in the world were just naturally brighter than me and I was unlikely ever to become one of them. My clouded views of Shakespeare, and my lack of confidence, or enthusiasm to explore and uncover the hidden truths that Shakespeare was launching to go 'blowin' in the wind' got pushed to one side and filed away in a folder marked 'unexplained' in my mind's memory banks.

Macbeth, particularly, was lost on me, despite the fact that I must have read and discussed, even acted parts of it, in English class at school. I had a latent resentment, that Shakespeare's presentation of Macbeth, somehow maligned Scotland as treacherous, deceitful, ruthless – quite distasteful chaps whose hospitality was better avoided. This scepticism that I felt was endorsed by the later discovery that Shakespeare's Macbeth had no historical veracity and was a terrible fiction that, somehow, became more widely accepted as fact, than did the truth which lay unnoticed, because Scottish history was not a priority in the British Empire of a post World War 2 era.

The truth was that Macbeth had been a stable king who had governed Scotland well, for over a decade, and had no direct hand in Duncan's death.

I also did not understand the relevance of the Three Witches with their cauldron of 'hubble, bubble, toil and trouble', which seemed to be some injection of the occult – black magic or witchcraft – that had a foundation or, at least, a presence in Scotland.

Hey Iain, for something that wasn't digression, that was a wee bit of a detour!

Now, I still have to explain the 'ladies I have loved' comment, so I will park that with Frank, for a while; because Frank is both the past and, I now realise, a starting point for the future that I visualise plotting a course for. I know, time zones, parallels and time travel becomes very confusing. Back to the Future. indeed!

In the real time of this morning of Friday, 8th October 2021, while sitting on Anna's bench in Kirrie Hill cemetery, communing with you, I saw the pieces of the jigsaw as various generations of 'covens'. Last night Sheila had a ladies evening when she entertained. Gail and your Helen; a benign happy little coven as they stirred the pot, as ladies do, and put the world to rights. I have a little coven of three generations of ladies in my 'to resolve' file, which qualifies for the cauldron stirring description and, I have the three ladies I knew through bereavement or traumatic experience who inspired me through their ability to stir the hubble, bubble and trouble out of their particular cauldrons; a little coven of faith and hope.

The essence of the matter is the ladies, and their depiction as witches – particularly as three witches stirring up a cauldron of broth, which may not be to your taste. And I thought, "How chauvinistic of this so-called Christian Era!"

We have reviewed the problems and opportunities of this tragedy of crucifixion, this possibly fictional account of a tragedy, in terms of the three male characters and totally ignored, or suppressed the involvement and essential part played by the ladies of the piece. God the Father and God the Son and God the Holy Ghost – the Holy Trinity, are all male orientated characters.

Where is the Holy Coven? Where is the leading lady? – the Lady Macbeth of the Scottish tragedy, which might be a model of the Life size tragedy of the Christian Era.

Do you know Iain, the word, or name Macbeth derives from the Gaelic and interprets as 'Son of Life'? A lot of people don't know that – as Michael Caine would say! Isn't it interesting that Shakespeare writes a play in 1603 or 1604, just when a Scottish king is about to unite the nations of Scotland and England, and depicts, for an essentially English audience, that Scottish kings are deceitful and treacherous monarchs. And for his scenario, he creates a fiction about a real king, named 'Son of Life, whose tenure of Scotland was almost exactly one thousand years after God sent His Son of Life to unite the world, but who was killed off by a manipulation of public opinion.

Not taking that anywhere at the moment – just thought it a wee bit interesting and eerie!

So, back to the coven; where is Lady Macbeth, the wife of the Son of Life, in our Christian Era fiction? The Eve of Adam, the Blessed Mary who carried God's child, the Virgin Mary who held the Church of Christ together, when there was nobody else, by complementing St Peter, who was only supposed to be the foundation 'Rock' and not the Captain of the ship.

Where is God's leading lady, the earth Mother, or Mother Earth, who kept the belief in her Son alive for almost two thousand years; and now, like Tinker bell protecting Peter Pan, is slowly dying from the poison fumes that the humanity of this Christian Era has forced her to consume.

Oh Iain, the picture on the jigsaw puzzle box lid is the Earth – or, at least, it is the half of the sphere that can be depicted from a single perspective. And this particular view of the Earth is contained within the geography and time zone of the thousand years of the so-called Roman Empire, which contains the birth of Christianity to be united with a rebirth of Islam, and combine with Judaism in a Holy Trinity of a monotheistic religion that would spread the word of God, not sure which one though, eastward and westward until the message encircled the Earth – like the Great Circle of the Equator; which doesn't pass through Glasgow. But if the word of God, Mankind to save His Beloved Partner, Mother Earth, doesn't get transmitted through COP26 from Glasgow in early November, we are all in trouble!

Mother Earth – the coven of three distinct female personalities, bereaved by the tragic death of her Son. The wife or partner of the creator of life, the mother of the son of life, and the spirit of humanity that is circulated through God's great magnetic field and returned to mankind as positive energy; the positive spirit that makes mankind unique among the living creatures on Earth: the ability to think and avoid becoming the Christian Era's dinosaurs.

And the depiction of three witches is not something that I have suddenly stumbled across; I first became aware of this line of thought away back in the early seventies, remember, at the time when I told you I had waded out of my depth in Karnes Bay, at Millport, when I attempted to rescue my young son. On that holiday, I found a little book, which a previous occupant of the flat must have abandoned; 'What do you say after you say hello?' a book on psychology or psychiatry – I am never quite sure where one stops and the other begins – written by Dr Eric Berne, an eminent psychiatrist who was attempting to explain the workings of the human mind for the layman. The human mind – not the God mind; an earth mind, essentially influenced, and programmed as a result of the experiences and impressions of any generation of earth mothers: a long dead grandmother could still be influencing family attitudes long after her demise. Apparently psychiatrists still use this concept today, although my experience is that they don't totally understand it. or always apply it. And yet it explains so much of what ails the modern world.

My goodness Iain, the words of the story, the revelations are pouring out the wee doors in my head faster than I can pick them up, and record them as a letter that you can understand and interpret at your own pace – and begin to believe; because that enlightenment will be a quantum leap of belief, after two thousand years of Christians being programmed to believe a contrived mystery story that needed unfankling and rethinking to be viewed as the Truth.

Well Iain, I have reached that point in 'A few Good Men' where Jack Nicholson shouts "The Truth Sonny? You couldn't handle the Truth!" And, I couldn't handle the truth, the conclusions, that our version of Diarmuid's Quest presented me with.

Remember Iain, away back in one of our earlier letters I suggested that Satan wasn't after all a bad guy; he was simply the Chief Engineer, that second most senior crew member, the essential crew member who organised and fuelled the ship from below decks......in a Biblical sort of language 'the underworld'. Iain, there is no underworld, there is only the World! The Universe, which is still expanding and, from our perspective, as the centre of the Universe, the World, our world, this planet Earth, presided over by Mother Earth, Goddess of the Earth, God's Chief Engineer Satan: the Truth that I have had so much difficulty coming to, skirting around Shielhill Road avoiding this Truth.

The same problem that J.M.Barrie had when he invented Peter Pan – perhaps Pan of the underworld of mythology – to create the link between a beloved mother figure, the Fairy Godmother and the earth creature, Mother Earth with the instincts for procreation and survival invested in any animal being, given the opportunity to people God's little Garden of Eden with thinking animals who have tasted the fruit of the tree of knowledge.

Now Iain, we have, sort of, completed Diarmuid's Quest; we went looking for God and, at least found some sort of truth, which might help to give Mother Earth some comfort along with the Hope that the applause from

COP26 in Glasgow will revive Tinker bell; and keep Peter Pan alive for another thousand years, and learn from the history still to be uncovered. Which reminds me; somebody has hidden a wee bit of the truth somewhere and I would still like to know who that somebody is. Who depicted Satan as a demon and educated Humanity, through the three monotheistic religions to fear and despise Satan, the mother of mankind? Maybe that is another cold case we could look into after we complete this Great Circle.

Anyway I have to get home and clean out Satan's altar, and see if I can fit a few more pieces into this Jigsaw of a Christian Era,

Talk to you tomorrow,

*Ed*

**Saturday 9<sup>th</sup> October 2021**

*Hi Iain,*

I won't tarry long today; we are going down to Edinburgh to have dinner with Sheila's daughter Sarah and her husband; so I have a bit of preparation still to do.

I realise that I left you yesterday with a bit of a teaser; pulling the thoughts of Dr Eric Berne out of left field – as the New World baseball enthusiasts would say – and not developing any explanation or interpretation of how his theories apply to this so called Christian Era.

Actually, if Dr Eric Berne explained it well enough for a wee fat Glasgow man who doesn't think of himself as particularly bright, then it should be easy peasy for a bookworm like you, with a University degree, to read and absorb, so I will take a couple of those quantum leap giant steps for mankind to put my interpretation.

Basically, the female of the species, Mother Earth, is the source of Life, and of love and for preparing each generation to cope with the pitfalls of life, based on her own experiences; and she has to adapt the message dependent on whether she is attempting to modify the developing behaviour of the male or female offspring for whom she is responsible. So, say in the example of the Christian Era, the mother of a son, tragically and cruelly killed, might blame the father who should have provided protection, or blame herself for her inadequacy in not preparing her son for the dangers or alerting him to the warning signs.

Whatever impression she has of the effectiveness of her love, she modifies her loving behaviour, henceforth, to the male side of her family. She may extend less love to a husband who appears to have failed as a protective father, or smother a surviving son within a cocoon of protective love. She also modifies the advice and guidance she transmits to her daughters and grand daughters who have the responsibility for creating the loving environments and relationships for the future.

In effect, by thought, deed and verbal communication she instils a programme, a script for living, in her children which she hopes will equip them to face the challenges of life, based on her own experiences and to help them avoid the pain and suffering that she experienced with this one massive tragic event of the death of her son. Consequently, whether she has elected to love more, or love less, or provide love with conditions will create patterns which will determine how her sons and daughters behave, and love and make the best of their lives. within the constraints of the ingredients that the 'witch' mother, or the 'witch' grandmother adds to the cauldron of 'bubble, bubble, toil and trouble' to create a, sort of, mental vaccine to make them alert and immune to the pain that she experienced.

And to cope with the memory of the pain, she buries the memory deep in her soul, so that she can try to take care of her new, or surviving, children with as much love and positive upbringing as the burden of her tragic memory will allow; the cross we, apparently, all have to bear.

At this stage, in this early twenty first century, when the love of God is remote from a lot of people, Mother Earth is ailing, because her family, the current generation, have not been programmed to take care of her. And, Mother Earth, or Mary, Mother of God is now experiencing post traumatic stress disorder, which used to be the special preserve of shell-shocked soldiers; but is now affecting a young generation experiencing the mental illness of depression that they did not realise they were at risk from, because their computers and I phones have not been programmed to alert them to the dangers of negative grooming by hackers or internet predators: or indeed from the religious leaders and teachers they believed they could trust. So, everybody has a cross to bear.

Sorry Iain. Wee Glasgow man on a bit of a crusade there.

By the way, did you know that our little personal war cry 'Via Veritas Vita' is forged on the metalwork of the gates of Glasgow University? In Latin, obviously, so that the old Roman Empire gets the message! And, in plain language, plain English, so that everybody gets the message, the motto of the City of Glasgow is contained, in short form, under the City Coat of Arms;

Let Glasgow Flourish! But the full motto reads "Let Glasgow Flourish through the preaching of the Word and the praising of Thy Holy Name"

I know, I know, Michael Caine would say "A lot of people don't know that!" We used to get taught it at school – I wonder if that is still the practice.

You know, Iain, Glasgow is a wonderful example of an evolving piece of history that has avoided becoming a dinosaur. The original Dear Green Place was transformed, quite dramatically, through the Industrial

Revolution to become the biggest industrial city in Britain, then got a grip of itself and gradually exported some of its talent to the 'new worlds', and is tidying itself back down to the manageable Dear Green Place once again.

A wee bit emotional there, Iain; but, like I said, "You can take the boy out of Glasgow, but you will never take Glasgow out of the boy!"

Anyway, the boy and his wife are going to Edinburgh today, so I'll need to get home and clean out Satan's Altar, get some petrol in the car – hybrid, of course – and pack my stuff for the sleep over,

Talk to you tomorrow,

*Ed*

**Sunday 10ᵗʰ October 2021**

*Hi Iain,*

I really did not see this coming. As I told you, Sheila and I are visiting Sarah and her husband in Edinburgh, Portobello actually. This is where we ran a successful hospitality business, before our move to Kirriemuir; just in the last year of the twentieth century, before our world, everybody's world, seemed to change with the new millennium.

Anyway Iain, we had a really enjoyable evening in the town last night; what a vibrant busy place it is: hard to believe we are in the middle of the same pandemic as Kirriemuir. The pubs and the restaurants are full, and people aren't stepping two metres away from by-passers as we still, pretty much, do in Kirrie; masks and hygiene measures are evident but, well, my goodness it is a busy place.

We had a few drinks, as you do at family reunions; but, of course, as you wouldn't Iain, being a life long abstainer. I often wondered how you coped with the numerous celebrations you must have attended, where you were the only party goer with his sensible head on, while tongues loosened and inhibitions became less restrictive as the night and the drink wore on. Last night was one of those nights where we touched on family matters; in our case, two families actually, Sheila's and mine, where the timelines started to merge, over thirty years ago, with the odd little fankle in the merging. We had a good few drinks so I cannot really remember if we unkinked. any of the fankle.

This morning, I am up and about early, strangely 'un-hungover', and heading down to Portobello Promenade for my, now compulsive, life preserving morning walk! I won't, of course, be able to visit you in your wee slit trench today but, already, as I head down King's Road towards the beach I feel that this is all part of our continuing story; part of Diarmuid's Quest, part of our moving backwards through history to carefully pull off the layers in manageable sections without disturbing the Truth, too shockingly, or tipping out the entire contents of Indiana Jones' Lost Ark in a rush of revelations that overwhelms us with ugly truths, that some people will not accept, or accommodate – or even cope with.

At the bottom of King's Road I tum Eastwards, along the Promenade;

funny how an easterly direction keeps featuring in this Quest of Diarmuid: even in the model world scenario of Kirriemuir the route to the historical truth was in a north easterly, swinging east through southerly direction before coming round westerly to connect again, in a full circle with the modern real time world of today.

Today's Portobello seems a much improved from the tired place it had become twenty years ago; particularly when you consider the past eighteen months of pandemic when everything seemed doom and gloom and business failures and food banks! Portobello is looking quite spruce, with old pubs refurbished and new little bistros, and cafes with open air seating where there previously had been boarded up sites and tired looking buildings.

This is 'dreich Scotland' in October, and yet the weather is mild, the Promenade and the magnificent Portobello Beach are alive with people exercising, or dog walking and the little cafes and coffee shops are doing a roaring trade with folk out enjoying a Sunday morning al fresco breakfast.

As I continue eastwards, Portobello merges into Joppa and I realise that this is a 'smallish quantum leap' backwards in time to, if not the beginning but, certainly, another start point. Iain, you and I have enough to contend with in our little model world that Kirriemuir represents as our model of the so-called Christian Era. But, of course, my big complaint about the Christian Era is that it does not have a precise start point in time. I suspect I may be about to experience another little kink, or bight, in the time line that we are unfankling.

The walk eastwards into Joppa takes me into a model of the so-called Holy Land and a pre Christian era that you and I are not ready to explore just yet. You know, Iain, my theory about historical events all happening at the same time, but replicated by model events at some previous or later date seems about to receive a little nudge of confirmation. As I progress along the Promenade I realise some significance in that I am turning back the historical clock, ever so slightly, to the brief period of a life that Sheila and I inhabited immediately before our move to Kirriemuir. I can see that my little sorties of time travel flights with the benefit of hindsight and, in being high enough to see the current time parallel I can also catch a clearer glimpse of the adjacent parallel of events of the previous time line.

Well Iain, the Portobello and Joppa promenade was looking pretty good until I reached the last grand building on the prom – it becomes the Esplanade, from this point until the end. This last building, until recently trading as the Dalriada had been, until 30 September 1998, the Templehall Hotel, which Sheila and I had run fairly successfully for thirteen years, then affectionately known as The Temple: now, lying empty with boarded up windows The Temple is looking pretty sad!

Anyway Iain, our whole 'Testaments' scepticism overlapping with my experience of this tired looking building have me clutching at straws 'Just Blowing in the Wind' that are too relevant, even significant to be ignored.

Within the grounds of the Temple lies a little stone built chapel – allegedly commissioned by an early owner, of a Masonic persuasion, who found himself, and fellow local Masons, remote from any other conveniently located lodge; the little chapel was named Hebron Hall, and was shown as such on an early Ordinance Survey map of the area.

Now, I know that I clutch at remote coincidences and straws in the wind but, after all, we started out looking for God and the Truth about the Christian Era; how can we ignore such a concentrated dose of coincidences, right here in what was once my back garden?

Hebron, near Joppa, in the Holy Land is the location of the Cave of The Patriarch, wherein dwelt Ibrahim and his wife Sarah, the mother of Judaism But Ibrahim had also fathered Ishmael previously by Hagar, a serving girl, apparently with Sarah's approval. Ishmael is the founder of Islam.

Iain, I find myself being drawn into the fankle of another well spun story that, as I said, we are not ready or equipped to even contemplate at this time. But I have a taste for this Truth searching now, and perhaps you and I can have a go at opening another Ark of the Covenant on some future quest.

Meantime, to bring our Diarmuid's Quest back into the Christian Era. and also in the real world, would you believe that not far from the Temple in Joppa lie two little housing estates; the Magdalenes – built on the site of an old Magdalene Laundry – of ill repute – and the Christians? I haven't uncovered any clues as to the naming of the Christians, but I am always intrigued as to why the Church of Rome keep trying to discredit Mary Magdalene; first by hinting that she was a prostitute – only once was it suggested, but the mud stuck! And then the modern slur, in the updated depiction as the Patron of the cruel order of Nuns, who managed and staffed the Magdalene laundries, which effectively enslaved young Catholic girls who had fallen pregnant and were held hostage to pay for their sin of having brought a new life into the Church. Doesn't compute!

In truth, Mary Magdalene did not feature in the scriptures after the Garden of Gethsemane, so why the modern Church revived her existence, simply to discredit her again, is a quandary to me. Perhaps after two thousand years her non – disclosure agreement was approaching termination date and somebody had the foresight to brand her as an unreliable witness. I certainly think it was something more sinister than any mother in law, daughter in law friction. Some devious Vatican advocate has spun a little deception to render Mary Magdalene's testimony unreliable or inadmissible.

One thing, from the brief dabble in the Cave of the Patriarch, is the realisation that Sarah was the earth mother, or Mother Earth. of that version of Holy Land testaments.

You know, Iain, before I type these letters into an acceptable legibility I have written them out in my little notebook; and. when I look at the written page, from a short distance, my handwriting looks incredibly neat and orderly: straight vertical margins and precise, almost attractive, lines of script. Then I try to transcribe it as typing and I find it hard to decipher my own writing. Some words, somewhere between mind via pen to paper, have degenerated into a hurried scrawl. Only because I know the story, and the context, can I decipher my scrawl and interpret what I have tried to record.

Iain, I realise that the same problem must have been present thousands of years ago, when writing was still a new skill, and badly formed writing without the benefit of being transcribed into legible typed script would be even more difficult for a latter day scribe to decipher and translate any ill formed letters or words. I could give numerous examples of words, in my own writing, that I would transcribe quite differently were it not for the fact that I wrote the jottings quite recently, and the memory of what I am attempting to convey is relatively fresh. Think of the number of transcriptions of the New Testament before it became the 'Authorised Version' after twelve hundred years; or the 'Chinese Whispers' effect on the Old Testament during the seven thousand years of recording, translating and transcribing.

Anyway Iain, I'll cut to the chase! The word, and the context, and the seemingly illogical or unacceptable connection is Satan and Mother Earth, or any Earth Mother, being one and the same person. But, in the Cave of the Patriarch, Sarah was depicted as Mother Earth, the Earth Mother of the birth of Judaism. Is it possible that in early writing, that was even less legible or precise than today's, or in verbally communicated legend. the definition of words became imprecise so that Sarah, in oral or written communication became slurred into who presided in the world below heaven, which by interpretation became the 'underworld' from which the anger of post traumatic stress could erupt and thus appear like the anger or mischief, the evil, of Satan who was God of the Underworld?

And all the time it was Sarah, Mother Earth, angry with Ibrahim for his infidelity, or Mary, mother of God's child. angry with the murderous world He was trying to save by showing the Way, the Via to the eternal life, the Vita that required the truth, the Veritas that the human species has to evolve to sustain eternal life on planet Earth before attempting to escape to some undiscovered world in the Universe. Or, is it perhaps the developing mental disorders of today's young people, suppressing the fear and frustration, that this magical substitute brain of an 'I phone' does not have imagination or instincts to save their planet, which a recognised genius, Sir Isaac Newton, calculated and predicted could self destruct this century, within their lifetime?

Just a thought, Iain. But it frustrates me to observe the decision makers of the World looking on this 'Apocalypse Now' as if it is an entertaining disaster movie lasting a stimulating three hours; and after the credits, the stars and the cast of thousands even those who played dead, will reappear in the next epic blockbuster disaster movie. Not if we don't save Hollywood and Bollywood from being consumed by Fire, Flood or Pandemic, they won't!

Anyway Iain, today, in real time, the 10th of October is the anniversary of wee Frank's departure from this mortal coil. And today, my visit to the Temple reminds me of my move to Kirriemuir and the start of this model adventure in which Frank featured so heavily during the ten years before I met you. It seems we have come round in a circle moving forward from 2010, ten years until you took your leave, but then circling round on a parallel of latitude that takes us through 29m March 1999, the day I moved in to what had been The White Horse and coincidentally, the Monday of Holy Week for that year – another memorable Easter; and, I now assume, destined to uncover some more historical interpretations before we complete the model circle in Neverland, at 2010 again.

Talk to you again tomorrow,

*Ed*

**Monday 11ᵗʰ October 2021**

*Hi Iain.*

W̶hen I left you yesterday we seem to have reached, roughly, the year 2000 which, again approximately, is about when I was beginning to experience a bit of turbulence in the anticipated life of comfortable retirement in Kirriemuir.

On reflection, now, the eagerly anticipated new millennium proved to be a bit of an anti-climax. The new beginning for the world turned out to be something of a damp squib! The world had not suddenly become the promised land; it was business as usual – the rich continued to get rich and the poor did not become any less poor: and the tax paying middle income earners seemed to have to work harder to subsidise both rich and poor in this 'cross we all have to bear' Christian Era.

You know Iain, I had not particularly wanted to leave The Temple just at that time but, thirteen years of searching for the pot of gold at the end of the rainbow had lost some of its magical appeal. The new beginning in Kirriemuir, the Fairy Tale world of Peter Pan, held great promise.

But, after a few months of relaxation and lots of do-it-yourself jobs I was missing the demands of some purpose to my life. A wee pub was up for sale and I was, after all, a successful publican, having also been a successful senior sales manager after having been a successful navigator. With all this success in my C.V. what could possibly go wrong. My daughter would manage the day to day running and I would be a sort of director, just drawing the occasional advance of dividend on profit between a few administrative chores and frequent holidays.

However, I fear that I was wearing rose-tinted spectacles when I had anticipated my prospects; the transfer of the business proved to be an untidy and costly experience and the first two years of trading were equally costly and extremely demanding; some of this due to unforced errors, some to having planned while wearing the rose-tinted spectacles and some of it just bad luck which I wasn't prepared for. Sod's Law!

This fairy tale world of Kirriemuir was not behaving as 'happy ending' fairy tales should. I recalled an old marketing maxim – every problem presents an opportunity; well Iain, I seemed to be inundated with opportunities to an almost suffocating extent!

I recall, during those early days, a local worthy asking me how things were going. I replied, honestly, that progress was less exciting than I had hoped. He explained the problem with, "Ah weel, ye see, you are driving a Jaguar!"

I replied, "It's a twelve year-old second hand car," "Aye, but it's still a Jaguar"

"What difference does a Jaguar make?"

"Weel, Kirrie folk dinnae like tae see a body getting' too far above himself!"

So, it seemed as though I was being cut down to size for my modest success in the Temple as represented by the ageing Jaguar I had made do with for eight of its twelve years.

You know, Iain, it is only now, in 2021, with the benefit of an awful lot of hindsight (and I do mean an 'awful' lot) that I can see that, for some reason, I had brought a similar ton of shit down on my own head, and those close to me. as you and I experienced in 2014 without us having realised it at the time.

Once again. a member of my family seemed to be the victim of a particularly vicious kind of retribution. After the 'saving Caledonia' episode, when Roddy was a 'first born' target, now Lindsey, who was managing the pub, became the target for some extremely nasty attention.

All the scriptural or historical precedents flashed through my 'blowin in the wind' brain; Herod's slaughter of the innocent first born, Rome's brutal revenge on Boudica's daughters for their mother's defiance in the name of freedom – any situation where the innocents appeared to have become the target or collateral damage of some mysterious conspiracy or a more obvious retribution meted out by a tyrannical power. "Get Real" I told myself "This is the twenty first century, not a re-run of Culloden or the Glencoe Massacre!" Even so, Lindsey had to be evacuated back to the safety of Glasgow and supportive friends.

I recalled having watched the epic film of 'The Battle of Britain' about the RAF fighter squadrons resisting the domination of Hitler's evil empire, particularly the scene of the climactic battle that broke this Armageddon-like siege; Winston Churchill asked Dowding. Chief of Fighter Command, "When will you bring up the reserves?" And Dowding replied, somewhat ominously "There are no reserves!"

That was how I felt, and we all had to pitch in to 'try harder' and realise we 'could do better' to convert all those opportunities that were presenting themselves, and piling up about our feet, disguised as problems!

This was another occasion, like our experience in 2014, when the going got tough, the tough had to get going! Sheila stifled her disappointment at being dragged out of blissful retirement, and cooked for the pub, stood shifts or invested her magnetic personality in adding sparkle to quiz nights and feature nights we organised to stimulate interest and keep business alive.

Frank, my most regular and dependable customer, also swapped sides of the bar, on occasions, to help out; the only condition being that, after any particularly carousing Saturday night, he wasn't expected to carry bowls of soup. on a Sunday, with any expectation that the contents of the bowl would survive the shaky handed journey from kitchen to table!

Frank was one of the good guys; because when he was good, he was very, very good – to his family and his customers and his friends and acquaintances: and when he was not so good, well, he wasn't particularly awful, except perhaps to himself! He was a good friend to me during ten difficult years.

Like you Iain, he was born into the Roman Catholic faith. but fairly early on, when he started to think for himself, he found too many anomalies, in the history of the Christian Era, that he was expected to accept without question. Like me, he wasn't programmed into accepting the fairly rigid disciplines of Roman Catholicism and felt that, somehow, the Roman aspect had a greater influence and presence than the faithful, unquestioning Catholic adherents were free to examine.

Like Dr Eric Berne's programmed mind philosophy, Rome knew exactly how to condition humanity to accept the Empire's plan to dominate the world or, in fact. to achieve Universal domination. The clue is in the title – Roman Catholic; after all, the definition of catholic is universal.

Speculation about any Roman Universal domination was a bit too fanciful and spiritual – other worldly – for a little gay, alcoholic hairdresser from Kirriemuir, and a wee fat Glasgow man to consider in any depth, when there were real world pressing battles to fight, like surviving recessions, keeping ageing kitchen equipment operating or fixing the leaking roof and broken window pane of this tired old house of a pub.

And yet, there must have been some spiritual influence permeating our thoughts, even then. I had changed the name of the pub from 'Kilt and Clogs', as any Dutch connection or relevance had departed with the previous owners, and had only been the identity for a fairly short five years.

The name which had been the building's identity for centuries was 'The

White Horse Hotel' having been carried on when this new structure replaced the previous building at the start of the Victorian Empire era.

Iain, you know how I get these fanciful thoughts – the thoughts that get me considered a bit eccentric, or even a crackpot; well, I couldn't stop some sort of Biblical wisps of thought just Blowin' in the Wind. through my mind. as I considered changing the name back to The White Horse. Even then, I visualised a sort of spiritual Kirriemuir, with the little round courthouse, on the edge of the square, which is now the 'Gateway to the Glens' museum and tourist office, settled at the entrance of this model. or microcosm of the real world; this courthouse which in historical times would have been visited by the Bailies, the judges, from Forfar, to pass judgement on the recalcitrants of Kirriemuir.

Lying at the top of 'Bailies' Brae'. which through word corruption is now Bellies' Brae, behind a natural entrance flanked by the notional twin pillars of Life and Death; on the one side The White Horse of 'Revelations' eternal life, while opposite the Pale Rider of Death in the presence of William Lyall's undertakers office.

But, Iain, those thoughts did not convert into any money earning science fiction project; there were too many pressing real life problems, to convert into opportunities, to waste time dabbling with the occult or spirituality.

Frank must also have had some fanciful thoughts, without exploring them too deeply. On the occasion of George 'Dubyah' Bush declaring 'mission accomplished' on the dodgy Iraq War, when he was embellishing it with some of those born again pronouncements about Apocalypse and Armageddon, Frank had muttered "Well you better be quick!" He reminded me that the Second Coming was predicted to occur between 2008 and 2021; only a couple of years in the future.

We also had a shared interest or, in fact. a shared scepticism about the recorded history of Scotland, and the dismissive attitude accorded to any impact ancient Caledonia had on world history as it was being lived, and acted out at the beginning of the Christian Era The fact that the mighty Roman Empire had failed to subjugate Caledonia, despite naming it as a Roman province, in three hundred years of military campaigning. and then withdrawn behind Hadrian's Wall, declaring that this inhospitable piece of real estate was not worth the effort is, to say the least, questionable.

The further fact that the military presence in Caledonia, as the army relaxed its grip. was gradually replaced by a religious presence which seemed, suddenly to endorse and encourage the existing friars and monks that the Roman controllers had dubbed Companions of God, Celi Dei, from which the name Caledonia was constructed, was also mysterious. However, those earlier monks and friars were swamped and homogenised into the vast influx of newly ordained clergy arriving from indoctrination in Rome, to exert a gentler and more persuasive control on the spiritual sensibilities of this stubborn people, who could resist the inevitability of a military exerted physical domination, by the Empire which had enslaved every other corner of the known world of that era.

And Iain, Frank and I, with our shared passion for cryptic crossword clues and anagrams and 'sounds like' words, found a rich harvest of historical subliminal messages in words of that era, that have survived, without explanation or interpretation – like Pict People, from the Latin 'painted people'; dismissed as a mysterious people who inhabited Scotland in the Dark. Ages. How can you have a strange, mysterious people appear and disappear without some logical explanation in the midst of a time line, which otherwise, was pretty meticulously recorded by first the Army of Rome and latterly by the Church of Rome? Who decided such a significant presence should remain mysterious?

Even today, the Celtic people are described, pretty vaguely, as originating from some Indo-European source – but no specific ethnicity defined! Could the Celtic 'word' not be attributable to the same Latin derivation Celi Dei – the Celideic people of Caledonia, and by communication through differing languages of people who followed an old religion, the Companions of God. the Via that Jesus was trying to restore, become the Celtic people, the refugees from Roman domination who fled to Caledonia, the last bastion of freedom in a Roman world? Just a thought, Iain.

But, Frank and I had other little cryptic fantasies such as Pict sounding like Picked; and maybe another opposite of the obvious applied......instead of God allocating a promised land to a chosen people, maybe those early Companions of God. the Celideic or Celtic people 'picked' Caledonia as their land of promise to enjoy freedom from oppression. Just another thought, Iain; but before you say "Ah, but you are spinning words to suit your argument!" A wee bit of Weegie rhetoric, perhaps?

Well, not really. Frank and I were trying to unspin the fankle, in the time line of the apparent change over from the Roman Era to the so-called Christian Era. When Rome rebranded itself to stay in control of the market it had dominated for eight hundred years and was now adjusting to accommodate changing tastes with an, apparently 'light' variant, like Coca Cola, 'the real thing' becoming Diet Coke, and still remaining 'the real thing'! So the Roman Empire which had captured the earthly human world by full strength military presence now targeted the spiritual human world by capturing and controlling the souls of humanity through holding God's son hostage on a promise of a magical return of the prince of peace when we could all live happily ever after.

Iain, I remember your lamenting that when the Roman Empire abandoned Caledonia, it turned the clock of progress back one thousand years. Maybe so! But perhaps Romulus. the man of the City, or Capitalism, had progressed too far without the steering oar of a spiritual Remus that it had left for dead in 34AD and was going wildly off course, or just round in circles stuck on that one parallel of time.

You know, Iain, when I started this letter today I launched straight in to a continuation of where I left you yesterday; I didn't follow my usual pattern of picking you up after the climb up Gordon Park and Douglas Street to the Episcopal Church of St Mary, which is still lying empty, without a vicar, on West Hill Bank: then the final climb up the Roods to Hill Rise at Shielhill Road where I had left Frank waiting. He had obviously become impatient and come back a couple of paragraphs to meet me. My moving finger was obviously not writing fast enough to get to where it should have writ!

I suppose that the thoughts I have now communicated in this letter are those that emerged in the subsequent walk along Shielhill Road, down East Hill Road and westwards towards Cemetery Road. I suppose I must have been in a dwam, as we say in Scotland, and I have only wakened back into this world, or time, as I tum into Cemetery Road to find the steep hill before me is empty! No black Audi or wee red Fiesta to mark the top of the hill opposite your gate.

Remember Iain, this is in real time now – not a memory of a past experience or a time travel vision of some historical event, some cold waking the dead reconstruction. Something is different about today; change is always a little disconcerting.

I start my climb, watching my feet, one step at a time; there is no challenging end point to this climb, today, to look at anyway. I just concentrate on the road under my moving feet, and suppose I must have drifted off into another little reflective dwam when I become aware of voices ahead of me; I assume it must be folk crossing over at the intersection with Strathmore Avenue; I don't look up until I realise that as I cross Strathmore Avenue, the voices are still ahead of me further up Cemetery Road.

About the same time as my curiosity became too much, there is some shouting – a woman's voice commanding "Mungo, come here, Mungo!" A woman who had been accompanying two children to school was in hot pursuit of a lovely little puppy, all innocent and happy and friendly, running towards me, with the woman holding an empty dog leash, shouting "Mungo, come here, Mungo, no! Don't jump up!" But Mungo had reached me and jumped up, and I bent and lifted him; he was delightful.

The woman started to apologise, but I was more than impressed by the coincidence of this encounter "No, it's OK, I reassured her" as I returned Mungo to her safe keeping, "Love the name. Do you know that Mungo is the name of the patron saint of Glasgow, and your wee Mungo has just run to a Glasgow man to be picked up?"

The coincidence being that I had just spent my morning walk thinking about the Roman Empire and the Celi Dei and how the Church of Rome gradually diluted these unique holy men into the priesthood; I would have considered the original Mungo was a Celi Dei, a companion of God, because the Roman Church which held sway, in those days, subsequently absorbed Him as a saint with the name Kentigern, but he will always be St Mungo to me.

I noticed that one of the children was dressed in a bright green hooded top and the other was wearing blue jogging bottoms. I couldn't resist a bit of wishful thinking of these bi-polar colours of a present day 'old firm' Glasgow united in one family, who have chosen Mungo as their new symbol for family love and affection.

I know as if I have made this up to fit the theme and direction of these letters, but there is a lady, who lives in Strathmore Avenue, who can testify to this minor Veritas.

I decided that this was enough spiritual meandering for one morning and simply gave your wee slit trench a wave as I hurried home to attend to Satan's Altar,

Talk to you tomorrow.

*Ed*

**Tuesday 12ᵗʰ October 2021**

*Hi Iain,*

In this real world of 2021, there are so many of different little stories, falling out of the box that it is difficult to know which one to grasp and concentrate on. I feel it is a bit less sinister, or frightening, than the depiction of malignant evil that Indiana Jones anticipated when the Lost Ark was opened, in a great cavern in the Holy Land, where it had lain hidden for thousands of years.

But, I still caution myself. with Denis Wheatley's warning about taking care when dabbling in the occult. Since that morning of 6th September, when I first introduced Frank, and experienced a touch of indigestion, the slight tightness which appeared to be similar to his approaching symptoms of the fatal heart attack, I have taken extra care; but I am pretty sure it is only the effects of my early morning exertions before breakfast. I also wonder if the cause of my slight discomfort is a little bit of stress as I contemplate the relatively short duration of our association and see all the tight kinks and bights in our hampered log line, our time line of history that should have miraculously unfankled and straightened out, functioning smoothly with the positive influence of the fabled second coming!

You know Iain, there appear still to be so many kinks, in what should be the period of the promised happy ending, that I fear a bit of digression is necessary to investigate why there are still kinks hampering the free streaming of our log line, in a second coming duration that was predicted to begin in 2008 and be complete in 2021. Like the Battle of Waterloo, Revelation of the Second Coming seems to be generating all the uncertainty and tension of that similarly 'near run thing!"

I have been swithering about on this same parallel of latitude that J. M. Barrie reached, 120 years ago, when he wrote Peter Pan, but didn't quite know how to make the quantum leap to the top of the Hill to, I suppose, the second coming, when the threat to Neverland from the evil pirate band, would be removed.

Peter had united the world of Neverland; the indigenous people, depicted as Tiger Lily's Braves, and the Lost Boys, presumably the freedom fighters fleeing oppression elsewhere, and the children of the real world Michael,

John and Wendy, all inspired to action by Peter Pan to fight this threat to the existence of Neverland.

At this moment, in the real time world, close to the end of the so-called Christian Era we find ourselves nineteen days away from the start of COP 26 in Glasgow, planning, perhaps, the final battle to save our own twenty first century Neverland.

So, what happened to the second coming, that was presumed to be the overture to the new beginning of the thousand years of happiness and prosperity, after two thousand years of the purgatory of the cross that we have all had to bear? And where is the box to contain the evil, whatever evil is, but presumed to be Satan – presumably another Ark of the Covenant – observed by Indiana Jones? It should have been big news after a two thousand year wait!

Yet, Iain, during this real life period, the run up to the predicted second coming in 2008 I, along with my wee pal Frank, who was incredibly knowledgeable about Biblical and Historical fact, was fighting to preserve my own particular Neverland, this pub that had once been called The White Horse. but was being buffeted about by the realities of life in these latter days of the Christian Era.

As people tend to do, when they have known nothing else, we just had to accept 'well, that's life!' and make the best of it, and bear the cross that we had been presented with!

In our real world existence, oblivious to the parallel worlds, or model world of Kirriemuir that we were actors in, Frank and I continued to puzzle over crossword clues and share a fascination for word sounds, like the phonetics of Pict people sounding like Picked people, or constructing clues of anagrams like 'new Romans landing on the beach' 7 letters – answer 'Normans'. And our suspicion, which we shared only sketchily, that the Roman Empire hadn't faded away and died, like the authors of history would have us believe; bearing in mind that the authors of history are reputed to be 'the victors', or controllers, at the time the history was being recorded and written: it doesn't take a quantum leap of evaluation to identify who was in control, as history took the relatively small step of moving from BC. into the so-called Christian Era, that became a giant two thousand year leap for mankind!

Iain, I know that you and I agree to disagree, agreeably, on certain interpretations of history, and on our individual perceptions of the spiritual continuity, and influence of a presence, humanity defines as evil, in this lifetime or era; we are each conditioned by the spiritual teachings, the presentation of faith, we were first introduced to: you to the discipline and obligation of the Roman Catholic religion, while I was introduced to the same faith, without the rigidity of Roman discipline or the Catholic obligation and, somewhere, in that slight difference of interpretation is a giant side step for mankind!

You know, Iain, as a youngster growing up during and after the Second World War, as you also did, my big influence was American movies; Westerns with cowboy heroes, where good always triumphed, in the end: but originally the war films, like 'Wake Island' and 'Back to Bataan' and 'The Sands of Iwo Jima' in which we knew all the good guys were not going to survive, but that Good would triumph in the end. But, as those young good guys hit the beach, I used to envy every other GI who prepared to storm out of the landing craft, making the Sign of the Cross to give himself that extra protection, as he blessed himself, before leaping onto a hostile beach, and charging towards an evil enemy, like some latter day crusader.

Iain, much as those Catholic GI's faith impressed me, I couldn't bring myself to view the cross as protection; I couldn't separate the vision of that first pain-racked GI, that I carried about in my mind – loved even – pinned to that cross for eternity, with His grief stricken mother forced to endure that same agonising eternity because, without Her determination to not let Him die, and Her strength to hang on to God with one hand, while She kept Peter, the Rock of the Foundation anchored in the Crypt, there would be no Mother Church!

It is the same faith that we share, Iain, just in different religions, from slightly differing perspectives. The big problem of looking at these differences is, like the so called Good Book says, in the beginning was the Word, and the word was God. And God is the great umpire of the Universe in the game of Life, the competition between the words LIVE and viewed from another perspective its mirror anagrammatic image EVIL. The good God who plays by the rules and the mirror image God who can change shape, through the sting in the tail ability to reverse the L for love, or become Veil or Vile as the people who choose not to play by the rules of the majority, and spin the words to confuse and take advantage of the faithful. who have been programmed to believe that the goodness of a promised heaven is available in the world of NOW. In the game of life, in the world of NOW some people seem able to flaunt the rules without penalty or the excommunication of a red card.

Iain, the only rule books of words that we, certainly in the Western side of the world have to live by are the Scriptures of the old and the new Testaments; and the Koran. the most recent testament, written around six hundred years later than the Testaments. But we, you and I, in our Diarmuid's Quest scenario, are concerned mainly with the New Testament words. that affect and condition us in this so-called Christian Era

You may have wondered why I keep referring to this era as the so-called Christian Era. I do not believe that Jesus would have called His faith Christian, the word being either too specific to one religion or, the opposite of this obvious, too random to define a course or a path to follow to the goodness of life. His purpose was to bring the World, the game between Good and Evil, back to the rules, the Way of Life that, the Via, the way that God had intended the great game of the Universe to be played, by the rules of fairness; after all life is supposed to be an enjoyable game.

But, here we are now, in the twenty first century of this beautiful game, with the Umpire's Son held hostage and the team of EVIL scoring goal after goal with no regard for the rules, and little fear of penalty or red cards while the umpire's son remains a victim.

And Iain, you are still in your wee slit trench, on Kirrie Hill, and I can only do the best I can, to report to you the developing situation; I recall, in an earlier letter, saying that I needed only to convince one person of the Truth, the elusive Veritas, and that person was you – The Good Man of Kirriemuir!

And, of course, Iain, I am not conditioned or constrained by any hard and fast disciplines of faith I feel obliged to believe. Like my instincts on Caledonia, I feel that this ship we call the Christian Era is about to founder. as Isaac Newton had predicted, some time around the year 2060, unless we recognise that the old infallible sounding machine of the Scriptures is giving faulty readings and the good ship Christian Era is caught in some adverse, negative current that we have never been alerted to before, without precedent and, therefore, a mystery that allows us to plough on towards imminent disaster.

Iain, those are the two specific subjects where you and I agree to disagree, but agreeably. Well, really I agree with your observation of the positive realities of the good of those cases, but we fail to agree, or even discuss too deeply, the spiritual negatives of two historical eras.

Those two subject areas are Israel, where you admire the determination and resolve of the new 'Israelites' to create a little jewel in the crown promised land in a fine piece of real estate at the eastern end of the Mediterranean Sea, the centre of the old Roman Empire, which you also admire; and you feel that Scotland, Caledonia as was, turned the clock back one thousand years when the Roman legions withdrew, allegedly, to defend the threatened Empire at the head office of Capitalism located in Rome.

Iain, as we have agreed throughout these letters, we have enough to contend with in dealing with our scepticism about the Christian Era, which overlaps the Roman Empire, without delving into the Cave of the Patriarch to understand the origin and spin of scripture that records the development of Judaism. However, I will quote my recently discovered champion of historical cryptology, on his view of the claims within the Hebrew condition, the bard William Shakespeare.

In the Merchant of Venice, old Shylock was portrayed, somewhat critically and unfavourably; although I was unaware, until quite late in life, that a couple of hundred years after the new Roman or Norman Conquest, the Jewish settlers of southern Britain had been viewed as unwelcome immigrants and refugees, and severely persecuted –

As Michael Caine would say.........'a lot of people don't know that'

In Shakespeare's 'snapshot' Shylock held a contract for a loan to be repaid in settlement by cash or by a pound weight of the debtor's flesh.

In the ongoing spiritual world of the Hebrew nation, Israel claims a contract with God that guarantees a promised land for the nomadic Children of Israel to settle and call home. And, Iain, in 1948 a valuable, but undeveloped piece of real estate was allocated to the Children of Israel by God, directing the Western world – the old Roman Empire and its new colonies – to honour the contract and provide a promised land; or, with the benefit of a little scriptural word spin, a land of promises.

But, like Shylock's contract, when calling in the debt, the promised land, the pound of flesh is awarded precisely, "not a drop more, not a drop less!" And, Iain, in today's real world the contracted pound of flesh of a promise land has to be collected precisely – no little careless cuts of additional real estate because the God, who drew up the contract, was created in the Old Testament scriptures, written by early scribes, and a little judicious editing will condone a little careless butchery, that slightly exceeds the agreed 'pound of flesh' promised land.

The Roman bit? Iain, of course I admire the ability and achievement of the Romans, and their ingenuity to survive and develop, way ahead of and beyond where evolution was supposed to take us at that time of the beginning of Rome. But, Romulus and Remus were the "fairy tale' of a previous pandemic like Covid 19; the dinosaurs of the pre-Christian Era.

The twins, the first mutation, were like any life form evolving from a basic living animal source, had the instinct of any animal the hard-wired will to survive, the kill or be killed motivation of all living creatures. And through evolution, especially with twins, where one develops the survival instinct and the other inherits the more compassionate traits, which the priority for procreation invests in a brain, the successful virus has mutated – the quantum leap – to a human level. The process is, obviously, long and covers millions of years of evolution. But, just like all the fairy story allegories to mark the beginnings of any era, from the 'in the beginning' Garden of Eden, through to the so-called Christian Era Easter story, and the birth of Judaism and Islam in the Cave of the Patriarch followed by the Roman Empire, the combination of animal cunning and compassionate thinking has been a balance between good and evil. And Iain, in all those allegories of historical beginnings, the mythologies of pre-history humankind, twins have been involved, fathered by a male God – except in the case of the Roman twins; without explanation they appeared, already born, and were raised by an Earth Mother, a she wolf: the ultimate survivor, through communal pack living, adapting to the changing environment while other species became victims to extinction as the world changed and evolved without them. The fabled foundation of a Roman Empire is the point where the refined animal instincts, of the democratic wolf pack, were complemented by the ability to think beyond one dimension of survival; the point where the earth animal with the single polarity became bi-polar with the ability to choose between fight or flee, life and death, good and evil and survival of the species or extinction.

You know Iain, how Sheila is sceptical of the possibility of any universal power directing life; the NOW era of any one human life is all there is, except what survives through the life script, or way of living you bequeath to your children; and Dr Eric Berne would endorse that view – up to a point. But, similarly to me, Sheila hears and responds to music, perhaps not 'blowin in the wind', but current or modern music playing on the car radio; she particularly likes "Are we human, or are we dancer?' written and performed by Brandon Flowers of The Killers pop band. Apparently the grammatical irregularity of that line is intentional, designed to be a little cryptic and oblige the listener to consider a profound subliminal aspect to the question. A subsequent line in the song states 'And I'm on my knees, looking for the answer' leads me to consider that the song, and the question, has religious or spiritual aspects to be identified – a cryptic clue to be unravelled. I found Sheila's attraction to a song. which seemed to depend on prayer to identify some deeper spiritual interpretation, both mystifying and interesting, considering her rejection of any life era other than a NOW existence.

For me, the cryptic aspect was a challenge, particularly since it seemed to contain all the ingredients of the very clues that you and I have been trying to interpret anyway; to me there is no big mystique and, as the unravelled clue is almost too simple to be believable or acceptable to people who don't enjoy crosswords. With a little bit of 'sounds like' influence, and a little bit of melodic tongue work in the singing, poetic licence, the phonetic sound could become 'are we human, or are we dinosaur?' Seems, to me, to be a reasonable question to be praying to be answered at this stage in the so-called Christian Era, when world leaders are dragging their heels about any action needed to secure the survival of the species. It also occurs to me that, this close to the end of the Cop 26 conference, and the end of the prophesied period of the second coming, humanity hasn't quite grasped that the Planet Earth will survive, in some be it 'too hot' age or 'too cold' age......it is humanity that will struggle to survive and exist on an overheated planet.

Anyway Iain, back to the fabled beginning of Romulus and Remus, the founding fathers of Rome, who were suckled and raised by a she wolf. I sometimes wonder if this is some early representation of Dr Eric Berne's theories of instincts and operating parameters programmed into the brain and hard drive, and the operating system designed as a script developed from previous and current experiences updated to keep the brain equipped to address the ever changing challenges of any age or era. Iain, I know that you are a better Latin 'scholar' than I, but, did you ever evaluate the significance of meaning, of any Latin word or phrase, once you had made the translation?.

For example, Romulus translates as 'man of the city', and his twin brother

Remus is the Latin word for 'steering oar'; as is usual with Latin in free translations, such as 'guiding hand' or 'navigator'. Do you see any bigger picture emerging here, Iain?

Romulus, the man of the city, the first Capitalist, kills off his twin brother Remus. in a provoked animal rage because Remus tactlessly criticised the slow progress Romulus was making in building his Capital city. Romulus killed off the rational, more cautious side of this twin, bi polar partnership, the navigator, the guiding hand that would have kept Romulus on course to avoid disaster.

Romulus was the original survivor, who followed his predatory instincts to survive and develop ignoring the rules of evolution, like the dinosaur, but who bad been partnered with a guiding hand balancing polarity who might have warned him that once he had gobbled up all the other creatures as his survival instincts became more predatory until there were no potential victims left, except other Capitalist members of the wolf pack who would tum on each other and keep devouring any victim to survive and their survival instinct would see them gobble their way to extinction.

Remus' way would have been better, in the democratic comfort and protection of the wolf pack, cooperating and sharing and adapting their little world, to accommodate and adjust their way of living, to the little changes in their environment as the world around them evolved.

You remember, Iain, when we were wee boys and joined the Cubs and the junior Boy Scouts, and we earnestly gave our pledge to Akela that" we would do our best to do our duty … and follow the rules of the wolf cub pack and do a good deed for somebody every day!"

Whatever happened to that early promise, Iain?

Have to go, need to check where I am after all this digression!

Talk tomorrow.

*Ed*

**Wednesday 13th October 2021**

## Hi Iain.

Here I am once again on my life preserving walk – still trying to find words to close the gap on this final parallel of latitude.

Iain, I suddenly realise that, I have become so engrossed with the content, of each varying historical time era contained in each parallel of latitude, that it is too late to keep jumping from one historical parallel to another to find the precedent or the common factor that might be represented in our little model world of Kirriemuir.

Iain, there is no precedent! We, humanity, are on that final parallel of latitude. the great circle of the Equator that girdles the Earth; and while I am trying to find the words that make the connection. or the overlap or the similarity between each historical era, there isn't another parallel of latitude for humanity to jump or fly to. As the Rubaiyat says, "The moving finger writes. and having writ moves on!"

And the moving finger is moving for us, inexorably. around the equator until we find ourselves at the end of this great circumnavigation of when the Christian Era ends in its present form and Life, of some sort, goes on; a new type of life has to evolve, a new era to adapt to the new dawn of evolution on the great circle of time.

Iain, I have to make a quantum leap out of my digression and dithering, in trying to find historical parallels, and positions on models, to explain the position we are in. This is the point in the story where Butch Cassidy and the Sundance Kid have to make that leap of faith, into the abyss of hope, to escape the fate which will overtake them, if they don't jump now!

Iain, while I have been space hopping from parallel to parallel find the common factor, I have completely forgotten that it doesn't matter which parallel of latitude we are on; it is Time, after all, which is the common factor: Time that is the same in cutting and linking every age. every era, every parallel of latitude. It is the meridian of longitude. any meridian of longitude, connecting Time; linking the beginning of Time through the Judaic Era, and the Roman Era and the so-called Christian Era. It is a meridian of longitude that links the North Pole to the South Pole on this bi-polar Earth that finds itself, at this moment in Time, suffering from severe Bi-polar disorder!

And, Iain, I have been starting from the bottom, trying to combine or connect all my little sample eras; the day when I take my walk and think out the content of that day's letter, and the later time, perhaps a later day. when I collate my thoughts and make the notes, and then the day, perhaps some few days later, when I transcribe my handwritten notes into typed legibility, and deliver the letters in the hope that they are timely, and make enough sense to inspire your animal instinct. your fight for survival determination: remember, our original challenge was, to give your nemesis a fight, to stand up to this Cancer that afflicts this Christian era and take the leap of faith in your own fight for survival.

Iain, you did that! You extended your own life by another ten per cent, a further seven years after the seemingly tactless consultant pronounced an imminent death sentence on you. Have you ever considered the 'opposite of the obvious" that we discussed, of the Lord working in mysterious ways His wonders to perform? Maybe the tactless one did you a favour, by goading you into a fight back, by making you angry, and forcing you to choose between the fight or flee adrenalin of your animal instinct immune system, which gave you the incentive to decide, "I'll show the bugger he's been in a fight!"

In real time terms, this letter is being written at the witching hour on Wednesday 3rd November; we are already on the fourth day of the Cop26 conference in Glasgow and Glasgow is only 4 degrees West of the Greenwich Meridian – the point where the world, our World, completes the great passage of time on the great Circle of the Equator at zero degrees latitude in any direction. And, it doesn't matter that the Equator sits at O degrees latitude, and Glasgow is on 55 degrees North. and Kirriemuir, our model world, is on 56 degrees North, the end of time – the end of this Christian Era is when the historical parallel comes round full circle and crosses the Greenwich meridian; which in our model terms is both the Alpha and the Omega of time – but we have to reach the Omega before midnight, and the new Alpha starts.

So, where do we go from here Iain? Well, in distance to travel, our little model world of Kirriemuir is 25% ahead of the time that the Christian era has left; Kirriemuir is 3 degrees west of Greenwich while Glasgow is just over 4 degrees west, and behind our model. And, Glasgow is where the decisions are being made that affect the earthly habits – as Dr Eric Berne would say – agreeing the script to define the actions for the next generations.

In our world of Kirriemuir with you in your wee slit trench directing operations, and me sitting on Anna's bench, reporting back from each covert expedition.........oh, my God, Iain, what a fading. ridiculous pair of SAS men we make; one already dead, and the other, at 85, congratulating himself each morning, as the Kirrie Hill cemetery gate clangs shut behind him, next to Barrie's Camera Obscura. You know, Sundance, you have to laugh!

I said, in one of our previous letters that I didn't have to convince the whole world – just the one man, you, to feel I had achieved communication. You were such an example of good, from an early age (apart from the fate you planned for the cats shitting on your flower beds!) that you wanted, like me in the Boys' Brigade, to believe in the goodness of your religion's presentation of faith and you saw the best attributes of Judaism, in the Israelis' fight for survival, and in the best influences of the Roman Empire on human development and achievement.

The reason that I find you such a challenge to convince, and, of course, a satisfaction in that you find my correspondence interesting. is that you are such an intense and questioning. enthusiastic reader. And yet you accept the positive contributions of Judaism, the Roman Empire and the Universal Church based in Rome without becoming alerted to the anomalies in their writings, within their own records of their respective histories, and without examining the flaws and corruption of words in, even, their own accounts that their historical PR departments have made available to us. Those same flaws and anomalies that have been identified by other writers, whom you admire, whose works are so impressive that they survive throughout history. even influence history, for generations after the era of their initial publication.

Great writers like Shakespeare inserting little subliminal warnings in his text, for example, on Judaism 'a pound of flesh, no more no less!', and on Rome 'the evil that men do lives after them'. or closer to home, his subtle denunciation of a Scottish king's suitability for accession to the throne of the relocated Empire's seat of power. You read the words, and applauded the mastery of the communication and entertainment, without absorbing or interpreting the subliminal message tucked between the lines, or perhaps 'just blowin in the wind!'

Iain, you are the good guy because you, the devout adherent to the faith, eventually became embarrassed by the evidence of the corruption that had permeated your church – the evil of a long dead Rome that, lives on – with its accumulation of riches and worldly goods in apparent indifference to the teachings of its founder. Or the tolerance, and protection the church extends to the predators, supposedly in its service, masquerading as benign guides of the little innocent minds they are leading to the fostering care of Christ, while they abuse their innocent bodies on the journey. A wee bit of spin on 'suffer the little children to come unto me' has crept in there Iain; and all the time the original model of a good guy has to watch with impotent rage, this abuse of His church, while His hands and feet remain impaled to the old wooden cross!

You know. Iain, Rome did not die away and embrace the Christian ethos of goodness and mercy in the Way, the VIA, that Jesus was trying to promote. I suspect Constantine's miraculous conversion and attempt to relocate the Head Office to Constantinople, it is Istanbul now, was simply an attempt to advance Rome's imperial domination eastwards.

At the beginning of the Christian Era, Rome had conquered most of the known world, in every earth covered direction from the 'middle of the earth sea', the Mediterranean, with of course, the exception of Caledonia, which it walled off, declared worthless and tried to isolate and ignore.

The cost of maintaining control of this vast empire by military presence, the original survival and predatory instincts of Romulus, honed and perfected to a highly efficient degree, was proving cumbersome and unaffordable. Transporting slaves and produce back to the Capital, from far flung provinces, was time-consuming and costly – severely reducing the net profit value of the enterprise. The old example of control that Judaism seemed to effect, with some magnetic influence on the minds and souls of its people to follow their leaders, without any apparent physical coercion from the leaders, provided an example of how Rome might control the extremities of empire without the cost of maintaining a military presence, while establishing local slave manufacturing in the provinces and returning only the profit to the Capital.

In modern marketing terms, Rome needed a new mild variant to replace the old strong-tasting product, the military presence, which people were starting to resent as damaging to their health. Like when cigarettes were modified from full strength to mild, or extra mild, or fizzy drinks from, say, 'The Real Thing' to Diet Coke, or Budweiser became Bud Light. And the example of this new, lighter brand of Judaism, being presented as The Way, seemed to be having great success and appeal through a small company marketing faith, under the leadership of some guy called Jesus Christ

Business is Business – the same rules and attitudes were alive and kicking at the start of the Christian Era, just as they are at this end of the era; there were honest traders, but the successful big boys were just as devious, just as ruthless, just as corrupt! The cunning and predatory instincts of Rome kicked in. and launched a bid to take over the Company of Christ which was marketing The Way; the same old Way that, presumably, Moses had tried to return the wayward Children of Israel to, when they were corrupted towards false gods. Rome quickly rebranded this new Faith as Christianity, with the charismatic leader established as the brand logo, and distributed throughout the Roman world by an army of spiritual salesmen, to capture and hold the minds of Roman citizens whose physical existence was already controlled by the more costly measure of military presence. The new army would be called clergy, wear a habit of uniform and operate in orders and Sees, reporting in a military hierarchy, through bishops and archbishops, to the Vicar of Christ, who was the only person who could communicate with God.

Iain, you and Father Neil, your Franciscan friar friend, often talk about the Culdees, who were an anomalous group of priests, within this apparently new and enlightened clergy recruited and trained in this new Roman Catholic church. But Lo and Behold, as might have been said in those days – the Culdees were the latter day adherents of the original belief in the Way that Jesus had been trying to revive and restore; the Culdees were the original evangelists of The Way, who had settled in Hibernia and Caledonia, and were originally named Celi Dei, Companions of God, by the Romans who could not suppress their faith: the faith of the Celi Deic people, the Cel'tic people of Indo-European origin whose ethnicity seems so difficult to define. The same Celi Deic or Celtic peoples who sought freedom from Roman subjugation, by fleeing along a route of Celtic mountain strongholds all the way from Kurdistan to the last outpost of freedom, beyond Hadrian's Wall in Caledonian Rome, with its capacity for cunning and spin, gradually diluted the effect of those Celi Dei monks by homogenising them into the general priesthood, and corrupting and softening the pronunciation of Celi Dei through to Culdees, until the identity and the word lost any impact or definition, like a wavelet that has finally lost its power and merges back into the ocean swell.

By the end of the first millennium, the Culdees were suppressed into appearing no different from any other priest, and their effort to spread the truth, the Veritas about the way, the Via, that life should be lived in freedom, which Jesus and the Celi Dei had been trying to promote, was swamped and diluted by the New Testament ethos, of everybody having a cross to bear, and distributed throughout the Roman world as The Scriptures, by a mainly honest clergy who believed that they were delivering God's script for the Vita, the life that brought salvation.

Iain, I could never get my head round the fact that, during this remaining six hundred years of the Roman Empire, Christians were hunted down and persecuted while the Empire appeared to condone and tolerate the head office of this new Christian Church, which had been clearly opposed to the Imperial oppression of Rome, becoming established in Rome as the Vatican.

Iain, Rome did not fade away and die; Rome saw that capturing the minds and souls of humanity was the ultimate control: and holding God's Son hostage for eternity was the opportunity to subdue the Companions of God, Mary and Mary Magdalene and the Twelve Apostles by using the psychology of post traumatic stress disorder, and programming future generations to follow a script of obedience, concocted in the three witch cauldron, to control Mother Earth. With the apparent endorsement of the Earth Mother of humanity, the eternal city could spread the beautifully spun story that brought generations of new enthusiasts, to search for the mythical Garden of Eden, the Promised Land, the Paradise for which the earthbound capitalists in Rome held the title deeds!

And, of course Iain, you are right to admire Rome, and the Roman presence, albeit tenuous and brief, and the positive influences it exerted in the Roman Scotland of Caledonia; because Rome was the ultimate dinosaur of its day, with the earth creature's hard-wired instincts and will to survive, almost at any cost to avoid extinction or accept the submission of domesticity.

But, Iain, for all its ingenuity and power and, indeed animal cunning, Rome lacked the inspiration and vision that Romulus had killed when he slew Remus, the steering oar; the Caesar's repackaged an old habit in a new image without having the inspiration or the vision to consider that this new Way, or the old Way restored, would actually provide eternal life: the eternal life of a self sustaining democratic world. freed of the constraints and strictures of a pyramid sales hierarchical structure which invested all the profits in maintaining and developing the Capital at the expense of the Provinces.

Covered a wee bit of ground there, Iain; and while I was digressing through a bit of speculative history, our moving finger clock leapt forward to real time 6th November 2021. COP 26 in Glasgow has completed a week, with lots of brave. enthusiastic speeches and good intentions – you know, like the paving on the road to Hell! The little nations who have only people and life, to worry about are keen to get on with saving the Planet; but the big boys, holding the purse strings on the world's capital, the big population nations where lives are expendable for the protection of profit, are dragging their heels: some have just not bothered to attend. Maybe they think they are watching a disaster movie and life goes back to normal at the end, after the planet has self combusted and all the people and all the saved money have burned together.

And Peter, Paul and Mary waft another little line from their warning message 'just blowin' in the wind' … "How many times can a man turn his head and pretend that he just doesn't see?"

All the Neverlands, from my letter writing, the model of Kirriemuir, the real time world of today, any day, and the historical time worlds of any era, all in the big cauldron of broth being stirred by Macbeth's three witches; the three dimensional mind of an earth mother as defined by Dr Eric Berne. The experience as a wife, a mother or a daughter, that any woman – Mother Earth to Earth Mother – is influenced by, as she writes the script for her daughter to follow, in the hope she can avoid the worst experiences of a life where she has suffered the pain of bereavement, rejection or brutality, as a cross to bear by being part of this humanity; and the script will be handed down through the generations, dictating a reaction to life which may not always seem appropriate, even to herself or, to those closest and dearest to her. As a safeguard, in the event the script does not provide total protection, there is the temporary morphine of post traumatic stress, which suppresses the pain of the worst experiences until time removes this comforting 'amnesia' and the searing memory of the shock resurfaces and erupts as post traumatic stress disorder.

Male scripting also occurs, making Man equally conditioned to follow a planned course, as parent, provider and protector, and equally as vulnerable to post traumatic stress when the challenge or the experience, particularly of failure, or impotence to meet the challenge, proves too overwhelming for his mind to accommodate, without also hiding the shocking memory in some secret mental memory bank as post traumatic stress. And occasionally the bad memory resurfaces to torment his loss, or revive the guilt of failure through the same disorder of unreleased stress.

As you know Iain, I am not a fire and brimstone church-going practitioner; I believe, like you, in the Via Veritas Vita, but, not entirely in the spun versions of the truth within the faiths we have, pretty much, followed. Regrettably, there is no freedom of opinion within the Testaments therefore, I guess I would be considered a bit of a heretic, by the fire and brimstone dispensers of the Faith.

I still see the earth as a bi-polar entity and mankind, the children of Earth, are constructed to that same bi-polar pattern; we have the basic instincts of every living creature, powered by direct current that ensures we survive so long as the batteries last: but, in addition, humanity has the opportunity to plug into the main power supply, which gives the magnetic inspirational power for man to think beyond the dinosaur existence and evolve, to stay within the constraints of a finite earth and sustain humanity's survival, in the eternity of a universe we have all the time in the world to explore.

I think one or two witching hour shifts may have gone into this letter – easy to lose track of time when you are enjoying a bit of space hopping.

As I said it is now 6th November, 2021, and I have my life-saving walk to enjoy; people are so surprisingly friendly around 7 a.m. and I am really quite impressed by the drivers in cars who take almost exaggerated care, to show me they are giving me plenty of space on the narrow East Hill Road and endorse it with a wave as they pass by.

I will sit with you for a while if the wee bench isn't too damp in our Scottish weather.

Talk later.

*Ed*

**Sunday 7ᵗʰ November 2021**

*Hi Iain,*

I realise that most of what I have to say now is fairly current, or relates to recent history; the few years just before we met: my experience, I suppose, of the second coming that nobody else seems to have observed, or is prepared to admit to! Perhaps some people did feel something, but are too fearful, that a vengeful ancient Rome still has a spiritual presence which can detect a believer and deliver harm indiscriminately to any Christian to ensure the elimination of Companions of God.

I feel that an ancient .capitalist world that seemed just as impressed by, and reliant on deviously-worded contracts, would probably anticipate that in two millennia the statute of limitations would, at least have weakened their case. But I remain cognisant of Denis Wheatley's warning about dabbling in the occult, and keep a watchful eye on the loose floorboard or any other threat which might otherwise be dismissed as 'Sod's Law'. In fact, at this moment of typing, which is a couple of days beyond the event, I had received a caution from my daughter,. who had been advised by a friend, that my morning walk down East Hill Road before sunrise in dark clothing, was not giving motorists much opportunity to avoid punting me into that wee slit trench beside you. Iain, much as I enjoyed the cosiness and companionship of our allegorical joint occupancy of your wee trench, I am not in a hurry to restore that much cosiness, in fact, I changed my route, and may miss you some mornings, until I get a high visibility jacket. I still like to hear that Gate, at the Hill Rise exit from the Cemetery, clang shut behind me, with me on the outside. So, thanks Jane Grewar, for the 'heads up!'

Today is my grandson's birthday; I have just wished him 'happy birthday' on Messenger, which is very satisfying, despite my reservations about the dangers of this 'mechanical brain, effecting some sinister control over our young people: I have to admit that there are great advantages to the internet, so long as the 'bad guys' don't take control of our thinking. I am wary about the fact that some remote person can get into my mechanical brain of a computer, to analyse my activities and identify my preferences and thence to influence my thoughts and choices by subliminal selling in a direction of their choosing. Like some latter day sophisticated control, without the costly presence of a Roman Military to effect physical control, or a Roman Clergy through confession and discipline to maintain a spiritual control – this is the opposite of the obvious. This brain that I own and apparently control is accessible to some domain which can float subliminal messages to me, presumably in an attempt to counteract my 'blowing in the wind' communiques. Eerie!

Today was also one of those days when little happy coincidences occur. Sheila and I spent the afternoon with Helen, which was very pleasant; the coincidence was that I found out that today is also your eldest grandson's birthday. I am not going anywhere particularly with that, other than I find it interesting that Easter, the moveable feast, has held some mysterious negative for me, which seemed to have slightly jaundiced my view of anniversaries, my birthday included However, this happy coincidence of the eldest grandchildren of two such good friends, sharing a birthday, puts a happier perspective on my own anniversary; because my birthday is shared with my mother's two eldest grandchildren, my son Roddy and my brother's daughter Elaine. These were all happy occasions for my mother and her two sons, and the realisation has wakened me up again to the happiness of birthdays, and to the possibility that the Christmas to occur, within this period of Second Coming, might be a new birth without the interest and control of a Roman presence.

I have to think a bit more about the implications I am imagining, but the constant recurrence of coincidences intrigues me and somehow, endorses my theory that events replicate throughout history, packed together in parallels of latitude for their historical repetition; but also packed like Russian dolls from the smallest individual life-experience through various increasing sizes, like a bereaved mother being contained within a bereaved Virgin Mary being similar and contained within Eve, a tortured Earth Mother, contained within the Blessed Virgin Earth, the original mother in the Universe, as far as we know. And they all have a similar profile, and a shared tragedy which has to be put right before the end of this Second Coming, which is forecast to end six days after Christmas of 2021.

I still take my life-preserving walk around the 56th parallel that contains our model world of Kirriemuir but, this morning I was a little behind time and decided to save some minutes by taking the short cut along West Hill Road, which cuts out the stretch of Shielhill Road, and the long leg of

East Hill Road which runs along the side of Kate's Wood. And a wee door swung open with a wind blowin' in my mind.

You know me, Iain, with my obsession for coincidences and snatches of song, or Shakespeare works that seem to be a commentary or a signpost, to some historical anomaly that might be worth a look or two. Is this Kate, of Kate's Wood, perhaps a pointer to the 'Kiss Me Kate' of The Taming of the Shrew? Perhaps directing me to the brave or feisty women, that Dr Eric Berne was concerned about, acting out a difficult life script that had been handed down the generations from mother to daughter and granddaughter? Perhaps a second pointer or reminder. in case I had missed the significance of the Three Witches relevance, in the equally starring role of the Earth Mother, in this Christian Era drama. Or indeed, Iain, the significance of the other female lead in the real life biography that provided the ingredients for this Christian Era story, the Virgin Mary. Or, indeed, the other significant feisty woman that the New Testament scriptwriters were obliged to mention, but limited almost to a brief cameo role.

You know Iain, in this now, up to date world of me, the Herald seems to have a new crossword setter who very much favours fairly devious cryptic clues, particularly 'sounds like' words presented as 'on the radio' to suggesting a phonetic sound that transmits a different meaning from the spelt out written word; such as 'Sounds like the way, to anchor a plant, 4 letters-answer Root' or 'A warning to the quartet on the radio" 4 letters – Fore.

The significant feisty woman that I have in mind is Mary Magdalene, a star of the production, who was suddenly removed from the play, after her brief but essential scene in the Garden of Gethsemane. Now, this is the tricky bit, Iain; the bit that doesn't depend on some Old Testament type miracle, updated to create the giant step for a metamorphosing Empire. How about this for an alternative tale?

I think it possible that the controllers of the Empire had to 'not allow' Jesus to be seen to have died, if their plan to take control of the Church that He planned, was to succeed. And the best way to do this was to free Him from the cross before He died and have His wife, Mary Magdalene confirm that He lived; make a deal with His supporters, a non-disclosure contract, if they took Him away, secretly so that a miracle resurrection could be promulgated to premier the launch of this new faith of

Christianity in the Universal Church, with a board of directors based in the Capital of Empire in Rome.

Iain, did you know that one of the interpretations of the word Kirriemuir, from its earliest beginnings is 'Care o' Mary' and the earliest inhabitants were 'Care o' Marians', not much different from today's Kirriemarians – you know, a 'sounds like' clue.

Iain, I don't see that this little fantasy of speculation I am indulging in is any less credible or believable than the allegorical tale, dependent on miracles from beginning to end, that we have tolerated and accepted without rational explanation for two thousand years.

And, in the best traditions of a hostile take over bid, the board of twelve apostles received a large bonus, and key roles in the new company; with Peter retaining his role as General Manager and Mary (the Blessed Virgin) installed as Managing Director until Jesus recuperated and returned from sick leave to assume control. Mary Magdalene also signs a non-disclosure contract and is awarded a considerable cash settlement in the Garden of Gethsemane (I always wonder if some first century scribe was playing 'sounds like' games with Gets the Money!) to take Jesus out of Jerusalem, which has become pretty agitated because of the Crucifixion that had been voted through on a dubious very narrow margin.

She makes her way along the refugee trail, through the Celtic fringes, in difficult terrain where military deployment was difficult and Roman domination less effective, to the safe haven of Pictavia, in the Roman province of Caledonia which is still controlled by the Companions of God. The Empire is not overly concerned, since it controls most of the known world, and could soon hunt down and eliminate any who tried to break the terms of the non-disclosure contracts. To ensure secrecy the Empire would simply exercise its policy of 'kill everyone and you are sure to have eliminated your foe'! The same policy adopted by the Roman Church at times, the Inquisition or the Carcassone Massacre for example, to reinforce adherence to a faith that was supposed to be founded on love.

The new Church is established and given an illusion of independence, with its own management hierarchy, but ultimately reporting to the sleeping partner who controls it through a seat of Capital power based in Rome.

So Iain, what about the Second Coming? Well this is where it gets a bit difficult for the Empire to update its two thousand year old story;

even after establishing a Regional Office at Westminster, following the 1066 revival of the old Conquest script, corruption has infested the Universal Church in some of its previously most loyal and compliant areas, seriously disappointing and discouraging its most devout adherents. Even a disciplined and enthusiastic worshipper like you, Iain, became embarrassed and ashamed by the decadence and immorality of some clergy. The wealth and opulence of the hierarchy was in direct contrast to the millions of Faithful who remained poor, while their children fell victim to the paedophiles, who were attracted to join the clergy for the access it provided, and the freedom they could enjoy to exercise a malignant power, over the innocent youth entrusted to them for spiritual guidance.

I recall Iain, that you defined the situation, to protect the genuine dedicated clergy, "Priests don't become paedophiles, paedophiles become priests!" And nobody seemed to be doing anything about correcting this deteriorating situation. Maybe it was all happening during the period that Pope Benedict had concluded that God was asleep. Whatever happened to managing upwards, or Hands on management?

You know, Iain, that morning in early September when a wee bout of indigestion took me back to remembering Frank, I did my walk and my climb up the steep hill through the Cemetery, and I was quite pleased when the heavy iron gate clanged shut with me on the living side. I recall that there was a heavy mist and visibility was quite restricted; in fact the Camera Obscura building was hardly visible even the short distance from the Cemetery gate, but I could hear a woman's voice calling to her runaway dog, and out of the mist came Lynn MacGregor, who had owned Oslers Hairdresser, in the Roods, where Frank had rented a chair and they had worked as a team. I know it is a bit of a coincidence, but my experience during this period of Second Coming has a few coincidences peppered throughout.

Lynn is one of those ladies I have loved, in the most innocent of ways; she was bubbly, good fun and liked a laugh for the half hour of my once a month hair cut from Frank: Lynn and I would indulge in a bit of harmless "chat up' banter.

In late 2006 I was considered a good enough customer to qualify for the reward of an exclusive Osler's 2007 Diary; a wee book, with gold lettering on the front cover stating 'Compliments of Oslers' under the header 'legend which read,

'TEAMWORK together we achieve the extraordinary'

And inside, every week contained a quotation from a person – this week in November 2007 the quotation was by Harry S Truman, 33rd President of the USA.

"It is amazing what you can accomplish when you do not care who gets the credit!"

I still have the diary. and Lynn is one of my heroines because sometime during the anticipated Second Coming, her husband, Barley. took the dogs for a walk on a Sunday evening, along the Forfar Road; and just before Maryton, with no other cars or pedestrians in the vicinity. Barley was struck and killed by a skidding car.

A bereaved young mother of two wee girls, Lynn dropped out of circulation for a while, and we lost touch – but, when the going gets tough. the tough get going! She picked herself up, studied nursing and is now a community staff nurse; not only getting on with her life, but making a difference to the lives of others. And she is still bubbly and good fun.

As she emerged from the mist on Kirrie Hill, in her nurse's uniform, hurrying to complete her dog walk, we had a quick exchange of our usual banter, "How are you?" she asked.

Recalling my earlier bout of Frank's fatal indigestion I feigned "Oh Nurse, I have this pain in my chest!" But she just laughed and said,

"Aye, if you've just walked up that Cemetery Hill you're doing just fine!"

I took that as a positive prognosis from a health professional, while she hurried off to make a positive contribution to somebody else's well-being. I hurried home to clean out Satan's altar.

During 2007 business had improved considerably from the dire depths it had fallen to a few years earlier; there were no particular highlights and, certainly. no evidence of any preparation or excitement building for the impending Second Coming due to occur in 2008. No hint from Benedict, no encouraging speech to advise the world that God had awakened, to welcome and applaud His son's triumphal return; no enthusiasm from Canterbury. or celebratory street parties suggested by the Defender of the Faith in Buck House. And, to distribute this criticism fairly, no indication from the Moderator of the General. Assembly of the Church of Scotland, that he was organising the Culdees, and the Companions of God, as an Honour Guard to greet the return of the Saviour after two thousand years of promise and expectation.

Meanwhile Iain, at realism's level, on the streets of Kirrie was another of the ladies who impress me, and I care about. Fidelma who, like Lynn, lost her husband in a tragic car accident and, with a baby son to care for, picked herself up, packed her grief in a little package in her heart and tried to make a difference for others. Fidelma is one of those volunteers who tries to encourage youngsters to see a better way of life than relieving idleness and boredom through drink or drugs. or just becoming accustomed to idleness so that a wasted lifetime becomes a way of life. She counsels youngsters in this comfort zone of inactivity where they assemble in the streets of Angus towns.

Fidelma used to visit the pub for a Jameson or two after an evening counselling, however, as a combination of my reducing my evening hours and the pandemic lockdown, I haven't seen Fidelma for a while; but I recently received a little card of encouragement, signed simply F,.........x, which I suspected was Fidelma. Another lady I admired who got going when the going got tough.

You know, Iain, when I get a bit elevated, or view this Christian Era with a bit of hindsight, it makes sense of our speculation that we might be floundering in blissful ignorance through a sea of purgatory; an awful lot of good people seem to be bombarded with a load of shit that they don't deserve.

I have just thought about our joint reaction to the present era, or at least this final quarter of it; our reluctance to being drawn into the fast moving world of information technology: our concern about allowing a mechanical brain, which some controller somewhere else, remote from us, can influence and, even, dictate our thinking by analysing our choices, or our exploratory moves. and presume to design a package for purchase which it interprets will most closely fit the needs that it (IT) has decided we were expressing.

Obviously you and I had lived long enough, and still have enough brainpower to recall our last big fight for freedom against the domination by Naziism, which was supposed to release us into a better free thinking world, presumably to allow us to prepare for the fabled Second Coming which would guarantee that freedom of thought and choice for the next thousand years. What happened to that early promise?

Perhaps Iain, after the supposed free world nations united in a volunteer confederation, like some latter day Caledonia, to resist the expanding empire of Naziism, the little nations realised that they were already exploited by existing Imperial powers and started to agitate and create disorder to release themselves from the stress of paying allegiance to a demanding capital state distant and remote from where their individual life scripts were being acted out. Maybe we feel some instinctive warning, the fight or flee adrenalin, to alert us to this third millennium threat being gestated without the involvement of a supreme being, to create a humanity of machines controlled by an earthbound god who convinces mankind that he is happier, freed of individual thought or creativity, or inspiration to adapt his life script with a little variety or improvisation. The Empire of IT, that doesn't need a military presence or an evangelical clergy; just a little machine that each citizen has paid for and can't live without: and naively believes he controls, because he presses the buttons on this receiver of subliminal messaging. Eerie!

So Iain, are we human or are we dinosaur? Or are we still on our knees, praying for the answer?

I am hoping that COP 26 in Glasgow, the Dear Green Place. the birthplace of Mungo, a Companion of God. will provide that answer. And the second coming prophesied to occur between 2008 and 2021, did nobody notice? Benedict, could he not tell the difference between God snoring and God waking up angrily at what mankind had done to Mother Earth while he was mourning the crucifixion of their Son?

The disrespect for women and the abuse of children was rampant everywhere – even in the Church that the Roman Empire cannot fully control because a 'few good men' and one strong woman would not allow Rome to 'handle the Truth' – the ultimate Veritas that united the Via with Vita. Peter Paul and Mary are not some random accident of underground protest music activity. Rome, through its earthly domination believed it controlled the body of mankind, and while Rome held the effigy of the body of Christ impaled to a cross it believed it could also control the spiritual power of the Universe it sought to dominate.

But first. was the one small step for mankind; to be drawn to follow the Lamb of God into the Church that Rome had obliged Peter to found. as had been directed by Jesus. Managing upwards is no less difficult in spiritual terms than it is in today's, allegedly, democratic societies, and nigh impossible while operating under the oppressive scrutiny in a dictatorial Imperialistic domain.

The ace card for freedom and democracy in this entire exercise is the underestimated female strength and resilience and influence; the Blessed Virgin: the Mother Earth, who existed before God descended to create the beginning of Humanity. And in this Christian Era, she was the bereaved mother who held her son's church together. to honour his wish when he thought he was dying, while she held him alive in her soul, and refused to let his spirit die.

Iain, I haven't a clue what preceded the Big Bang, or indeed, the Universal developments which took place before the turbulence and disturbance factor settled in to the magnetic order of our Solar System, which lasted so many millions of years that measurement or, even, understanding seem almost irrelevant. And our, Mankind, existence in millennia, which appear significant to us is, somehow, infinitesimal in the Universal adjusting or balancing that appears to be an eternal contest between Good and Evil and beyond our current level of comprehension. Trying to interpret what our existence is about is a big enough challenge; trying to understand what the Christian Era is about is the immediate survival problem, if Isaac Newton's prediction of the world ending in 2060 is the ultimate Dead Reckoning position (to use another navigational term.)

So, my theorem is that, just as is happening with our earthly exploration of the Universe, trying to find a star or a planet which can sustain human life – the precedent is that 'Earth is just such a planet, perhaps, even, the only planet; the Blessed Virgin planet which could produce simple life forms with basic survival instincts, which developed from virus to advanced life form – dinosaurs – and then became extinct because of their inability to either sustain or contain their own evolution.

You know, Iain, it is a complete mystery to me that the spiritual authors of this entire Christian Era story, or serial, were unprepared for the next episode which they had been advertising for the two thousand years that the series has been running. Perhaps, as happened at the time when the Caesars were plotting against each other, the corruption that once pervaded the Roman Empire was creeping into the fabric of organisations. Nations, such as Ireland. which had co-operated with Rome, since its days as Hibernia when it extended hospitality to a visiting Roman military and the Roman interpretation of Christianity adopted without force or apparent subjugation, now felt betrayed by the indiscriminate abuse of its young people; particularly by the deceit of this clergy. the priests and nuns who were permitted access to the most precious recesses of a believer's conscience through obligatory confession, and also entrusted with the sacred responsibility for the care and preparation of the souls of the little children. Elite and exclusive seminaries run by respected orders of monks were operating like concentration camps of iniquity. Even in the great cities of the New World, Boston and Chicago in the US and Sydney in Australia evidence of this betrayal by trusted clergy emerging to shake the faith of the hitherto most faithful, the Church answered with denial or a wall of silence, and the guilty simply transferred to another naive parish; worse still when absolution was made available to these perpetrators of sin and their anonymity secured in a well-funded retirement out of public reach.

Even committed believers like you, born into the Roman Church and programmed and scripted for a lifetime of obedient dedication, were beginning to be embarrassed by the behaviour of the corrupt people and practices that were exercising control over the course this great ship of a church was heading. It seemed as though the Church that Jesus had planned was caught in a dangerous negative current and the old navigation instruments of the scriptures, the Standing Orders of Gospel truth were giving a false reading.

You know, the more I read or re-examine parts of the original story the more incredible it becomes; the rush of events in Holy Week with the triumphal arrival on Palm Sunday, the turning over of the money lenders on Monday and berating the scribes and the Pharisees in the Temple on Tuesday: Wednesday, presumably, preparing for the big briefing meeting on Thursday with the last supper in the evening and the main event of a public trial, presided over by the Governor of the Province, not to mention the significant journey, carrying a heavy cross to the place of execution followed by death and resurrection by the end of the weekend, well the logistics and timing seem impossible to credit. And, after resurrection, the young couple, the romantic leading roles in this whirlwind tale just vanish; until the female star is discredited some two thousand years later, for running a laundry in Portobello staffed by vulnerable young women, who required to be disciplined, for having flouted the Church's intolerance on indulgence in the original sin. This despite the evidence that clergy similarly indulgent, whilst also betraying trust, were given absolution and retained or promoted within the priesthood to perpetuate this abusive conduct with apparent impunity.

And if one tries to confirm the story and create a logical sequence of events, it seems that the timeline has a variable start date, being a moveable feast, and, at various reviews, theology experts, historians and academics cast doubt on Good Friday's events, which might actually have occurred on the Thursday to comply with prophesies and events which occurred in the Old Testament, which would mean the whole scene would have to be rewritten two thousand years after the original production had been premiered.

Yet, while the whole world exists in the Era of Now and deals, pinned down in fact, with the problems of this fast disintegrating Now Era, which is heading for destruction on an overheating Earth, the senior management of Christianity, the Defenders of the Faith at the top of the Sales Pyramid, and the Born Agains – the alleged new enlightened failed to alert us to the truth that the great pyramid of Faith Selling is actually an iceberg. floating on a sea of purgatory with the Christian faithful holding on to this vast bulk of the truth, that is frozen in a life held below a sea level of enlightenment.

You know Iain, another of the 'Blowing in the Wind' lines from Paul and Mary is "How many years must some people exist, before they're allowed to be free?"

And the answer has to be two thousand. because the moment has to be now; not the Era of Now, but the instant of now. before the great circle of the Equator reaches the Omega of this Christian Era at the Greenwich meridian

Need to get a move on and clean out Satan's altar again

Talk again soon

*Ed*

**Thursday 11ᵗʰ November 2021**

*Hi Iain*

You will see from the date of this letter that I have again jumped ahead a little. I visit you, as you know, almost every day, when I take my life-preserving walk – but I missed out today because I had an early appointment at the Kirrie Health Centre for my annual health check.

I don't know the results yet, but the experience was quite encouraging for an old guy. Face masks add a little to the mystique of being assessed by a young nurse, when all you can see is twinkling brown eyes with a little bit of humour and mischief lurking in the twinkle.

I was pretty much alone in the waiting area, which, as you know is quite large, when she came out to summon me for my appointment, but she walked past looking around the room, even round into the dog leg section, before calling my name, "Yep, that's me" I responded and she replied with "Oh, I walked past you; I checked your date of birth, and was looking for an old guy!" What a good start to a Health Check, I thought!

Anyway Iain, that gets rid of a little bit of digression for today's letter.

In the real world of Kirriemuir in 2008, my lot seemed to have improved considerably; business was buoyant and I appeared to have made up all the lost ground of the bad years – although not recouped any of the lost savings which were jettisoned to prevent the Good Ship Three Bellies from foundering. The Jaguar which had apparently offended the social conscience of the drinking class of Kirriemuir had long since been replaced with a modest Volkswagen for Sheila, while I inherited her old, small BMW to show that my feet had returned to more humble ground.

Now that business was more buoyant I felt that I could upgrade, also, to a new Volkswagen without stirring up too much disapproval, although this change was also commented on! But, in fact, the world generally seemed to be more buoyant; after the shock of the upsurge in international terrorism and the supposedly compensating victory in the Iraq conflict, 2008 seemed to be enjoying some encouraging forward momentum: certainly, at least, from my perspective in the, then, current world of Kirriemuir. But still, none of the religious leaders whose philosophy and Scriptures prophesied and anticipated a second coming of the Messiah, seemed aware of any Spiritual turbulence.

You know, Iain. for some reason the month of June had always featured in my life when something good or positive starts for me. Somehow I felt this same tremor of a lift beginning, particularly when it was heralded by a big bang – Glengate Garage, almost opposite our house, exploded with a really big bang and the building was totally destroyed by the resulting fire. The irony is that the Garage was the neighbouring building to Kirriemuir Fire Station. Allegedly the mechanic, Davy McDonald was welding a repair on a van, unaware that it bad a secret fuel tank fitted to use agricultural grade fuel which was subsidised for the exclusive use of farmers. The tank exploded, Davy was blown across the road and the flames ignited the many combustible substances present in a working garage and paint shop. Davy was assessed as sustaining no life threatening injuries, although his subsequent lifetime was plagued with the bad luck that suggests the now, commonly diagnosed, post traumatic stress disorder.

The road had to be closed and nearby homes evacuated until any risk of further explosion from gas bottles and fuel tanks was judged to have passed.

Sheila went to her son's in Broughty Ferry for the evening, but I had to stay with the Pub as this was traditional music night; so I spent the night in my pal, Frank Reid's, spare room.

My increasing buoyancy continued; whether the excitement of our local Big Bang or the lift from, at last, affording a new car, I can't tell. I had experienced such a lift a couple of times before in life, once in 1982 when I had attended a company-run motivational seminar, which involved a whole week of intense programming by a team of high powered American management specialists – William J Burke, Robert Miller and Bob Smith. We called it 'The Burke Course'. I was selected by Burke as his stooge for the week and, somehow, ended up as the star of the show. I loved it.

Back home that weekend the buoyant feeling persisted and I continued to experience the emotional lift. I was pretty high. I had never heard of bi-polarity, but now recognise that this was my first test flight (of fancy?) as the lid was lifted off all of the suppressed memories that had conditioned my life until that time; the highs and the lows, and the very lows! The anger and frustration at being too small, at four years old, to protect my mother from an assault from a bullying brute of a man; I had tried my hardest, and done my best to no avail: perhaps my first experience of a suppressed trauma, long before the impact of trauma, and its tendency to rekindle the extreme feelings of suppressed anger, fear, hate at a later date, without knowledge or apparent reason why one should be assailed with such negative depressive feelings, at this later stage in life without apparent cause.

I realise now with the benefit of hindsight, and, of course, the accessibility of knowledge on the internet that I was performing an amateur application of transactional analysis on myself. The other buried 'hurt' was the loss of my first-born son, Roddy; the time of much greater conscious input and out pouring of grief. and therefore less pain to suppress or soothe; I did not realise that failure as a father protector was also a guilt trauma that would be suppressed and stored in a mental recess beside the remaining pain of loss.

Iain, only now can I see the extreme pain of my wife, the mother of my children, who refused to release the spirit of her beloved son, but lived with the pain of this post traumatic stress, which occasionally erupted in some form of disorder. She turned the anger and rage in on herself for her part in contributing to Roddy's cancer having been told, somewhat tactlessly like your own experience, that the condition could have been present from before he was born; which of course meant, in the womb, thus making the blame and the guilt the mother's cross to bear. Despite this emotional burden she attempted to conduct and present a stable and normal life for the sake of her children and family to enjoy the sort of happy life that the loving personality of young Roddy had promised in his three short years.

Joyce did not find peace in her life, despite her love and the satisfaction she derived from her two children, until the moment her soul could be reunited with the spirit of the beloved son she had refused to release until she was freed to join him.

Perhaps, Iain, when we progress all those models of human experience through their reducing parallels, from the great circle of Mother Earth down to one suffering earth mother we can see the same parallel reluctance of any mother to release the creative living spirit of her son to be a victim a second time to the unenlightened single polarity predatory creature that man has evolved to.

Iain, one of the comments that Diarmuid made during his presentation, that stimulated our quest, was on his reluctance to understand or

accept his church, the Roman Church's depiction of the act of love,
of procreation as the original sin. Like Diarmuid, I could never quite
understand why the physical act of love and creation was defined as
something sinful or to feel guilt about. Perhaps, like the post traumatic
stress eruption of hidden, suppressed feelings there was some knowledge
that was introduced, and suppressed from a pre-birth spiritual awareness,
to erupt in a later generation as an awareness of sin and guilt with no
specific event or memory even, to connect or explain this feeling of
unacceptable behaviour, so it was labelled sin; and since it was beyond
living memory it was the original sin. You know, Iain, the picture that
would need a thousand words to paint-Adam and Eve and the apple and
the serpent! And even then be a difficult explanation.

Just supposing that, by the time mankind was able to communicate, by
speech or picture drawing or the written word, that human disciplines
and rules. for the best reasons, had evolved to where fidelity and love had
standards, defined and judged in the sanctity of marriage between a man
and a woman. Thinking and curiosity had also evolved to a point where
trying to explain the 'in the beginning' bit was a quantum leap backwards
which the enlightened of the day, seeing the truth behind the Garden of
Eden picture, decided was a heresy, impossible to explain to these simple
but disciplined people without causing some shocking reaction. The
moment of,

"The Truth, Sonny? You couldn't handle the Truth'!"

The fully formed Adam and Eve were the reality of mankind. And
trying to explain to the less enlightened that Man had actually developed
over millions of years from a self-mutating virus was a truth that would
not be easy to convey or convince. The further truth that would not be
handled, but considered a heresy was that the virus of creation of mankind
was produced by the Blessed Virgin Eve, this pictorial thousand word
depiction of Mother Earth, and the virus mutated either, by the virgin's
monthly egg-producing a male virus that could mutate by mating with
the original virgin virus or a twin egg producing male and female viruses
which could mate and mutate. And, as we have been told by today's
pandemic experts the virus can then replicate exponentially.

So. Iain. the truth that could not be handled by a mankind that believed
the Adam and Eve story, and had evolved to believe in the sanctity of,
effectively, a conventional breeding pair of fully formed adults, this truth

was that mankind evolved from an incestuous relationship between a mother virus and a son virus, or a brother virus and sister virus, and trying to make the quantum leap between the beginning and the now, the breeding was, by their standards, incestuous and the explanation was a heresy and better parcelled up as a little package of potential traumatic stress as 'the original sin' – the truth that could not be handled!

And, after ten millennia of accepting the Garden of Eden, Adam, Eve, apple and serpent mystery, nobody seems to question or throw light on the truth that cannot be handled.

I guess Iain, we will bring another ton of shit down on our heads for that bit of heretical speculation.

Anyway, back to 2008 and the prophesied Second Coming that all the monotheistic experts seem ill-prepared for.

I for one had great hopes for Barak Obama.'s developing campaign to be president of America. I thought that a mixed race American in the White House would be a giant leap forward for America and for mankind. However the promising development of good news seemed to be partnered by a counterbalancing development of bad news. I watched with growing trepidation the foolhardy game of blind brag that Fred Goodwin of the so called Royal Bank of Scotland was playing with Bob Diamond of Barclays in a reckless gamble using ordinary .investors' money. The prize seemed to be a dodgy over-mortgaged Dutch bank and the ultimate winner likely to have a Pyrrhic victory experience.

I have little financial expertise, but I have played the odd game of poker; I felt Diamond and Barclays were just toying with Fred, taunting his power grab mentality until he was overstretched, when Diamond would suddenly fold and leave Fred and the Royal over-extended with a bargain that had suddenly cost more than it was Worth. And Diamond did withdraw, but it seemed the irony is that the Royal Bank, having sullied the brand name of Scotland, has all but abandoned Scotland and effected its own second coming as the National Westminster Bank in debt to the UK taxpayer by some forty billion pounds which would have gone a long way to subsidising the NHS during this current pandemic.

Oh Iain, it seems I cannot resist a bit of digression when I have an avid letter reader as a captive audience.

And as this period of second coming progressed. it seemed that our politicians had found a new creativity – in the expense claims they submitted to run this tax payer funded Government; the creativity of the claims were such that in some cases, it left the generous salary almost intact to be creamed away as savings along with the other bonuses derived from lobbying. and the rewards of the celebrity, or second jobs, that their subsidised, occasionally part-time, representation of the people could generate for them. Even the apparently revered house of rewarded lordships could pick up an expenses supported £300 per day tax free allowance which is five times the value of the £300 weekly wage of a living wage taxpayer.

The Houses were rocked by the scandal – for a depressingly short period of admonishment.'

Iain, I cannot deny that during 2008, at my decidedly 'feet on the ground' level, I felt an excitement that change was in the air. And, with the benefit of hindsight I can see that my bi-polar anticipation had been aroused in this otherwise single polarity, neutral or negative world. I had got somewhat above myself, as the old Kirriemuir seer had warned a few years earlier.

The blow by blow details do not matter; the fact is that I recognised my symptoms and elected to seek medical assistance, perhaps a mild sedative to slow my mind down enough to keep pace with the world events I was racing ahead of. Iain, at this point in our real time of 2021, I have to take a quantum leap backwards to the situation in 1963 and 1964, through to 1980.

This was a prolonged period when, at various critical points, I had sought professional help for my – I now recognise – deeply traumatised wife; and none of the professionals seemed to be alert to the fact that the shock of bereavement deserved some element of therapy. We had to soldier on alone with living out slightly depressed lives, until carrying this latent burden of grief became the normal state and, consequently, the reality of life. On the surface Joyce appeared strong, confident and capable; particularly in those situations when I did manage to convince a health professional to attempt to observe the problem. Only in normal daily activity, when some perfectly innocent action triggered the memory of loss, did the pain erupt as anger or irritability, but in the privacy of our home and family circle where none of us were informed or knowledgeable enough to understand.

As the result of my experience of this effect of mental trauma on both our lives I had endeavoured to understand the workings of my own mind, and indeed, it seemed that most minds reacted similarly to specific situations; I felt I had attained a competence level of enthusiastic amateurism, which is where most specialities reach before they are elevated to professional status endorsed by qualifications. Meantime a professional branch of medicine had developed very quickly, to educate students in the recorded understanding of the brain to a level of degree qualification which separated the professional from the amateur; however, amateurs like me had the 'lived in' practical experience of the conditions, without having any qualification to support the assertion that their opinion might have a relevance. This was the situation in which I found myself in 2008.

Thus, when I presented myself as feeling a wee bit high, but could handle it if they would just prescribe something to slow me down and encourage sleep that was not possible! In the previously unenlightened speciality of the mind, only those with the degree qualification, apparently, had the expertise to judge; the alternative allowed for no grey areas or amateur awareness: the choice was between certificated enlightenment, or ignorant victim suffering from a disorder that was too complex for anyone but a specialist to understand. My insistence that I could handle it, with a little bit of help to calm the physical symptoms was clear evidence that I must be nuts; like the Jack Nicholson character in 'One Flew over the Cuckoo's Nest'.

I have kept a written record of my impressions of this particular influence on my personal experience during those early days of this second coming; I feel these impressions have some relevance in. our Diarmuid's Quest. at this stage, thirteen years after their occurrence: a little burst of hindsight while the memories are still warm!

Meantime I will get home to clean out Satan's Altar; although this recollecting of the Second Coming experience is reminding me of an eventful, but seemingly unrecognised period of human history.

Talk again soon,

*Ed*

**Friday 12th November 2021**

*Hi Iain,*

I am already sitting on Anna's bench looking across at your wee slit trench. Helen has decorated it with potted plants that are sturdy enough to withstand the rapidly cooling Autumn weather. A couple of really tall-stemmed plants, a bit like Irises, are waving steadily in the cold breeze, like battle ensigns, as if you are signalling, "Still here, bayonets fixed, and ready to move over the top!"

You know Iain, you really are something special. Nineteen months after your own particular Damian Roth of cancer delivered a mortal blow, you are still here on the front line, directing our fight from your little slit trench; and all along this Hadrian's Wall of defiance, around the World, people are responding to the instinct, to fight back against whatever form the cancerous thuggery of their individual Damian Roth manifests itself. As I took a walk along your section of the line on Kirrie Hill reading some of the names on the headstones. Many were just names that stirred no little coincidence of connection in my memory – but some were surprisingly relevant. Just along from you and Anna was a stone with a dedication to Joyce Valentine, whom I don't know; but in my cryptic clue 'sounds like' thought processes, Joyce Valentine sounds a bit like Joyce Ballantyne my first wife, and mother of my three children, who was my anchor on my first bi-polar solo flight into the occult atmosphere of recent Universal history. A wee bit of poetic licence, I admit, but there is a definite phonetic identity that would be difficult to ignore if the sound was blowing in the wind.

A few more unknown names and suddenly Frank Massie's name, unexpectedly appeared; almost missed it because the top name on the stone is his mother's maiden name, Boyd, then his father Frank Small Massie then my wee Frank at the bottom with 'Died 11th October 2010', which came as a surprise: Ian Christie and I remember his last day as Saturday 10th October, 10/10/10! But presumably the Doctor, who attended on Monday 12th October, elected to split the difference between our last sighting on Saturday and the morning of the discovery of his remains on Monday.

Frank would have loved the cryptic quandary this presented; if he felt well enough to undress on Saturday evening, why had he not even attempted to eat his Chinese carry out – his last supper, which still lay unopened on the kitchen worktop on Monday morning. Frank's death was a long time from Easter, in either timely direction – six months forward or six months back; and yet it seems as though this wee gay hairdresser from Kirriemuir had been allocated a moveable feast death just like the kidnapped hero of the main story of this Christian Era. Eeerie!

And Iain, despite all the permutations of timings, moving fingers and revision of calendars, such as the Julian and Gregorian calendars, and events from ancient Judaic calendars and eras, this moveable feast always manages to fall on a weekend! Every other major anniversary, Christmas, Remembrance Day, New Year's Day, American Independence all have to occur on the random day on which the chronological date falls … except Easter; perhaps the occasion, containing two bank holidays, was contrived and manipulated for some Capitalist purpose as one small step for capitalism, before the banks arranged the big bang bank crash of 2008, gambling on the bale out by billions of taxpayers' savings, which bankers achieved with relative impunity.

Not going anywhere with that, but, in the context of our big world of Earth being replicated in this little model world of Kirriemuir, I see a little parallel in Frank's moveable feast passing, and the events predicted to follow that original moveable feast occurrence of Easter 34AD.

Frank had no savings when he died – his family had to club together to fund his funeral expenses; which understandably was not a particularly welcome burden for all contributors: this inconvenience was certainly commented on as the arrangements set Frank's family back a few thousand pounds.

Lo and behold, as we say in miraculous circumstances, Frank's reputation was resurrected a year or so later, when it emerged that he had a 'not insignificant' pension pot, untouched, in the William Low/Tesco pension fund. There were sufficient funds to reimburse all family contributors their share of the funeral expenses, plus enough for a significant bonus to be shared by his family.

"Oh, you wee beauty Frank!" or "Hallelujah" as we say in such miraculous circumstances. What a happy resurrection and redemption for this apparently insignificant spirit in the model world of Kirriemuir. Seems eerieness can have a happy ending.

Also, Iain, still on the line of headstones just along from you, another coincidence, perhaps. The resting place of Andrew Irvine Simson, the original Coalman in the local purveyors of the fossil fuels which traditionally have provided the only comfort that Sheila will accept as enjoyable. Although the Simsons in today's fuel supply business are moving towards less toxic materials to keep Sheila's little Satan's Altar providing the level of comfort she finds most pleasing.

A few wee coincidences lurking in there, Iain. Now I have to get home to clean out Satan's Altar; it's like the 1940's when we all used to sing "Keep the home fires burning!" While our Dad's fought what we thought was the last Great War. I guess we all believed that Armageddon was just a fantasy and hadn't anticipated a wee virus having the potential to become a Dinosaur or Mother Earth suffering post traumatic stress disorder and erupting us all to another big bang.

Catch up tomorrow,

*Ed*

**Saturday 13ᵗʰ November 2021**

*Hi Iain,*

We covered a bit of ground in our review yesterday; except yesterday stretched from real time 13th October until real time 6th November, at the end of an awful lot of witching hours: there still seem to be a lot of relevant bits and pieces lying at the bottom of our own little ark of the covenant, jigsaw parts that complete a picture from earlier, or the little wisps of song and cryptic clues left in the writing of significant authors and thinkers from the time of the Gospel truth right up to the reality of today, when we are procrastinating about the choice between saving our accumulated wealth or saving the people and the planet!

There is a song blowin' in the wind of the current pop scene, "If you like the way you look so much, why don't you go and love yourself?" It doesn't matter which way I spin the interpretation of the words, I can make a comparison with our world situation today. A world that has become so corrupt with discrimination, inequality, child abuse, disrespect for women that the purgatory of this moment in time is awash with anger; and if that is what you, humanity, are happy with, then get on with it, but love yourself and self destruct without me. Or is it, perhaps. free yourself from the script. of generations of guilt from the beginning of this so-called Christian era, and love yourself for the real person you know, who is only acting out this angry role that you have been programmed or directed to play? Love yourself, and show the world how lovable you can be.

Do you recall, Iain, I commented a few letters back, how we can only see a quarter of the Earth, or of our Kirriemuir earth model, at any one time; that was simply an observation I made based on our experience. About the same time I was offering another, apparently unsupported, factoid that the name Kirriemuir derives from the phrase "Care o' Mary".

I decided to Google the name origin of Kirriemuir to identify any clues or confirmation; Wikipedia offered Kirriemuir as, in Barrie's depiction, The Wee Red Toon, followed in brackets by its translation in Gaelic as An ceathramh Mor; it wasn't clear if the Gaelic related to the word Kirriemuir, or to Barrie's depiction as The Wee Red Toon. In fact An ceathramh Mor is Gaelic for the 'Fourth Quarter'. Nothing and yet everything to do with Kirriemuir and The Wee Red Toon; this is the fourth quarter, the final quarter in our working model of Earth, that is fast approaching the Omega of the Greenwich Meridian, before we can start from the Alpha of a new beginning. If we can only free ourselves, humanity and Mother Earth, from the self-destructive script, the negative adverse current that has us on course to founder as we circumnavigate the Holy Land, where the problem, the Alpha, began two thousand years ago. The wikipidia offering suggested that, in ancient times, Kirriemuir had been an important site of cultural and religious significance; this would not be inconsistent with the possibility that here is the fortress of freedom that took 'care o' Mary' when she sought refuge with the ailing Jesus among the Companions of God; the confederation of Celtic peoples who united to preserve freedom from subjugation to Roman imperial domination.

Iain, I am aware that legions of theology students and experts will denounce such a suggestion as heresy, because it keeps Jesus and the spirit of freedom alive. without dependence on miracles and the magic of a God who performed miracles, but seemed to lose the magic touch just when He needed it most. This is the God who walked as a man, and asked people to follow Him on the Way, through the Truth to the better Life and two thousand years later, at the latter end of the prophesied Second Coming between 2008 and 2021 we are running out of time for this miraculous Second Coming. And all the theology experts from the Popes and Archbishops, and the Rabbis and Imams, to the lay experts, whose respective faiths depend on this twenty first century miracle have not uttered a word about its arrival, the progress of the resurrection or the imminence of the ending of this miraculous salvation of mankind, that is supposed to prepare us for a world of peace and prosperity that will last for the next millennium.

Had the Glasgow COP26 conference any significance in this second coming miracle? Perhaps, but it didn't seem inundated with interested Faith practitioners! In fact you would see more dog collars in Glasgow, congregated at the Celtic and Rangers ends of an Old Firm game, giving tacit support to maintaining old divisions, rather than preaching a Way of collaboration and unity to save the Planet, and preserve the freedom of all Jock Tamson's bairns to live in the world of peace and prosperity that was predicted at the Alpha of this Christian era.

Anyway Iain, I am going to tip out the ark, or the cauldron. to see what bits and pieces are lurking at the bottom; it is a year to the day when I was freed from my old life – trying to absorb a pub, that was once called 'The White Horse', of eternal life, into the twenty first century. My daughter Lindsey, in the middle of the Pandemic, took it it on, and is making a much better go of it, creating a hospitality venue that caters for the 'haves' through the Bellies Brae entrance, and taking care of the 'have less', as a Food Hub, through the Pier Head entrance to the rear.

As you know, our Kirriemuir model, of the world in this fourth quarter of the era, is a little higher in latitude than Glasgow – so we can see a little bit more of what may be before us; and, being one degree closer to the Omega of the Greenwich Meridian, we can, at least, visualise the final scenes in this Caesar's production of the Christian Era.

You know, Iain, I think back to some of the questions and the doubts and challenges that presented themselves to us during our eleven year cold case review of the so-called Christian Era – the 'Why us?'; obviously because we have been here a long time, beyond the three score and ten. that measures a reasonable batting average without incurring too many of the penalties of age that impair one's thirst for one more go at uncovering the truth. But, also because, between us we have experienced or observed every challenge that man has to endure – the cross that we all have to bear; except, in our case, we have carried it between us for the last eleven years which made the burden all the less or, at least, a little easier to bear: particularly when we could discuss our progress and not suffer, alone, in silence!

I could not understand why I left Frank – who was Christened Frank, the word for truth – at the start of Shielhill Road, and could not bring myself to complete this final circuit of the fifty sixth parallel of latitude which contains our model world of Kirriemuir. Only now, when the big decisions are being thrashed out in Glasgow, can I see that, sometimes, in contrast to the 'moving finger' philosophy we have to take two steps backwards before we start to move forward again. Iain, we have to see this so-called Christian Era in a more truthful light, and see the ugly truths of two thousand years of suffering and injustice, and clean them up before we store them away again in some latter day Ark of the Covenant. We cannot leave those imperfections festering, like some eternal box of disorder, which represents the traumatic stress of the Christian that breaks open every so often to allow the suppressed hurt to well up and torture Mother Earth, with the relived memory of events that she had to suffer in silence while she was obliged to get on with honouring her commitment to her earthly family.

Mother Earth did her best to prepare her descendant earth mothers, her daughters and their daughters by preparing a script for them to follow, a programme in their brain, which conditions them to follow the compliance of the female of any species to subscribe to the dominance of the alpha male or pack leader. There was no enlightenment or freedom to interpret the role beyond the constraints of a martyred mother, dedicated to her children because the father figure husband could not produce the miracle of preventing the death of the child she loved.

There was no enlightenment, or opportunity to believe, that in this fertile Garden of Eden, Mother Earth must have been the first occupant; Eve, the source of life that could produce eggs: the first pandemic to mutate and eventually produce twins, each with a division of the animal brain, one with a gentle urge to procreate and protect, and the other with an instinct to survive, by overcoming and suppressing any perceived competitor – and so the battle of the sexes was born. And, because the male virus had the more dominant genes, the male of the species presumed the leadership role – well.........maybe apart from your house and mine! And because of that first compliant female's instinctive script implanted, like a computer hard drive, into descendent females, those legions of feisty women have felt uncomfortable with this subordinate role they have been obliged to adopt.

So Iain, Man, like Romulus, was the first being, on earth, with the Imperialistic urge, and perhaps, with all the disturbance factors of individual freedoms. national freedom, ethnic freedom, gender freedom, creating turbulence in the world, it is time to review the role and negative impact of Empire. Certainly it is worth a look, before the Empire of IT dominates and conquers the hearts and souls of our youngsters, who think they are in charge because they can operate an 'I phone' without realising that a faceless somebody designs the programme, and writes the system or script, which they are obliged to follow.

Iain, somewhere along the line – the timeline – you and I have seen, and lived, a part of it all; you from your small comer, and I from mine; and we can each see our respective little lights and hope somebody else can catch a little enlightenment and freedom from the pervasive darkness.

And, Why Kirriemuir? Perhaps because it is the last place in these British Islands where witches were persecuted and dispatched! Can't resist a wee digress; when I was googling bits of information to confirm some of my assertions, in the Kirriemuir section there was an allusion to 'witches stones' which were inserted in house walls, apparently as protection. We, Sheila and I, have such a lump of granite lodged in our, otherwise sandstone, gable end. I think the contributor to Wikipedia has got it wrong, and the granite is a little witches' access point, where Macbeth's three ladies come in every night to remind me to write to you. Kirriemuir, of course, is just up the road from Glamis Castle where, in Shakespeare's construction, Macbeth, the Son of Life, was misrepresented and depicted as a threat to the seat of Imperial power, which had relocated to Westminster to be convenient to snuff out the last little light of freedom, held by the Companions of God, in the still independent confederation which had foiled ancient Rome's aspiration to rule the Universe.

Iain, been a wee bit of a tortuous witching hour tonight,
See you tomorrow,

*Ed*

**Sunday 28<sup>th</sup> November 2021**

*Hi Iain,*

You will see from the date that I have made another mini quantum leap of time – which is pressing! I can no longer indulge either of us in my trying to translate thoughts into analogies, or allegories to fairy stories; letters which I think will interest you and hold your attention with the purpose of prolonging your mortal life in your fight against cancer, long enough for you to hear the end of the story.

A bit of long windedness and digression worked pretty well with you by holding your attention for seven extra years while you only had one foot in the grave. And I have entertained myself these past nineteen months by visiting your little slit trench on Cemetery Hill and trying to convince you of the Truth of my deductions of where we are at in this moment in time.

Well Iain, at this precise moment of thought I am sitting on Anna's bench and reviewing and reevaluating this Truth. You already have both feet in the grave, because it seems that all my analogies, allegories and fairy stories have joined up the light from your small comer with the light from my small comer. But I feel that you, who captained our enterprise from the start, are still in charge, although you had enough confidence in my story telling to allow me to complete the watch and take this model world to the end of this particular leg of the voyage.

We have lots of models to review, to be sure that we can apply them to this real time situation on Mother Earth, close to the end of this so-called Christian Era. My ship model of Caledonia, the model world of Kirriemuir, the Russian Dolls model of Mother Earth consigning women to play a subordinate role in their exclusive earthly paradise that they were prepared to share with loving respectful partners; whatever happened to that early promise that man made in the marriage vows?

Like me, on Caledonia I could go on with the tactful observations that the course we are on is disastrous, when what I really want to say is "For fuck's sake Captain, alter course before we run aground!" You know Iain, in my little cryptic head, I often feel that my Captain Blair was living as Captain Blurr, until he eventually saw the light, that somebody who was trying to manage upwards, was shining for him.

He headed for the open sea, and then passed the command responsibility back to me to complete this 8 to 12 watch, the final quarter to where we would pick up the Pilot, who would navigate us safely into Aden. I never completed the story of that original ending of that night watch, as we rounded the bottom of the Arabian peninsula; because I was too miffed that the Captain had not specifically acknowledged my 'brilliant instincts and insight' in saving his ship. And yet, that was my job; to paraphrase the big RSM in 'Zulu' "It's why you're here, lad!". And Captain Blair did acknowledge my competence, when he returned his beloved Caledonia back to my temporary care, for the critical final quarter watch to meet the Pilot.

Iain, I am sitting on Anna's bench, having done my life-preserving walk, up past the Episcopal Church of St. Mary and round the 56th parallel of Shiel Hill and East Hill – and it was pretty hard work. It is a freezing cold morning, and I woke early and decided to get on with it; but the road surfaces were, certainly for pedestrians, pretty treacherous, and icy in parts: so avoiding Denis Wheatley's loose floorboard of a hidden icy patch was a tiresome, and tiring, chore. Strangely, the bench was dry despite the cold, and I sit here well wrapped up in my Barbour quilted jacket – Sheila's determination, to make a fashion icon out of a wee fat Glasgow man, is admirable but, perhaps a bit ambitious. I am wearing, also Barbour, the gloves that you never got to wear, after Helen gave them to you for your final Christmas; she passed them on to me and knows that I appreciate the comfort and, of course, this co-ordinated effort on my brand imagery.

A wee digress; we spent last evening with Helen, she is pretty good. In fact, I can reassure you that your contingency plan is working just fine. Helen is surviving bereavement well, and recalling the happy moments you shared, to replace the loss, and fill the empty space you left, when you moved ahead. Your family are playing their part to cover some of the responsibilities you would have seen to; your two grandsons are doing a fine job of keeping an eye on Grandma: Grant checks in daily, and Fraser was in last night to arrange to take Helen to a wee memorial service for you, and the other 'dear departed' who didn't get the 'full military honours' funeral from your Church, during the pandemic lockdown.

Back to me, and my final piece of Sheila's ambitious image improving comfort accessories; my extremely well-made Tommy Hilfiger Beany hat, with the tiny little 'H flag' Hilfiger logo on the front: well, one has to be careful, to make sure that it is to the front, and central, to look orderly and fashionably iconic! You know, Iain, funny how this fits in with my Caledonia story; because the H flag is the international code signal for 'I have a Pilot on board!'

At this stage I have to mix our metaphors or analogies or fairy stories a bit, because they are all coming together at the same moment in time, like the parallels of latitude, from the Equator to the Poles in both directions, north or south, all coinciding in time at the Greenwich Meridian. The Omega for this Christian Era, at the end of the quarter watch which contains the model world of Kirriemuir, in the now of real time, and my historical experience on Caledonia in 1960, as we approach Aden which is a subject of concern in today's real time, lying at the bottom of the Arabian peninsula; the bottom of the so called Holy Land, which gave me the creeps every time I sailed through it or around it.

And, in the real world of today, the big whole real Planet Earth, all the Captain Blurrs are deciding whether they should alter course to save the Planet, or take advantage of this troubled situation, to do a land grab, or pirate grab, of the good ship Earth in their limited Era of Now. As also is the crew of the Pirate virus Captain Hook, who will create a new Dinosaur Era on this Neverland as humanity allows itself to be overheated to extinction.

But, hey Iain, we are in the model world of Kirriemuir which is a few hours ahead of the time that both Planet Earth and the Christian Era reach the Equatorial Omega at the Greenwich Meridian. So, as I sit here, on Anna's bench communicating with my, now, spiritual best friend – you know, Iain, if I stretch out my legs on the ground, I am convinced my two feet make contact with your two feet in your wee trench – and we create a temporary fuse connection which might carry enough power to get some message across.

I started really early this morning, picking my way up the frozen Roods well before 7am – and there was already a council worker, in his little dinky, salt spreading snow plough, treating the walkways; I was well impressed with Angus Council's service on this cold November Sunday.

And now, I can hear the town clock striking out 7.45 am, the last quarter of the 4–8 watch, just twelve hours ahead of when Caledonia rounded Perim Island, and my 8–12 started, telescoping the entire so-called Christian Era into one dramatic scene from, Raiders of the Lost Ark. I check my Beany to ensure I am conforming to fashion iconism, thankfully before I bump into Gordon Elliott and Sheila's pal Aileen, on the summit of Kirrie Hill. My little H flag is central on my forehead.

I am glad I have the Pilot on board!

Talk tomorrow

*Ed*

**Monday 29th November 2021**

*Hi Iain,*

I think my deliberations yesterday, or my walk in the cold, must have been too much for me. I had been resolved to batter on with this last burst through my experience of the Second Coming, which is close to the end, but fatigue or procrastination overtook me; I kept falling asleep: I hope Benedict doesn't see me and make a judgement.

I'd had to return to Kirrie Health Practice to have my blood sugar levels checked – so Sheila is convinced that I am now experiencing a diabetic tiredness; she may be right, but it may also be possible that I simply succumbed to the heat from Satan's Altar: you know how Sheila likes to keep the home fires burning and emitting enough KWh to heat half the homes on Glengate.

In this real time, close to the end of the Second Coming period and coping with the real time presence of our ominous replacement Dinosaur, lurking in the wings as a Pandemic, there really isn't time to explain the detail or justify proof of why I see events of today, spread out over thirteen years being the expanded version of the recorded accounts of the events contained in one turbulent week in 34 AD. Or, the experience of a whole era, such as this so-called Christian Era, being shrunk back from a Universal magnitude of a bereaved spiritual God and bereaved Mother Earth on a great circle, of Equatorial scale being reduced through parallels in time and dimension to a bereaved Mother Church, made mortal in the depiction of Virgin Mary agonising below the cross of bereavement, to a real life mother and father, bereaved by the loss of their son, in terms that ordinary everyday people can understand and relate to. And all those events on different parallels of scale and different eras of time, from mythological to Old Testament history through Roman history and New Testament to this latter end of the Second Coming, transitioned from spiritual to mortal experience when God, or whatever Universal power, tried to restore the positive polarity of reasoning and re-creation to reconnect with the natural, or neutral, polarity of survival and procreation and restore the ring mains circuit of power that kept humanity functioning. This power circuit that was broken each time a negatively charged twin, such as Cain or Romulus killed the positive polarity of their respective twin, Abel and Remus and humanity was thrown into bi-polar disorder, complicated by the post traumatic stress disorder of a humanity, carrying the cross of bereavement, without the spiritual leadership, or medical science, recognising the universal scale of the problem. This is where we find ourselves in this NOW passage of the voyage of the Christian Era, which is reaching a crisis point of an erupting overheating environment, while our leaders are haggling over old scores or affordability. Meanwhile a great dinosaur pirate pandemic is waiting impatiently, to replace humanity as the new occupants of this Garden of Eden, which was ours for eternity until we became corrupted by power and the capital gains of empire. We have to unburden ourselves of the great cross of Roman Imperialism.

So Iain, I have to assume that you are totally on my wavelength, and we are communicating without too much need for explanation or interpretation. I recall that I once had a boss who was a wee bit slow to understand situations that some of us salesmen were explaining to him. The explanations would become more detailed and basic as we attempted to achieve some reception of understanding, when suddenly we, the enlightened, would be admonished as pedants with the irritated words "Aye, OK. Mister, I'm away ahead of you!" Thick as mince, but he was great at playing Eric Berne's Parent to Adult to Child communication Mind games. So, everybody in Britain, where this production of the play is cast, is aware of the key events of 2008.

There was no triumphal entry into Jerusalem, or Rome, or Westminster, organised by the inspired spiritual leadership of the various clergy after two thousand years of anticipation; but, really, there couldn't be, because the body of Christ was still pinned to the Cross of the Logo of the resurrected Roman Empire. And the spirit of Christ was hidden away, apparently without trace, despite the detailed records of events which were archived in the catacombs of the Vatican which, despite its wealth, had not the inspiration to effect a management buy out from the Roman Capitalists who hold the title deeds. And those capitalists of Rome, powerful, like Damian Roth, but too thick to work out the opposite of the obvious, as to where the spirit of Christ was hidden and still exerting influence, scoured the Empire, including Caledonia despite their fear of the power of the Companions of God, in the hope of capturing the elusive spirit of Christ to take possession of both the mortal and the spiritual, and have control of the hearts and minds of mankind. But the Spirit of 'something' started working through the steps and the events of an exaggerated or expanded holy week, that was prophesied to last from 2008 until 2021. Each day of the original Holy Week taking two years to effect in this real time Second Coming.

The tables of the Moneylenders were turned over and their greed and profligacy exposed to a world which had mortgaged its life savings to a Captain James Hook, the Eton educated pirate, who wielded the power of capitalism. And the scribes and the Pharisees in the Mother of Parliaments were exposed for taking advantage of people who believed their promises to help, and influence Captain Hook to provide just Government, only to find that they had placed their trust in Hook's pirates who rewarded themselves by stealing out of the expenses kitty, or manipulated policy to award themselves or their fellow Pirates great contracts which could, almost legally, direct great wealth to their secret shell companies with only moral indignation for them to suffer.

Meanwhile, to keep the hoi polloi too busy to afford even moral indignation, Government introduced the bitter pill of austerity to ensure that those who could not afford accountants, or off shore accounts to hide their wealth, paid their full share of tax to ensure Government could function and afford this generous expenses system of reward. You know it's funny Iain, how the middle ages swashbuckling stories were of Pirates, burying their chests of stolen wealth in Caribbean Islands. Wonder how anyone could imagine such an unrealistic fairy story; but I won't digress!

On a broad human scale, rebellion against oppression was erupting across the world; old ethnic scores are still being settled: but worse still are the internal conflicts of brother against brother, like the Cain and Abel or Romulus and Remus allegories. The evil of the Syrian conflict, and the single ethnicity of the Arabian Peninsula where the rich Arabs in the north are knocking seven bells out of the less rich Arabs in Yemen. Or the Taliban suppressing and abusing the rights of Muslim women; it makes some of the complaints about racial abuse seem, almost, the least of anyone's worries.

You know, Iain, when I took my little nostalgic visit along Portobello Promenade to the Temple in Joppa, I had a wee imaginary peek into Hebron Hall, the symbolic Cave of the Patriarch; the birthplace of the Holy Land: my goodness, what a complicated fankle of emotions and distrust and abuse is trapped on the cobwebs, spinning the truth in there! And they were the guys who wrote the history – the Old Testament – on which we founded many of our beliefs. Thank goodness Diarmuid's Quest inspired us to take a look at the past!

There certainly is a spirit of something sweeping round the world in this thirteen years predicted as the second coming; the 'Temple' of the Universal Church controlled by Rome, has had a strong blast of cleansing air blowing through it to lift the veil of Piety, and uncover the corruption that is concealed below the wealth that has been accumulated.

I can't understand, in an age when three disparate religions claim to have faith in the one same God, that nobody else has cracked a light about any of the stuff, that our little lights from different comers, have uncovered or picked up; why has nobody, from the leaders of religion, steeped in spiritual belief, mentioned the second coming? – during the second coming. While they claim exclusive communication with God, yet you and I can hear God-like messages just Blowing in the Wind, or lying about in the scriptures or Wikipedia for anyone to read ... some of it cryptic, but a lot in plain language.

Anyway, Iain, we are in the Christian Era, and by Isaac Newton's time scale, we have until 2060 before the overheating totally changes the earth that constitutes our world, so we have plenty of leeway to conduct the next five year plan you proposed a year or so ago; don't see why we can't do it from our current positions: seems to me we work pretty well exchanging views on Cemetery Hill – just so long as you don't play one of your wee games and try to change positions: I'll do just fine reporting to you from the comfort of Anna's bench. We can maybe have another look at Hebron, and a wee rummage into the obscured truth about Caledonia, the Nation, or check out the Garden of Eden. I am sure Damian Roth is lurking in there; but he isn't a decision maker-just somebody's thug. Oh! A wee digress, about Damian. He was bought in as Sales Director to my old Company, by the Managing Director (Another' bought in' of whom I was never entirely sure!). Damian Roth was introduced to the Sales Force at individual area meetings where he intended to chat, somewhat informally, to individual team members. When he left the Glasgow team meeting, Florence Gray could not contain her unease "Oh my God, did you see those dead eyes? If he came into my shop I would tell him to fuck off!" Out of the mouths of Babes and innocents!

I think the Christian Era inherited Damian from further back in history; perhaps Herod, of the Old Testament, or some of the 'heavies' from

Roman and Greek mythology. I always wondered why the baby of previous mythologies was thrown out with the bathwater of the Christian Era; were there truths in those mythologies, that the controlling Romans wanted to hide, which might have alerted thinking people of the first century AD to their true purpose in tolerating certain aspects of this new religion, while still seeking out and executing some believers in the Way of Jesus. There do seem to be events within those previous mythological eras which reflect the same parallel effects of repetition through the various eras of mankind from Adam and Eve, right through to to this NOW period close to the end of the current Christian Era.

Our current quest, our Diarmuid's Quest, is within this Christian Era from Easter 34A.D. through to to the end of this second coming, which ends at midnight on 31st December 2021.

We still have to complete our little allegory of Caledonia's passage from the Gulf of Suez, round the Holy Land to Aden; and just like any ship's passage we need an ETA, estimated time of arrival to ensure that the Pilot is waiting for us to navigate the ship into Aden harbour. In 1960, this ETA coincided with the end of my watch, at midnight. In real time, today's real time, tomorrow is 30th November, Saint Andrew's Day; the patron saint of Scotland, and the first picked Apostle; the first called Companion of God, who was, perhaps, despatched to the end of the Roman World to preach the Way of Jesus, the Via, before the Roman church was established to distribute the Roman Light variant product, that Rome marketed as Christianity.

We should pick up our Pilot, just after midnight, for him to navigate Caledonia to a safe anchorage, on the southern tip of the Holy Lands, at the start of St Andrew's Day.

Tell you about our other second coming coincidences tomorrow,

*Ed*

**Tuesday 30th November 2021**

*Hi Iain,*

Pre-witching hour, night-shift letter once again!
Feeling pretty good that we had got to this stage of Diarmuid's
Quest, and had an early night; but I suppose I may be reliving some of the
heightened tension of sixty years ago, that would accompany the changed
responsibilities and routines of picking up the Pilot: with the entire officer
complement of Caledonia at 'stations' for docking and mooring procedures
of arriving in port, and undertaking the different responsibilities for loading
and discharging cargo. No rest for a ship's company.

Back to 2008/2009 to our second coming experiences, two events
occurred which, even as they were happening, appeared to have a
tenuous connection, of a spiritual nature, with this second coming
that only Frank and I seemed to feel any awareness of; and, even our
interpretation of events seemed so isolated, from any evidence of a public
spiritual acknowledgement, so out of step, that we did not announce
our observations, in the absence of any inspiration or guidance from the
dispensers and defenders of the Faith.

The first of these events was when a very sprightly, well presented man,
in his mid-sixties appeared and became our most regular customer, in
the pub. He more or less told us his life story, by way of introduction, and
adopted a presumption of acceptance and intimacy – almost as if Frank,
Ian and Melanie, our barmaid, were close friends; and, of course, me. His
name was Peter, Italian born, but living in London, where he had been a
very successful hairdresser. However, he had met a Kirriemuir girl, many
years his junior and they had married; although she had become home-sick
for Kirriemuir, and he had given her the money to buy a house; she had
moved back to be closer to her family. It all seemed a bit like Grimm's Fairy
Tales to Frank and I, who were the two he most confided in. Especially after
two or three weeks, when he confessed that his wife would have nothing to
do with him, and reconciliation was no longer an option, and her family
had totally closed ranks to resist any contact with him. All seemed a bit
surreal to us, and while we were polite with him we did not reciprocate
the affection he was directing towards us; he kept telling us how much he

respected us, even to the point of saying to me "I really love you, man!": and inviting us to his retirement villa down on the heel of Italy on the Adriatic coast.

I went off on a week's holiday, about this time, and when I returned Peter had gone. But he had left two hundred pounds – four big red Bank of England £50 notes, for us to buy drinks for the pub. It was all a bit eerie, even the wife and the house she appeared to have conned him out of, remained a mystery of identity or address. But we were involved in the eerieness – particularly when we were looking for any sign that could have a spiritual connotation or connection to the second coming. Was this perhaps some symbolic, physical manifestation of a spiritual St Peter, who could now retire from the Roman Church he had been supporting for the past two thousand years? And to prove he was a redeemed spirit, he was making a symbolic return of three blood-stained nails and a blood red crown of thorns; now that the mortal remains had been freed to reunite with the spirit in this period of second coming.

The four of us, whom he had embraced as intimate friends, discussed the episode, and its eerieness, although I did not expose my little flight of Biblical fancy to the others. We all agreed it was strange, and he must have been a lonely crackpot. Nobody else in the pub really knew him, as he had spent any pub time with us, so we split the two hundred quid four ways and convinced ourselves that this was pretty well in accordance with his wishes.

Around this time I was also experiencing my little tremors of bi-polar turbulence, although I had never heard the terms bi-polar or bi-polar disorder before; even though I had experienced two previous episodes of the 'symptoms' I was now aware of; but, on my previous occasions I had pretty much controlled my feet back on to the ground with little professional help. I felt I could do the same again, although the hyperactivity was accompanied by sleep loss which I reckoned needed attention.

I consulted my GP, expecting a simple prescription for some calming, sedative medication, but it seemed as though mental activity had been catapulted from its non-event, low priority status in 1963 through interesting and worthy of some attention, in 1984 to, almost, urgent and emergency level in 2008. Sixty years ago I could not find any professional, who could appreciate the need for bereavement counselling for my distressed wife, who was displaying all the signs of post traumatic stress disorder, while in 2008 I admit to a bit of excited activity and receive emergency treatment despite insisting I could handle it. Now, in 2021, mental health issues, amongst the young, is at pandemic levels, possibly because of their lack of faith in any future, as the combination of a disintegrating Earth, and an all conquering virus called Covid 19 attacking mankind's growth capabilities. And today's youth already surrounded by a heap of shit before they are allowed to develop to dinosaur decision size; while the Roman precedent – Nero fiddling while Rome burns – world leaders are still fiddling about doing little things instead of doing the great thing of talking to each other to find an answer to this two pronged Armageddon that has transfixed the minds of our young people.

China is hiding behind its Great Wall, treating its own people like latter day populus vulgae, obedient to a communist faith that doesn't allow these ordinary people to see over the wall to realise that they are confined in an introverted capitalist empire. While Vladimir Putin is attempting a second coming of the Communist Empire by re-annexing old possessions and assisting new friends like Syria to commit suicide so that Russia can inherit the territory to expand their military presence on the banks of the Mediterranean Sea.

Anyway, Iain, while I thought I was marching in time with the band, because I had read Dr Eric Berne's book, the people who had actually studied his philosophy, and had certificates to prove it, told me I was well out of step ( how can you be well out of step? You are either in step or out of step!) I kept an account of my experience and attach this to let you read how I felt at that real time in the Cuckoo world.

Pick you up again after my Whitehills experience.

*Ed*

# Crossover

## January 2009 – Whitehills

E d sat In the waiting area of the hospital.

Whitehllls was a modem, purpose built version of the old "cottage" hospital – not large, but designed to suit the needs of the local community.

The reception area was laid out like the hub of a half circle – an open fan – with corridors, like spokes, running off to the various facilities and treatment rooms. He likened it to a small airport departure lounge, the waiting bench seats arranged facing an overhead departure board – one line only – which would light up and announce the next patient appointment; this accompanied by a voice-over confirming the message "'patient 120 please go to Room Number 10".

He had shown his appointment letter at the desk, been handed a strip of paper which showed he was patient 124, and directed to take a seat until he was called. The receptionist added the information that his appointment would be in Room 15, and indicated the general direction of his interview room.

The car park, as always, had been jam packed and finding a vacant space difficult – suggesting a busy enterprise; but there was none of the bustle of a big general hospital. In fact, the reception area was quite serene with only about eight or ten people waiting, plus a couple in the little cafeteria which was in a spoke off to the left. He wondered where all the people from all the parked cars worked or hid themselves down the spokes of the fan; the answer wasn't really important. Someday a Steve Wright factoid would probably emerge that "on the opening day of Whitehills Hospital 150 cars were parked and only 30 have moved on that day, or on any day since".

He looked around the waiting room but didn't recognise any of the faces. He had already had a quick glance at the magazines; they were all glossy Show-biz scandal rags telling how somebody "famous" had somebody's –

an even more famous somebody – love child, or beat the habit or punched a paparazzi.

How was it, he wondered, that if you are "famous" you have a love-child or, receive sympathy for your understandable addiction to drugs or alcohol due to the strain of being a well-paid celebrity, or were so hassled by the paparazzi, when they tripped over your outsize ego or inflated PR image, that you were obliged to punch out against this intrusion into the privacy that you had already sold to their colleagues for a cool million or two? How was it, he wondered, if you were on basic pay and from a deprived area, your love child would be deemed an unwanted pregnancy, your addiction would be perceived as irresponsible and self-indulgent and, if you punched somebody for annoying you the courts, and public opinion would not be understanding and sympathetic!?

The only real human interest story was about Jade Goody, the Big Brother Celebrity; her terminal cancer, her determination to optimise her Celebrity income to secure her sons' future before her end, and the positive impact her health predicament was exerting on the young women of the nation.

He didn't want to read the detail. He felt sorry for a young woman of 28 suffering terminal cancer – with an almost specific termination date – and he admired her guts for using her time and her celebrity, to capitalise on her own death for the future of her kids and the health of young women everywhere......but, he was wondering again! "How the fuck do you become a celebrity?"

He had worked diligently and fairly competently for 40 years longer than Jane Goody, and he hadn't accumulated as much as she was forecast to earn in her remaining three months, let alone the eight million she was reputed to have derived from her five years of dubious Celebrity.

All the featured stories of the stars seemed to have some tragic-comedic aspect, from the laughably self-indulgent to the developing tragedy of poor Jade's inevitable death. They all seemed to have shitty, complicated lives, with no improvement to be derived from all their riches. Maybe he was better off being diligent, competent and skint.

He would still have liked a crack. at some of the dosh, but he decided to pass on the magazines – Celebrity news was far too depressing for him!

He felt pretty good. Really good! In fact apparently he felt so good that he must be sick! That was the reason he was here.

He still had his appointment letter in his hand. The announcements on the "departure board" did not come up in sequence of patient number or appointment; patient 125 had already been called, but his own appointment time had passed. He checked his patient number and looked again at his letter to verify his appointment time 'yep, 15.15 hours, sure enough' ... for the first time he noticed the bold print at the foot of the letter –

PSYCHIATRY OF OLD AGE.
He hadn't noticed that before, maybe he had just read what he needed to read......date and time.

The declaration of the clinic's identity irritated him a little. He wasn't offended by it; he just thought that it wasn't entirely accurate or appropriate in his case.

He couldn't deny, at his age, that he was anything but "old". And he couldn't argue that it was some of his recent behaviour that had obliged him to attend this clinic. But his behaviour had nothing to do with his age, other than that after a life time of "wondering" about the influences that affected peoples' lives, he had discovered another little piece of the Jigsaw puzzle and, this discovery had triggered a Eureka reaction in him resulting in a couple of days of unusual behaviour.

He wondered if Archimedes, running about naked from his bath shouting "I've found it!" had been considered unusual or irrational. History tends to show that this was-the moment that Archimedes was confirmed a genius!

Ed had no such illusions of himself. He knew he wasn't a genius! He knew he wasn't lots of things that some others thought he might see himself as. He knew he wasn't a Celebrity – he couldn't be, he was still working in old age to provide enough income to keep himself until his clogs popped.

The "departure board" announcement had called some time ago for patient 118 to go to Room 15 – which was the room Ed was supposed to report to. He had not heard his own number called but heard the rapid click, click, click of stiletto heels and looked up to see Dr. Risemouth approaching the waiting area – her eyes scanning over the faces, back and forth, obviously looking for someone.

Ed presumed that he had missed his announcement and started to rise, raising his hand to draw her attention. She suddenly caught sight of him but motioned him to "stay", shaking her head to indicate that she was not ready for him. Instead she walked over to an elderly man and invited him to accompany her. She slowed her pace to match his and her manner was very considerate and accommodating.

Ed watched them move from the reception hub into the spoke that housed Room 15. He thought the old guy looked a bit dottery and he could not resist a silent chuckle as he guessed that the dottery old guy- was probably three or four years his junior – but by the look of him, coupled with Dr. Risemouth's tender manner "Psychiatry of Old Age" was probably entirely appropriate.

Ed found it much more interesting to evaluate the way Dr. Risemouth moved; not the "covert ogle" you understand, it was simply his investigative nature, his wondering again.

She was quite slim and tall – elegant, and a nice dresser. But for all her height she took short, precise steps – almost as if she were placing each foot on a carefully chosen spot: as if......as if her walk had been choreographed. He wondered if she had taken ballet lessons in her youth, or here – in the North of Scotland – possibly trained as a highland dancer.

He never got to ask her, or to have any sort of open conversation with her. He would have liked to have known her on a more equal level, social or semi-academic, and explored some of his theories and opinions with her without the threat of a psychiatric diagnosis hanging over him. He felt that if he disclosed some of his thoughts, in their present doctor and patient persona he would be sectioned, and in the funny farm before the sword of Damocles had a chance to part from its psychiatric thread and land on his trusting, bursting little head.

Consequently he wasn't particularly trusting. In fact he was a little inhibited, which put a bit of strain on him: he found playing the "devious diplomat" and having to choose his words to avoid misinterpretation or misunderstanding did not come easily, or sit comfortably with him. He knew that, in today's wider world, honesty seemed not always to be the best policy, but he would have preferred that it were.

Ed liked the Truth.

He presumed that it might be a further ten or fifteen minutes before he was called and he drifted off into more thoughts and evaluation of his "'condition". The "psychiatry of old age" niggled him because the thinking and wondering that he did had been with him all of his life. He was prepared to accept that, against Mr. Average he might be very slightly strange – a little eccentric, maybe? He could be very focussed, determined and stoical. He wondered if he might be very, very slightly autistic – he didn't mind his own company, although he didn't necessarily prefer to be alone or like to be alone all the time.

He wasn't a particularly high flyer – hadn't achieved academic brilliance (academic mediocrity, more like), not hit commercial heights. But he liked to do things properly, at least to the best of his ability. He had taken a couple of chances in his lifetime – calculated risks – but tried not to be reckless (bad luck seemed to find him without any assistance!). He wasn't highly entertaining – a better listener than a performer, possibly gave the appearance of edging slightly towards being a wee bit uninteresting; not edging quite as far as boring, at least, not all the time. 'By sticking to the rules he had managed to avoid Kipling's two impostors, triumph and disaster, and keep the ship on course. He had done that very thing as a young navigating officer – Third Mate – in the Merchant Navy almost fifty years earlier.

The departure sign was illuminated again, and the voice was calling for 'Patient 124 to Room 15 please'.

Ed walked along the corridor past Room 12 – which was next to Room 14! He stopped to check that the room numbers were ascending in sequence 10, 11, 12 etc., and that odd numbers were not assigned to the left of the passage. Sure enough, single sequence – with No 13 missed out.

It seemed somebody believed in unlucky thirteen, and he knew it wasn't him!

When he had been at school. in the 1940s, a teacher had explained to the class about the Scottish tendency to be negative about circumstances – he couldn't remember if she explained why Scots were 'traditionally' negative. He did remember that she had demonstrated the attitude of considering a glass to be 'half full', or 'half empty'. Scots, of course, being negative always had the glass that was 'half empty'.

At some point in his later life, when he felt that the 'half empty' characteristic was influencing his thinking, he had determined to think in more positive terms – see the sunshine behind the clouds, or respond with positive thoughts to greetings. People when they asked 'How are you?' did not really want to hear about the possible disaster around the comer, or about the problems you had brought from home and wanted to dump on them.

Also, in his own particular case, he was well aware that, when he wasn't actually smiling, his face lapsed into a scowl or frown. He could be feeling quite happy – but thinking or concentrating seemed to bring on a serious face, that looked unhappy, even angry.

He decided to think 'half full' and try to look less grumpy, when a friend or acquaintance inquired, he would tell them he felt "good" – without qualification.

He found that this worked – on himself, by keeping him in a positive frame of mind and on the inquirer, by giving them a lift or cheering them up.

Communication can be a real pain in the butt. The word he actually chose to communicate his positive feeling was "-Wonderful" and he would try to endorse this with an accompanying cheery smile.

"Always look on the bright side of life," said the Monty Python team.

He went into Room 15 where Dr Risemouth was waiting for him. "Well", she asked "And how are you feeling today?"

"Wonderful" he said and gave her a big happy smile. He knew immediately it was a mistake. "Not too wonderful, I hope," said Dr Risemouth. Her voice had that firm, but gentle quality of reprimand, which infant school mistresses use to encourage excitable five year old boys to calm down. It wasn't a communication of equals: definitely Parent to Child mode!

"Oh fuck", he thought, "'Did I walk into Room 13 after all?"

He endeavoured to hold the cheery smile while he considered his response to the challenge.

"Well, I took my blood pressure this morning, and it was fine! The Health Centre have confirmed that I don't have diabetes, or any of the other conditions you had them test me for so I feel quite healthy. If I have Alzheimer's I wouldn't know it anyway, so I feel......I feel quite good"

Dr. Risemouth continued to hold him in a steady gaze. She maintained the gentle authority in her voice, but relaxed the emotional positioning between them slightly. He was promoted from excitable child to mature student (well, student at least) while she descended slightly, and laterally, from disciplining Parent to patient lecturer, explaining the essential component of the equation that he had so obviously missed.

"No, I don't think you have Alzheimer's," she conceded in the same measured tones,"but lots of people with bi-polar disorder report feelings of ecstasy or euphoria – even having a feeling of omnipotence."

He quickly thought how this scene should, be played – she was the Doctor, he was the patient, so it wasn't a level playing field. He hadn't felt ecstatic or euphoric – but he had experienced a little glimpse of enlightenment. He had achieved this by applying skills he had learned as a Marketing Manager and in his previous life, as a navigator; he had considered the opposite of the obvious and confirmed his position from the available data, and seen some answers to a very old problem.

He had responded to this with a bout of uncharacteristic excitement, but, other factors had come into play which he couldn't explain – so he must have been manic!

He had not met God, seen God, nor had God spoken to him. He had not felt omnipotent!

"OK," he said, "I feel fine, I don't feel too wonderful."

He had been watching old episodes of Friend's and decided to use their stock answer "1 feel good!", in fact he decided to settle on good from now on, when he wanted to demonstrate that his glass was 'half-full'.

"Good," she said approvingly. Her adult to his adult!

He really would have liked to discuss his thoughts with someone – but maybe a Doctor who specialised in the Psychiatry of Old Age was not the most appropriate person to share them with. At 72 he certainly qualified for the 'old age'. But, every time he tried to explain his thoughts to people he trusted, or should have been able to trust, their reaction added the qualification for Psychiatry – so that wasn't a level playing field either.

Maybe his problem was communication again – maybe he had always said "Wonderful" when he should have said "Good" or, '"Terrible" when he should have said "Bad" or even "Half empty' when he should have said "Half full".

Dr. Risemouth had only said "Good" – but he wasn't sure it was a totally convinced "Good". Maybe psychiatrists sat on the fence a wee bit because they were dealing with hallucinatory, or tricky people.

Ed wasn't a tricky person – but in the last six months he had become a little guarded with the truth. Not dishonest – but he certainly was not about to disclose the "'whole truth" and push his diagnosis back into the hallucinatory bracket – like......"You know how St Paul had that wee eureka moment on the road to Damascus? Well I had a wee experience a bit like that!"

"Oh yes, keep talking while I press this little bell to summon the men in the white coats."

He hadn't really had a St. Paul moment, but he had become a little over-excited. He had seen nothing, heard nothing, nor imagined anything that wasn't available to anyone else to see, in the real world. His mind had raced a little, as if he had been driving a car too fast and got into a skid, lost traction, slightly, but managed to control the skid and reduce to a safer speed. He had been working very hard on various projects and had pushed himself a little too far. He accepted this and consulted a doctor to calm him down a bit. But he had done this voluntarily – it was his decision.

The truth that had been opening up to him was mind blowing. Yep! – He knew that! But it hadn't actually blown his mind. He had recognised the problem – but just like 50 years before on the bridge of RMS Caledonia the problem had to be there before he could identify it. He knew where his "ship" was and he could correct the course – but, because other people were involved or affected by his actions he had to advise them what he was doing. That was where the problem started; the people he was trying to convince, family mainly, were just as sceptical, as Captain Blair had been fifty years earlier, about the position he found his life, his ship, to be in.

Of course, on this occasion it wasn't a captain, a ship and an "obvious" matter of life or death – as in 1960. He had even less sophisticated navigational aids: this time they were all in his head, or on his computer and nobody else had observed the exciting 'revelations' that he was being exposed to. To the concerned observer, his heightened sense of awareness was accompanied by a heightened activity level stretching in to slightly erratic behaviour.

He knew he had to slow down and check his position so that he could convince the professionals, who seemed to know more about his mind than he did and, also, the sceptics who, in this case, also seemed to know more about his mind than he did.

He knew exactly how Jack Nicholson felt in 'One Flew Over The Cuckoo's Nest'

Dr. Risemouth continued slowly. He noticed she spoke very slowly, very measured – not at all what he might have expected from someone who walked with short, sharp, choreographed dancer's steps. He presumed the slow delivery was the professional modus, to accommodate the reception speed of the old aged, who needed the psychiatry appropriate to their years, and the pauses or intervals in delivery were to provide time to gauge reaction, from these less active or confused minds.

"You were quite ill you know!"

Ed did not contest. or attempt to qualify this· assessment. He had been through all this six months earlier and hadn't managed to convince the professionals or the sceptics, during an entire week of intense discussion and reassuring, that had only served to stoke up an already active (over active!) brain to extreme frustration levels.

He wasn't about to argue; she was the professional, Room 15 was her particular cuckoo's nest, and he wanted to be able to fly out of it at the end of his allotted thirty minutes.

But he couldn't leave the statement suspended between her patient, waiting stare. and his own blank, non-committal expression.

"Well some of the symptoms you identify as contributing to this condition have been with me all my life – nobody thought it strange in the days when we might be afforded only a three hour stretch of sleep, because of watch-keeping duties."

"Yes, so it is not necessarily unusual for you to sometimes have less sleep! But, you were hallucinating!" The buffers…Slam! The gates shut. He did not think he had been hallucinating – he had tried to be a little bit creative, like J.M. Barrie dreaming up a Peter Pan, and it had back-fired a little.

Part of the story, his experience, would have endorsed her opinion. But, he felt, the whole story, to guarantee her acceptance of his sanity and self-control, would have necessitated a story of book proportions. His thirty minutes in Psychiatry of Old Age didn't present a potential nutcase with the opportunity to narrate a story of book proportions.

"Well, I know that I did a couple of strange things while I was hyper- if that's hallucinating, I have to accept that. But that was months ago, and no recurrences."

"And the tablets?"

"I haven't taken the last lot – they were making me sleep: I could have slept for Scotland! I feel fine. I have to run my business, so, I decided to take Bill Clinton's advice – 'if it's not broke don't mend it!'"

Bill Clinton obviously doesn't hold a degree in psychiatry – the allusion to "taking Bill's advice" had caused an almost imperceptible movement in the fairly static gaze. He felt a little admonishment coming, and the gaze became tighter, slightly less tolerant. back in parent mode, as it communicated,

"Careful......I am making an assessment of you, and you would be well served to treat it seriously-. After a short silence – as he withdrew to the other side of the emotional 'no man's land' – she obviously decided to stop the assessment and move on.

"Anyway you feel fine, you are sleeping well?" Ed nodded, "'So that's good." She gently bounced the. palms of her hands off the arms of her chair – "'Well," the interview was ending, "Can you come back and see me one more time – in February?"

"Yes," Ed replied – but he let it hang like a question ("'one more time?'")

"I am retiring in March •••••••• I'm just taking my first option. I can retire at fifty-five and the NHS pension is very good!"

Ed raised his eyebrows slightly at the fifty-five: he genuinely thought that she was younger – a bit, anyway – but didn't want to sound corny by making flattering comments about her age. She seemed to recognise the silent compliment, for she smiled and explained' a little about the job and the stress of having done it for thirty years. He smiled silently to himself, wondering if there was an unspoken, subconscious acknowledgement in her comment.

Ed felt that he had been doing the "job" that had brought him to sit in front of her, for fifty years at least, and, possibly, his whole life. He had performed many roles in that time and the only consistent thing about it was the fucking stress, and wondering what life and faith were all about. Now that it was getting interesting, and he was beginning to enjoy it, some fucker was trying to prove he was nuts.

Of course he chose not to tell her all this, smiled cheerily and said "Right, see you February" and left. He was quite relaxed. He was confident that after a kick-start, a practice run, and a dramatic lift off, he had the power to get the job done.

The car park was just as busy but he had located his car easily. He liked cars, and he was pleased with his – a new Volkswagen Passat, which he had bought last July. One of the problems of bi-polar people apparently, is that they can land themselves or their families in debt. Ed certainty had debts, but he had incurred them anything up to seven years before this "diagnosis". He didn't think his lovely car or its finance was a symptom of his illness – and, anyway, he didn't give a shit! Ed loved his new car.

He also loved the significance and the symbolism of it! Sheila, his new wife – Oh God! His wife!! They had been happily married now for twenty-two years – had bought him a personalised number plate for his sixtieth birthday. She had put a lot of thought and effort into getting the right one. His birthday was on the sixteenth – so she had chosen the plate to reflect this, B for birthday, 16, and his initials. He had loved it, and rushed off to fit it to his Jaguar (he had been moderately affluent in those days) He was slightly taken aback when he realised how the number plate read from a distance BIG ED – a wee bit pretentious for a "little Glasgow man!" Then he loved it all the more, and started to think of himself as BIG ED(W) the Wee Glasgow Man!

As he drove back. the seven miles to Kirriemuir he started to reflect – well he resumed reflecting: It seemed he spent all his time reflecting at the moment – on the events that had brought him to Whitehllls "Psychiatry of Old Age" unit when he was fit as a fiddle and, he knew, as bright as a button.

## Real Time Kirriemuir

Ed parked his car beside Sheila's in the little drive-in off the lane to the rear of the house. He always found this description 'the rear of the house' something of a contradiction. The main entrance, well the only entrance, was on this side with the 'back 'of the house 'facing' the main road. It all seemed back. to front. He could see the logic in the arrangement: the front door faced south with the small garden laid out before it, therefore the benefit of both the sunshine and the garden were instantly available when one came out the door. But compared to the conventional arrangement, fairly universal in the large cities of Glasgow, Edinburgh and Dundee where the 'front' of the house was presented to the main road and therefore, to the world, and the rear of the house was the secluded, private area, the Kirriemuir arrangement meant everything personal was kept private and secluded with an expressionless 'back' presented to the main road and the outside world. Most of the older properties In Kirriemuir were arranged this way, or had some other feature to preserve the privacy of the family home. It seemed very sensible – just a bit unusual. A wee bit arse over elbow.

The house was Sheila's – lock. stock and barrel. She had bought it for a specific purpose and they had never intended to live there permanently.

Because of their separate and respective families they had decided not to complicate matters by combing their heritable assets, and thus avoid any messy extended family disputes at some future date. The arrangement worked well. Today, Sheila had obviously been attending therapy – retail therapy. There was a Ralph Lauren top with a T.K.Maxx tag on it declaring that its recommended price was £140.00, but marked down to £35.00. It also had a little label announcing that it was 'last season's stock' – but 'what the hell!' it was a designer label bargain! ~ were a few other pieces of evidence of a successful days forage through the best fashion outlets in Dundee. Also a pot plant for the garden, to keep some general perspective, and a kitchen utensil to prove that the outing hadn't simply been an indulgent forage for wardrobe fodder.

"How did you get on at the Doctor?"The question was more conversation than inquiry.

"OK. She had a trainee – well, an observer of some kind with her, so full conversation was a wee bit inhibited."

"Why, what would you have said otherwise?" – Sheila liked every detail ironed out for inspection.

"Well, nothing too heavy – it's just … well, you know how I am usually fairly careful about specific words I use? Well, last visit I had told her about being on holiday, and waking up. a couple of nights feeling anxious. I thought I had been quite specific about the word 'anxious' – but she recalls that I said 'depressed', says she even wrote It down,"

"Well, I remember you using the work 'anxious' – but anxious, depressed! What's the difference?

'I wasn't depressed, I was on holiday quite buoyant! I had simply wakened up during the night feeling anxious – as if I hadn't attended to something, or had something to resolve."

"Well, does It really matter?"

"It does to me, particularly at this time. Depression is a psychiatric condition whereas I see anxiety as a human reaction to some unresolved challenge – like being a bit unprepared for something. I wasn't depressed."

Sheila either accepted this or had decided he was ironing out the details far too flatly. She was silent – there were no juicy bits, no exciting triumphs or disasters in his visit, so he added, "I didn't press the point. She said she had written down 'depressed' so I just apologised and said I must have used the wrong word. I didn't see the point in arguing in front of a third party

263

who was her colleague."

"When do you go back?"

"Next month, but that will be my last – she Is retiring – apparently on a generous pension."

Sheila considered the relatively young age of the Doctor – eleven years her junior, and the prospect of having a generous pension with so much life time available. There was obviously a bit of lateral thinking coming into play as she thought of where she could dedicate all that time, with a generous pension to fund it.

The switch was instantaneous. Ed thought it was no different from an evening watching TV. when Sheila had the remote control in her hand. (Right, I'm bored with this medical programme where's 'Catwalk?") Click!

"Wait 'til I show you the little top I got today."

Bi-polarity, it seemed, was no match for a Ralph Lauren bargain.

**Tuesday 30ᵗʰ November 2021 cont'd**

*Hi Iain,*

Just to finish off that episode where I appeared to be cured, and yet I am still bi-polar, and don't recall anyone checking me for post traumatic stress disorder, or any historical influences that might be contributing to my excitement. Also, in a World, and in a nation that professes to operate to a Christian faith and endorses this by celebrating the Birthday and the, let's say, farewell party of the Saviour, why should somebody be considered nuts to be excited by the prospect of an imminent reunion.? It's in the Book; the Good Book, the Gospel Truth. Is this the professional opinion of somebody, who has certificates to prove the certainty of their judgement, that somebody who believes the Gospel Truth is, almost certainly, loopy!

Still, we were in the early part of the Second Coming. And a lot of attention was directed towards the United States. The youngest kid on the block, like all teenagers, thought it had discovered all the answers to Mom and Dad's problems and could cure the World of its ills.

You know, Iain, I watched enthusiastically as Barak Obama became the first mixed race president of the United States; I thought he was some kind of second coming that would transfigure the World. Well, how else was the Saviour going to reappear? He couldn't amble down the motorway between Damascus and Jerusalem on a wee donkey, dressed in the white robe and sandals – and hope to be taken seriously; he would have to be a man of our time who was going to make an impact.

I have to indulge in a little bit of artistic licence here, because it wasn't until Obama's reinauguration for his second term that I realised the impediment to his destiny of transfiguring the World.

As part of the ceremony there is a rendition of The Battle Hymn of the Republic, written by Julia Ward Howe. Now, when I spent my thirteen years at Jordanhill School, where I could have done better or should have tried harder, I used to love morning assembly, where I became part of a magnificent five hundred strong choir of young voices who could belt out those rousing hymns with a passion and a precision that would have given any choir in the world a run for its money.

The Battle Hymn of the Republic was one of those belters; but, in Scotland we sing it to a different tune – not the 'John Brown's body lies a'mouldering in his grave' version. But it was the words that took me aback; at the reinauguration ceremony Beyonce sang beautifully, and the first verse was fine – but the second verse;

> In the beauty of the lilies Christ was born across the sea,
> With a glory in His bosom that transfigures you and me.
> As He died to make men holy let us die to make men free......

Oh God, I thought, she's got it wrong: in the Church of Scotland Hymnary the line was

> As He died to make men holy, let us live to make men free,

Sheila scoffed at my stupidity – 'Its their song, they know the words!' I Googled it, and sure enough it read 'Let us die to make men free!'

I couldn't help thinking 'What an ethos to programme into yonng minds!' Why die to make men free? Why not live to make men free, then we can all pursue the American dream of the pursuit of happiness! You can't pursue anything if you got yourself killed in the process. Maybe that is why legions of American teenagers are going to school, armed with automatic weapons, to do their classmates the favour of shooting them to death, so that they can be free all the quicker to pursue the dream of happines, by dying to make men free.

I prefer the Church of Scotland version.

Jordanhill College School's rafters would ring as our five hundred young voices sang, with a trained choir's discipline, the forte and piano sections, with a magnificent descant from the Senior Girls, as we completed the verse,

> "As He died to make men holy
> Let us live to make men free
> His truth goes marching on
> Marching on!"

Lived it and loved it!

And, Iain, I have to stick in this little bit of advice to those free world leaders, from a young New World; set a good example by sorting out

America's death wish, in the heritage of the gun. Northern Ireland has been a 'problem' longer than America has existed as a Nation, yet possibly, more kids have been killed by their pals, in American schools than are victims of an internal struggle in Ireland.

And learn that Ireland, the Hibernia that co-operated with the original Romans, is the Emerald Isle, which to a great degree achieved its independence from Westminster years ago. Why is it that American independence from Westminster rule has been celebrated every 4th July for 245 years, and Irish independence from Westminster is approved of, by American presidents, yet Scottish divorce and freedom from an abusive 417 year relationship with Westminster is discouraged by such a freedom loving Republic. Check your facts, and your ethos and show your old Dad how much he has matured in the past 245 years.

Sorry Iain, a wee bit of 'Glass-cow' – almost sounds like Glasgow – indigestion erupting there!

So Iain, what about the Second Coming? Well, as we discussed many letters ago, The Truth that we have been seeking does not permit any magic or miracles. There can be no cross over between God and Man, other than spiritual inspiration – which can be influenced for good or corrupted by evil; and explained by some human activity or understanding. And, during our period of wondering if some of the world events, or little local happenings had any relevance, we, Frank and I, had another eerie experience.

On a Tuesday evening, a youngish man and woman came into the pub for our traditional music night. The guy had a certain presence, an 'I can handle myself' air, and the woman was dark haired, attractive; as a couple they were noticeable, and made themselves known to Frank and I at the bar. Even after the music finished, and the pub cleared, they stayed chatting for a little while; the woman lived at Maryton, and the man, Paul, was an old friend visiting while on leave from missionary work in Africa. He had been a bit of a tearaway in his younger days, slightly involved in the drug scene, but had seen the light, and now distributed copies of the New Testament in parts of Africa.

A couple of days later he re-appeared, ostensibly to say cheerio, but he added "This is for you!" and handed me a little red copy of the New Testament. Frank feigned 'hurt' and asked "Don't I get one", and Paul replied "No, only him" and with that, he was out of the door and gone!

I know, I know, it sounds a bit manufactured, a convenient coincidence; we had a Peter, retiring to Italy, a Paul with a friend who lived at Maryton, each leaving us with gifts that require a degree of examination and interpretation to understand the possibility that there is some cryptic truth hidden in their actions. I wish I could have said the woman was 'Mary' who then sang a protest song with our musicians, but there was nothing more coincidental beyond that she lived at Maryton. In terms of witnesses, well, Frank has gone, but Ian Christie, and Melanie Crawford who lived at Shielhill Park, each had one of the blood red £50 notes that Peter left; and I still have the pocket sized New Testament that Paul left: in fact, Sheila recently made a joking reference to her friend Gail, about my practice of carrying this wee red book on holiday. I do, but only because a holiday gives me time to check anomalies that may occur to me, and sift through the cryptic clues that obscure the Truth – that you and I might be able to handle!

Talking of holidays reminds me that we have one due; you know how Sheila loves the heat of a sunshine holiday, or Satan's altar blazing out the thermal units on a cool Kirriemuir evening. The priority at the moment is a Canary Island holiday, which was cancelled twice during the pandemic. The apparent easing of restrictions has allowed us to confirm this pre-Christmas holiday, which strangely fits in with our developing story. We head closer to the great circle of the Equator and return at the Winter Solstice, 21st December, as the Sun starts its journey back towards the North Pole, arriving home on the 22nd, just in time for Christmas. I always wondered about the North Pole with its eight degree wobble, which meant it had a variable position, just like the variable timing of Easter; perhaps the wobble is actually the loose connection in the positive power supply, and just needs tightened up to restore bi-polar balance to the world.

You know, Iain, I could never see Easter as the joyous occasion our spiritual leaders insisted we should; but a Happy Birthday, or Happy Christmas – that is worth celebrating. Particularly since this Christmas beats the end of the Second Coming by six days. Maybe somebody 'up there' has worked out how to beat Herod's thugs, targeting expectancies for 1st January, by arriving a wee bit early to coincide with the Christmas tradition.

Anyway, again, I have a few more circuits to complete around this model of the 56th parallel of Hillrise in our little world of Kirriemuir before I head off to meet the Sun and bring it back North.

Talk again soon,

*Ed*

**December 2021**

*Hi Iain,*

I am actually writing this on 15th December, although it covers the period from Wednesday 1st December; I have had a really busy start to this final month of the Second Coming. I am finding it difficult to assimilate some of our interpretations of the various 'truths' of mythology, history and the gospel truth, to arrive at a credible understanding that satisfies the experience of mankind, in this 21st century, and parallels down from the experience of one Universal family, at the beginning of the era, to the real life experience of a typical family on this ripple, or concentric circle of time at the latter end of the Christian Era. The same problem, I suppose, that the Gospel writers experienced, whoever they were, or whenever, in creating a digestible story that became the miraculous Garden of Eden, and for our era the three in one God who miraculously overcame death to maintain a positive spiritual influence for what is good in mankind.

The Garden of Eden is the World embracing story that Mankind finds itself in, at the moment; but the family I see, in our Era, is my own family in 1963 when our son was afflicted with cancer, and died after a short illness: except, my wife refused to let her son's spirit die and kept him alive in her heart, until her own death re-united them in the universal spirit world. The same spirit world that is scoffed at by realists, and yet has billions of dollars invested in space programmes for mankind to unite with these other inhabitants of a universe that seems to be alive but......spiritual!

I see a parallel, in the Virgin Mary of the Gospels depicted as the Mother of God, with the ultimate parallel, for our world, of the Blessed Virgin of Mother Earth who could produce the human virus, unaided by man, as we know him, and therefore by God as we imagine Him, except God might be Her – the Blessed Virgin, who had to be here first!

So, although I cannot imagine, yet, what preceded the 'big bang' I am quite content, within this short voyage of the Christian Era, to accept the existence of a universal God who delivers a positive power that elevates the 'earth animal' from a single neutral (or negative) to an enlightened bi-polar state. Like the aura of magnetic field that surrounds the planet Earth and completes the electrical circuitry which sustains the human animal and prepares him for an eternal life; and eternal life for 'mankind' on earth if he can recognise – as some ancient philosophy must have – that this Earth is the Garden of Eden, which is self sustainable with careful husbandry, while also recognising that Mother Earth, Eve of the Garden of Eden was actually here first and has to be given her place, with careful husbandry, in an equal society. The power game is that Man has developed to be the Alpha male, who can dominate Earth for a short time, if that is his obsession; but only for a short time, because, if he does not keep Eve, Mother Earth alive and functioning there is no sustainable future, and Alpha closes with Omega fairly quickly in Universal time.

Like our Earthly great circle of time, on the Equator, this girdle of continuity is held together by Omega chain-linking with the Alpha of a new era which can be sustained for ever, in a continuing great circle of time with enlightened management.

Perhaps, Iain, this enlightened management is what the Glasgow COP26 was all about; and the poorer nations, those most threatened by the slavery imposed by climate change, are the ones standing up and crying "I'm Spartacus!" while the various Roman Empires of the Capitalist and Communist powerhouses and the Roman controlled Church do little to redirect their wealth or power to ensuring that the chain link of Omega to a new Alpha remains intact during this final period of Christian Era, which is impacted by Pandemic and potentially fatal Global Warming.

You know, Iain, on my power walks, round this 56th parallel that is Kirrie Hill, I am constantly impressed by the coincidences of events and the use of words which link historical events; like the Sod's Law that bereaved three young women through freak accidents, in otherwise safe conditions, on empty roads: or, this new term, 'the perfect storm', when three unconnected conditions unite (is 'conspire' too fanciful?) to create a catastrophe. Like today's great world threatening events; the impending end of the Earth, through Global warming- that people still deny, the end of mankind through the self sustaining virulence of Covid 19 and the end of Faith, and our place in the Universe through our religious leadership fumbling about in the dark with their eyes shut!

So, Iain – what about this Second Coming?

Well, you have to remember that all of this, after the Crucifixion, has to be spiritual; and we have seen the Holy Spirit sweep through the corruption of Capitalism in the banking system, and the corruption which pervades

Government, and a Church corrupted and controlled by the capitalism of evil Empire. You know Iain, you really have to hand it to Shakespeare – he said it again beautifully in Mark Antony's speech at the burial of Caesar, "The evil that men do lives after them…", and so it did, as Rome tried to control the hearts and minds of mankind through a highly skilled army of clergymen.

Maybe it is time to put Mark Antony's observation into reverse – do the opposite of the obvious – preserve the good, and let the evil be interred with the bones! After all the effort that Peter, Paul and Mary – the Companions of God – have made to keep the Spirit of Christ alive within a tightly controlled organisation, it is time for the Universal Church to shed the Roman Cross it has had to bear for the past two thousand years.

Like the people of this world who are suffering the effects of corrupt Government, whether it be the corruption of Capitalism, or a misguided Communism that serves the rich, or a Faith usurped and controlled by a Roman ethos powered by negative energy, it is time for the ordinary people to realise that it is their Mother Earth that generates the positive energy to keep the Earth turning with a self sustained supply of power.

Maybe it is time to recognise that the Blessed Virgin of Mother Earth is replicated in the Blessed Virgin Mary, Mother of God, who is not about to release the Spirit of Her Son, crucified by a Roman controlled Universe, while that same Roman ethos still pervades and controls the Church that She has held together, with the other Companions of God, for almost two thousand years. And Mary, Mother Earth is now being poisoned by the fossil fuel energy which the Imperialists of Capitalism, Communism, State and Church refuse to condemn to save this garden of Eden bequeathed to our care.

Maybe Iain, back in our little model world of Kirriemuir, J.M. Barrie envisaged Peter Pan, the boy who wouldn't grow old, as an eternal spirit for good protected by the motherly spirit of Tinkerbell who refused to let Peter consume the poison that would have killed hope for the freedom loving people of this Neverland.

Is it possible, Iain, that with some inexplicable prophetic vision of this point in World history, Barrie perhaps predicted this perfect storm of Mother Earth overheating, the turmoil of the Blessed Virgin reliving the post traumatic stress of the Crucifixion and reluctant to release the spirit of her son, the Saviour, into the Roman controlled world; the added threat of

Pandemic, the new Dinosaurs, waiting to replace humanity as the custodians of this Garden of Eden we appear to be treating so badly? Maybe, after all it, is time to listen to the music and ask ourselves again, "Are we Human, or are we Dinosaur?" and stop looking for the answer on our knees – but stand up, like Spartacus, and believe we are human, and that eternal life is here, for mankind, in this self sustaining Garden of Eden that Barrie called Neverland.

You know, Iain, as we approach this end of 2021, there is an awful lot of coincidence bubbling up; like in the cauldron of Macbeth's three witches, Mother earth, Earth Mother and Mary, Mother of God. And, in timing, the end of the Christian Era, remember 2008 to 2021, the end of the Earth as we know it; and the end of humanity, if the Pandemic of new Dinosaur beats us. And you will recall that we agreed that God works in mysterious ways His wonders to perform; and that God is obliged to play by the rules that Evil can bend or break without apparent penalty.

Oh, Iain, I have to indulge in a little bit of fanciful digression here. Man, in the image of God is the companion of Eve, the first woman, sharing a love between them; and in this puzzle, with crossword clues peppered about, love can be represented by 'O' or by 'L'. And this loving God, with Eve's love becomes 'Good'; and Eve, with the love of God invested in her becomes a mother, therefore doubly blessed with love, the L for love of a husband and the L for love of a son: so God is Good and Eve stays Level, with this balanced contentment. But a bereaved Eve, with the cruel loss of the maternal love that fills her head and her heart becomes Evel; a 'sounds like' evil clue: and so we have the eternal battle of this Christian era as a bereaved Father and Mother struggle to restore the creative unity of Faith, Hope and Love.

Is that too cryptic, or corny, too contrived – or, perhaps, too much like a Fairy story? Maybe too much digression into imagination; but the thought occurred to me, and, since you and I are searching for the Truth, I thought it bore a passing resemblance to my own experience of a bereaved Mother, who became angry and 'eveL' with the rage of loss and self blame, and refused to release the spirit of her son until she could join him in his afterlife.

You know, Iain, I can't tell if this is one of my blowing in the wind fantasies or, perhaps, a spiritual message to fine down the Gospel story to one man's experience, and incorporating a song and events which permeated his thoughts with God's experience two thousand years ago. I have told you my impressions as I climb Cemetery Hill to spend time with you – and of the black Audi, accompanied by the little red Fiesta parked at the top of Cemetery Road. The Audi has X66 in the centre of the number plate; the little Fiesta has 63, and I can't help remembering, in this somewhat spiritual environment of Cemetery Hill, that '63 was the year that we, my wife – an earth mother, and me – Edward 'the lord protector', lost our wee son who was such a bright promise to celebrate – a wee Fiesta, perhaps.

And Iain, before he was even born, I had a 'blowing in the wind' song during my childhood by a singer who was pretty dominant in the early and middle twentieth century – Al Jolson, who made the first 'talking movie', The Jazz Singer! He would be totally non politically correct today, as his 'persona' was to black up to appear as an African American and sing songs of the American South, that delighted the World at that time. His second talking picture 'The Singing Fool' featured the song that, somehow, haunted me from my childhood, almost twenty years before I had anything to feel haunted about. Jolson portrayed a singer who was devoted to his infant son who, tragically, died quite suddenly; his grief depicted in a scene where he sat with his dead son and sang 'Sonny Boy'.

"Climb upon my knee, Sonny Boy,
"Though you're only three, Sonny Boy,
"There's no way of knowing,
"There's no way of showing,
"What you mean to me, Sonny Boy.

"When there are grey skies
"I don't mind those grey skies'
"You make them blue, Sonny Boy.
"Friends may forsake me,
"Let them all forsake me,
"I still have you Sonny Boy.

"You're sent from Heaven, and I know your worth,
"You made a Heaven for me, right here on Earth,
"But, the angels grew lonely
"Took you because they were lonely
"I'm lonely too, Sonny Boy.

I know Iain, it sounds like another one of my convenient coincidences – and perhaps, in the cynical times of today, too much of a schmaltzy weepy to be taken seriously. And yet, the words were there in a song in a film, about a bereaved father, which was distributed in 1928; eight years before I was born, and thirty five years before my son died, and I see the suggestion of a coincidence. Anyway, we have been searching for the truth, and this is the truth about my thoughts as I walk around our 56th parallel, and climb Cemetery Hill each morning, to sit on Anna's bench with you for a few minutes.

I started penning this letter on 15th December, when Sheila and I are already in Tenerife; the holiday we cancelled at the start of the Pandemic and, it seems, we have managed to slip into a little gap of tranquillity, before the turmoil of the Omicron variant, which is waiting to greet us when we return home. Of course, you, Helen, Sheila and I have spent a few holidays here together, at Los Gigantes. My goodness, how hospitality here in the Canaries is suffering – it is very quiet. And, while the pandemic isn't spoiling our holiday, mask wearing is a pain, and also our first couple of days were dominated by tying down the preparation for going home, by identifying the restrictive, and subject to change procedures for Covid testing, and certification to travel home safely.

I suppose that there is a significance in my recalling our holidays together, here at Los Gigantes; that would be around the time that you and I accepted the challenge of Diarmuid's Quest, and started to examine our individual interpretations of faith.

Helen, a good Catholic lass, happy with the religion she was born into, and finding strength in the discipline and reliability of ritual and convenience; she accepts the Christianity, without questioning why the Church is based in the Capital of Empire, or how it was allowed to survive through three hundred years of Christian persecution by that Empire. She doesn't want to hear your sceptical criticism of some of the present day practices, and the corruption that you observe that has spread, like a virus, through the Church. Helen accepts the Church that Peter, Paul and Mary have held together for two thousand years. And, I suppose, in that context, along with millions of other good Catholics throughout the Christian Era, that faith has kept Christ alive, in the church, unaware of the pervasive presence and control of a negatively powered Roman spirituality. And they have borne the Cross obediently, because there never was any other way available!

The positive spirit of Christ is there, protected by the Blessed Virgin, who will not release Him until the negative Roman threat is removed, and a neutral polarity restored to link up with the positive polarity of a reborn Christ who will lead the Way.

Sheila, in her NOW era, 'this is your lot, enjoy it' is, of course, also correct. If we don't beat the Pandemic, or release Mother Earth from her fossil fuel nemesis then, this is our lot! And her prospect of one's spirit living on through the children, or grandchildren, is severely limited to another two generations, if Sir Isaac Newton's prediction is to be believed.

And, you and I, Iain; two Christians brought up in different disciplines of the same religious Faith – but sharing a belief in a path for life that Jesus was trying to restore, The Way, when he was kidnapped and held hostage by a negative Empire of Capital power; Jesus's Way, the Via, that would lead to the truth, the Veritas of eternal life, the Vita that is now obscured and pinned to a Cross in time. The Way that the Religious and World leaders seem to be making such a bad job of managing, without the charge of positive energy that relies on people power connecting with the Universe.

This Christmas of 2021 is the critical time of the Perfect Storm for our humanity; World leaders procrastinating about how, or whether to save Mother earth from suffocation: Religious leaders lacking the faith or the courage to proclaim that the prophesied second coming is upon us, and the new Dinosaur of Pandemic already competing to replace a Humanity that cannot see the light of Christ's Via, Veritas, Vita!

You know, Iain, I have covered a lot of ground this December, and in the course of producing this letter. So much rushed out at me, like the contents of Indiana Jones's Lost Ark. But, unlike those contents, it was not all evil and destructive; there was good amongst the jumble and fankle, it just required a bit of patience to sort out. The December we had planned provided plenty of time for that; our Christmas preparations complete in early December, our holiday to bring the sunshine back north, and then guests for Christmas dinner in Edinburgh: but Sod's Law ( maybe my old adversary, Damian Roth) was lurking in the wings! As Robert Burns so aptly put it "The best laid schemes of mice and men gang aft agley!" And, sure enough,' Agley went or best laid scheme'.

We had been pretty much spared any direct impact from Covid 19 but, in early December, it was apparent that we had not avoided the collateral damage of Pandemic: Sarah was suffering the exhaustion, a side effect of pandemic, which hit so many after eighteen months of restrictions and home working, and the concerns of mothers about the future for families, in the final stages of this perfect storm. Sheila decided that this needed a bit of Earthly Mother management, and immediately switched our Christmas from Edinburgh to Kirriemuir and we birled from being guests to becoming the hosts, in one fell swoop!

Iain, it was heavy going, particularly for Sheila who had the bulk of the catering to finalise in the two days before Christmas. But as she has demonstrated before, "When the going gets tough, the tough get going!" Man, we had a great Christmas: maybe there is something in this NOW philosophy, because you have to achieve as much as you can in the limited time you have allocated yourself before the big bang of a Kirrie Christmas!

Talk again in a couple of days,

*Ed*

**Friday 31st December 2021.**

*Hi Iain,*

Hogmanay 2021. Last day of the year; last day for a lot of things! Last day of a difficult twelve months for a lot of people; last day of the Second Coming that nobody, apart from you and I, seemed to have noticed: certainly, if the Chief Rabbi, the Chief Imam, the Defender of the Faith or the self proclaimed Vicar of Christ are aware of it, they have kept it a bit of a close secret. Maybe they think that this is the truth that "You couldn't handle the Truth, Sonny!" meant, and just leave all us millions of Sonnies around the World floundering in the dark purgatory of a Roman controlled Christian Era.

Even the Moderator of the General Assembly of the Church of Scotland – what a mouthful – has been silent about this momentous occasion, that the freedom from the Roman domination which the Companions of God, in Caledonia, fought so successfully to preserve, is about to be restored and extended after two thousand years. Perhaps all those religious leaders think that the Pandemic is the Second Coming, and are awaiting a Parliamentary Dinosaur reshuffle to find out which of them will head up Coronavirus, and the Delta variant or Omicron, or whatever position is available to exert their control over the obedient faithful they have failed to enlighten to the Truth.

This is the last day of Diarmuid's Quest, and also my walks around the 56th parallel of our little model world of Kirriemuir, that seemed to contain so many clues to events, or parallels of events that shaped the world during this so called Christian Era. And yet, the moving finger is still moving on towards Isaac Newton's predicted date for Apocalypse; and the significant world leaders, who could make a difference – who should make a difference – are sabre rattling, and arguing about sanctions and territory; arguments which will be academic in another forty years if the agreement to contain Earth's temperature is not reached very soon.

I watched Mary Robinson, the Chair of The Elders who try to make a difference, become quite emotional when she described the procrastination or ignorance of the powerful nations to understand the science of global warming, or the consequences, and act now to avert the inevitable disaster which is developing. And, meantime, the new Dinosaur of Corona virus, and all the allied viruses, is whittling away at Mankind, determined to replace us as the inhabitants of Earth when we render it uninhabitable or unsustainable for our species.

You know, Iain, I recall during the early days of our friendship, when we were having one of our agreeable disagreements, I suggested that you might actually be the Devil's Advocate; you certainly questioned any theory, and examined any preposition I put to you. But I realise that you have put your own faith under close scrutiny, and examined the Church which delivers religion to you, and become disappointed by the increasingly negative or, at best, neutral current that appears to be corrupting the balance, of positive and negative energy, which is necessary to produce a healthy power supply of faith. to sustain humanity as a life force that can avoid extinction.

We have examined the so called Christian era, and have a strong suspicion that, to ensure it's own survival, Rome, like some spiritual parasite or virus has hitched a ride on the faith – the Way that God designed for humanity, the chosen life force, to survive; and Rome kept the faith trapped, but alive, because if Good dies then so does Evil: the balance between Good and Evil has to be maintained to keep this bi-polar earth, the model of a bi-polar universe, functioning and spinning on it's polar axes, to generate the power to sustain the Spiritual life force. This unique life force that gives purpose and motivation to God's chosen people, Humanity.

You know, Iain, like the example of the Russian dolls, with each little model or replica of the bigger doll which encloses it, growing like the Universe with expanding concentric circles of circumference represented on 'model' earth by parallels of latitude, tight at the poles and expanding in circumference, until the two bi-polar movements become one great circle on the equator. And this same pattern and repetition of experience is replicated in the experience of one real life everyday human family inside the 'God in Human form' and 'Virgin Mary down to earth' Holy family, which replicates the bigger enclosing family image of Adam and Eve and their tragic sons, which tries to explain the beginning of time as God planting the fully formed Adam, in God's image and creating Eve as a companion......except that the Blessed Virgin Earth, Eve, was here first, and fertile enough to produce a life form, which needed the spark of Universal power to promote the basic animal dinosaur to the thinking being, Mankind, which can work out how to avoid extinction, and achieve eternal life for the species.

Throughout this Pandemic, this most pressing threat of our perfect storm, we have had daily briefings by experts and leaders, urging us to follow the science; which is searching for the truth, the solution that will save mankind; that search for the truth that is really us, 'on our knees looking for the answer' to the question 'are we Human, or are we Dinosaur?'

Following the science is simply a process of trial and error, until we get it right. It is a bit like our Diarmuid's Quest, say, for the Christian Era truth, and we could not find a true beginning, because it was variable, obscure as a moveable feast; so we had to work backward, from where know we are now, always cognisant of Omar Khayyam's moving finger of time.

You know, Iain, Mankind had two thousand years to prepare for this Second Coming, and thirteen years to identify the events that indicated that the process had started, and nobody seems to have noticed; not the educated, who presume that they are enlightened: and the enlightened, who haven't the educational credentials to prove that they can handle the truth of enlightenment, nor the credibility or celebrity to demand to be heard. And now we are on the final day of the Second Coming on this final day of December 2021. And, we have had almost four hundred years to prepare for the Global Warming crisis, since Isaac Newton's prediction – which gets referred to every so often, but ignored. And now, with only forty years left to take action, the most influential players in the world, Russia, China and the leader of the World's dominant Christian faith failed to attend the critical COP26 meeting in Glasgow, and left Mary Robinson, of The Elders who hope to make a difference, tearful with frustration.

Your idea that we might share our thoughts, even although they were not science and we are not celebrities; and our credibility sometimes comes off second best, even in our own homes in the eternal battle of the sexes: but it seemed a worth while try!

I had to go back to my old navigation disciplines to decide where our 'new beginning' should start from; no more moveable feasts! The most notable fixed point was Christmas Day – always reliable, always a Holiday, always on 25th December, And, anyway, this will actually be the first real Christian Era, considering that the 'so-called Christian Era turned out to be an extended Roman era, in fact, extended twice, if one accepts the 1066 conquest by the new Romans, and their establishment of a new capital of Empire in Westminster. So, with any luck this should be the end of the Second Roman era, and a new beginning for Jesus's Way, that has become known as Christianity.

I remember you and Father Neill, your Franciscan friar pal being excited that the new Pope, in 2013, had taken the name of Francis, the first time a Pope has used the name; notable because Francis, the Franciscan friar was dedicated to helping the poor and needy. In fact, it is almost as if he took his ethos from Jesus contention that a camel would go through the eye of a needle easier than a rich man could enter the Kingdom of Heaven.

I've often wondered if that condition also extended to rich Popes and mega rich Churches.

I know you also had the feeling that a few Vatican paintings, sold to subsidise the poor, would hardly be missed. After eight years in charge, Francis doesn't seem to have done a lot to clean up the Church or to emulate his chosen namesake. Maybe somebody should whisper that Francis of Assisi wasn't simply for the birds! He could make a start by expelling the Roman image and control, that the oppressive Empire continues to exert through the Cross that we all have to bear.

And the rest of us slowly enlightening folk, in the World, like the delegates at the COP 26 in Glasgow, who applauded the intention and effort to keep Mother Earth alive......you know, Iain, like J.M. Barrie's fairy tale of the audience keeping Tinkerbell alive, when she was dying to save Peter. Perhaps the ordinary people of this World should start clapping and cheering, and make their voices heard that they want to save our Tinkerbell, Mother Earth and keep our Peter Pan, the Spirit who won't grow old, alive and functioning, freed of the oppressive attention of Captain James Hook, the Eton educated Pirate, and his band of buccaneers who want to take over Neverland and keep all the riches and Goodness for themselves.

We haven't had a wee digression for a while! Another wee 'sounds like' crossword clue; have you ever tried saying J M Barrie, quickly? Jayembarrie, Jayembarrie. Sounds like Jamboree – a World gathering, a Celebration. Maybe Barrie was trying to communicate his vision of a Neverland, under threat from oppression and corruption; in the hope that a world audience would be sufficiently enlightened as to come together, and have their applause save Tinkerbell from the poison that would have killed Peter: the boy who wouldn't grow old, the timeless Spirit, who prevents the evil of Captain Hook, the virus who hopes to dominate Neverland.

H'mmmm, maybe too much of a Fairy Tale; and yet everybody, determined to be heard, seems to leave their messages in fairy tales and songs, just blowing in the wind.

You know, Iain, I always had a difficulty with the, so called, ultimate Fairy Story – even before it got to the 'miracle' stage. I couldn't believe the run up to the travesty of a trial and the tragedy of the verdict, the sentence and the intended execution. It was some of the detail that confused me … like the so called betrayal by Judas, and the unexplained denials by Peter. Poor old Judas just did as he was told, by his boss. And why was it so necessary to emphasise that it was Judas, the Jew, who betrayed the saviour of mankind?

It doesn't compute! In this production they were all of the Jewish persuasion, intent on persuading mankind – those chosen by the goodness of God- to follow the Way, those 'paths of righteousness',that Moses had also tried to persuade the hedonistic, party loving wanderers not to lose sight of!

So, whose sinister intent was it to spoil the party for the Jews? I mean, Judas didn't have to indulge in betrayal for thirty pieces of silver; he was the company accountant for a successful Sales organisation on the rise to market domination, for God's sake! He could have fiddled away millions into an off-shore account if he had been in it for the money.

Judas the Traitor? It definitely doesn't compute! In fact, Iain, I thought it might have been Peter, who made the three denials, who betrayed the cause because he fancied the top job in the Company as a subsidiary of Rome. Fortunately our research during Diarmuid's Quest gave me a fresh interpretation that preserved the Good that men do and parked the evil in somebody else's hidden agenda. Peter, and the Church he founded in Christ's name turned out to be all good, apart from the Evil influence of Rome's continuing negative spiritual presence.

You know Iain, I have another theory to put to you, for your Devil's advocacy to scrutinise, and determine the feasibility. Supposing God has re-evaluated the original Holy Week, and decided to avoid making the same mistake again; no razmatazz of a triumphal palm leaf strewn entry into a Jerusalem in the grip of an occupying, alien Empire. And to risk no more sons in the hope of saving mankind: I can tell you Iain, from bitter experience there is no father on Earth who would sacrifice his dearly loved son to the possibility of crucifixion; and I do not believe there is a Father in Heaven who would act any differently from the little earthly model of a father's love. The evil that was Rome took advantage of God's requirement to play within moral rules, and Rome tried to take His Son out of the game.

Rome would not understand the subtlety of God the Father and God the Son living in the same Spiritual being.

God would not make this same mistake again, with the big celebrity treatment, which alerted the Evil of Rome to the fact that Good was about to 'show the Way' to tip the balance of power, and put Evil in a box for the next thousand years! No charismatic leader of twelve loving followers who thought only of love and tolerance, with little experience of the evil and corruption that pervades a negatively charged world. God needed a new plan for this second millennium.

I guess that is where you and I came in; the two unlikely, ageing special forces guys – Celi Dei: two, poles apart, Christians who believed in the single Way of a Life learned from seemingly opposing directions of the one Great Circle of Faith. Between us we had observed, or suffered, most of the afflictions of body and soul, in two lives that extended well beyond the age point where most of our peer group were either stagnating in a care home, or already the subject of obituaries; we had little to lose and we could even cope with the broth of the cauldron, that the three witches of womankind stirred so vigorously!

Somehow, we were the unlikely advance guard, who cleared the minefield of deception, to create a path of truth, Diarmuid's Quest, towards a new start – a new Christmas!

As we discovered, seeing the truth with hindsight is fine, but we can only live the truth by keeping pace with the moving finger of time, as it keeps moving forward; and the Second Coming had, until this last day of 2021 to complete, in line with the prophesy.

You will recall how we agreed that God moves in mysterious ways His wonders to perform.

And Westminster, it seems, cannot resist the old Roman Empire philosophy of privilege for the Patricians to which the Plebs are not entitled; like, last Christmas, when all us Plebs were obediently observing lockdown to 'save mankind', the Gods, in Mount Olympus in Downing Street were celebrating a privileged Christmas party reserved for a Patrician Government Hierarchy. In fact, once the Truth started its snowball roll, it appeared that, during seven days of Advent, a small multitude of Cheese and Wine essential meetings and extended 'working lunches' were held, presumably to discuss the penalty for Plebs breaking the lockdown curfew;

or how the NHS would cope with the burden of mental health issues, experienced by the Plebeian classes who were suffering distress from home working, and the legal necessity to avoid gatherings such as family funerals and weddings, and indeed celebrating Christmas. Not easy to justify a working lunch, on Government expenses, for Granny, Grampa, and the kids, and their kids on Christmas Day.

This year, everybody celebrated Christmas, and God's plan came into effect. Just like political party central offices shovel out all the little bad news under the umbrella protection of some disastrous news – like happened when Princess Diana died, God effected the opposite of the obvious to perform His wonder. Quietly, while we all celebrated Christmas and Family contact, God released the Blessed Virgin from the post traumatic stress that had kept her Son's spirit protected for two thousand years and a reborn Jesus slipped discreetly back into the world six days before the prophesied deadline. You know, Iain, it never ceases to amaze me as to what people power can achieve.

And, Iain, you know how I like my little coincidences! You will recall that, early in this second coming, I experienced the guy called Peter, who returned the four blood red symbols of Capitalist domination; and Paul, the missionary from Africa, who presented me with the little red New Testament, and I regretted that I could not contrive a Mary to complete the Peter, Paul and Mary coincidence. Well, Iain, four days after Christmas, on 29th December, Sheila and I drove to Edinburgh to attend the funeral of Mary; a mother of seven children, who had lived all her married life in The Christians, the little housing estate that lies somewhere behind the Temple, in Joppa, with Hebron Hall in the back garden.

You remember Hebron, where the Cave of the Patriarch is located, in the so called Holy Land. I reckon another wee cheek into the Hebron Cave will uncover a few interesting Gospel Truths.

And, talking of the Holy Land – we left RMS Caledonia docked in Aden, at the bottom of the Arabian peninsula; we have to get her back to Glasgow and seek the Truth of how the Caledonians, the Celi Deians, Companions of God, resisted the might of the Roman Empire, and sent them homeward, to think again!

Talk again soon

*Ed*

## Scottish History

The history of Scotland,
As taught at school,
I feel, Is incomplete, tinged with deceit,
It, somehow, isn't real!

The timeline seems quite cock-eyed;
It starts ten sixty six:
A thousand years of England,
Scant mention of the Picts!

The thousand years, before Macbeth
Or, Harold, on the beach,
Unless it's Boudica's defeat
They somehow do not teach;

How Caledonia stood alone
Before the Roman might!
How Ceiledeic people
Put Godless Rome to flight!

Two thousand years ere Tony Blair
Used spin. to great effect;
Or Russia and Donald Trump
Were careful to reject,

The truth. the whole truth. nothing but!
Spread doubt-through every nation,
The Empire of the Caesars
Had devised 'misinformation'!

Mons Graupius. decisive?
It seems we didn't win
Hispanic Legion? Disappeared!
In air, that's very thin!

The Vikings and the Irish?
Absorbed, or settled here!
Northumbrian troops – just vanished,
In a bog at Nechtansmere!

Despite our internecine wars
We managed to unite,
A proud confederation
Putting enemies to flight!

And yet, dismissed, "Barbarians!"
Us? Hardly worth a mention!
If that were true, why are we due
Such negative attention?

# EPILOGUE

*Hi Iain,*

I really thought that I was finished this series of letters when I completed the 'last day' letter on 31st December. How naive of me.

Despite the number of times that I have mentioned it, during these past eleven years, I forgot about the moving finger; you can't write an account of a day while that day is still in progress: only hindsight can provide an account of an event and, indeed, the impact of that event. And, by the time we say, in our case, the letter recording the event is written, the event and its impact have occurred and we are already dealing with the consequences of afterburn. The impact and the consequences might actually be the message we are supposed to receive from the event.

This epilogue situation appears to be one of those occasions when we have to keep jumping from the big picture, or big event in time, down to the little picture, or model of the real time event, which encapsulates the big picture that seems to be too mundane, because we are living it; too ordinary to be profound or significant in influencing history. I think I may have got above myself, like the Kirrie worthy warned, all those twenty years ago; in this real time situation my enthusiasm to make the letters interesting, jumped from me recording Truth, and reporting real events and coincidences, to attempting to create a miraculous perfect storm of life changing events, all occurring on Hogmanay 2021. Those three events were The Second Coming, the end of the so-called Christian Era and the saving of Mother Earth by mankind answering the question, 'are we human, or are we Dinosaur?'

Iain, there is another song, which drifts into my consciousness and seems to help elevate the little picture to giant screen proportions; 'if a picture paints a thousand words, then how can I paint you?' The picture I see, at this Ides of January, is the press photograph of our bereaved Queen alone, sombre in her black mourning weeds, at the funeral of her life companion. The Pandemic, and the Westminster Government's direction for resisting the infection, dictates that the head of the most powerful family in the country, must mourn alone, uncomforted or even accompanied by family, who are obliged to set an example of social distancing, for the rest of the Nation to be convinced that this is the right thing to do.

This realisation that the Queen, the Defender of the Faith, and head of Commonwealth that was once Empire, is obliged to follow the rules designed for the Plebs, is something of a revelation; while the Eton educated Pirates who control a Government established in Westminster, after the new Roman incursion in 1066, parties – work parties or party parties? – to a special set of Patrician rules, denied to even the Head of State. It seems that there is a parallel, between our speculation that the Catholic Church of Christ was obliged to operate under the negative direction of spiritual Roman influence, and the government of this rapidly disuniting kingdom, operating to a single negative polarity, reinforced by the Roman Empire resurrecting itself twice, and now making hard work of this third attempt, after the birth of a new Christian era slipped in unnoticed, on Christmas Day 2021, just before time was up for the Second Coming.

And the Three Witches with their cauldron? The three faces of Woman, as visualised by Dr Eric Berne, perhaps Eve, Mother Earth, wife and mother, and daughter; the parent, adult, child personality locked in every 'mother's son and daughter'. Where is the parallel, as the Roman Empire endeavours to have every last vestige of freedom pay homage to the Capital? We know the first attempt at Imperial domination was unsuccessful as the Empire failed to hold, even the damaged body with its indomitable Spirit of independence and built a massive wall to contain the Celi Dei in Caledonia. The new Romans, swept up the country from Hastings in 1066, establishing their Capital at Westminster, and once the brute force of Manpower had brought Southern Britain, Wales and Hibernia to heel, and turned its attention again to Caledonia, this predatory Empire tried to dominate Mother Earth, in her three personalities, to influence and convince her children to bend to the will of this abusive and domineering Roman father figure, who wanted to rule the Earth. Caledonia remained a work in progress.

In a re-run of history, like Cain and Abel, Romulus and Remus, brother fought brother, by fair means and foul, until the Tudors emerged dominant with Henry VIII's predatory lust for power, prepared to execute anybody, even the mothers of his children, to secure absolute power over the hearts and minds of his subjects. The spiritual being, that was Roman Imperial power, was aghast at this accelerated repetition of the abusive and aggressive nature that had caused the original predatory Roman deity to rethink its plan for world domination. It had taken the spirit of Romulus almost two thousand years to progress from basic animal survival instincts to, almost, controlling the hearts and minds of this last significant boundary of the known world. But, Henry VIII was getting above himself, presuming some imagined God-like power over life and death and a divine right – Dieu et Mon Droit – to behave with the impunity of a God, above the rules of the masses who believed that they were living in a just world.

His decision to secede from central Roman power, by establishing his own Church, had less to do with the Protestant movement, which was stirring in Europe, and everything to do with his own desire for divorce from anything that restricted his baser animal instincts, which were influencing his reckless behaviour. Arranging the murder of the mother of his child was the last straw. The symbolism of this action was so apparent, to the spiritual instincts of a Romulus descendant aspiring to rule this Universal world. The spirit of Romulus didn't want to kill Mother Earth, the spirit of the Wolf pack; he needed her alive, and in his control: he had to ensure that Earth survived to ensure his own survival through Eternity. Henry VIII was not sticking to the plan. The spiritual Rome had to do something quick to restore the balancing influence of female power in the Universe, without creating too much fuss and disorder. Elizabeth, the Virgin Queen, daughter of the earth mother that Henry had despatched, was quickly confirmed as the Head of State of the recently established new Roman Empire at Westminster, and Defender of the Faith of the new Church based in Canterbury. But, a Head of State who had to absorb the trauma of a father, who treated women abominably, discredited her mother publicly and arranged for her execution by decapitation. And this young Virgin Queen had to grow up nursing the sentiment that she had not been born a male heir, and had to bear the cross of living in the 'weak and feeble body of a woman!'

I know, Iain, it is kind of rewriting history with another fairy story. But, not really; like a crossword puzzle, or collection of cryptic clues, the basic truths don't change, only the interpretation with the benefit of spiritual hindsight; when the afterburn has settled, and all people can do is learn from the example, and try to prepare for the next spiritual disturbance factor. Rome was aware of this necessity, to prepare for the next ambitious male trying to do his own thing, and built in a mother earth, who was controlled by the new Roman governors in Westminster, and who would exert a mother's calming influence as Romulus' negative power continued on its Imperial quest.

Victoria, the next blessed virgin who ticked all the boxes for the Imperial ambitions; a fertile earth mother producing many children, who spread this imperial blood throughout the ruling houses of Europe and Russia, while expanding Empire by exploration, backed by military presence if necessary, and ultimately by religious conversion, all in the style of the original Roman model of the early so-called Christian era. Empress of India, and still Defender of the Faith, but all that power and apparent control did not prevent all the brothers and cousins, of the Imperial houses of Europe and Russia, squabbling and fighting over territorial gain and national control, just as the Plantagenets and their descendants, and the Tudors had done when the new Romans embarked on their second conquest in 1066, in an attempt to bring all the Companions of God to heel. And, at each stage of this Imperial conquest Mother Earth or the earth mother who was appointed Head of State, suffered some trauma as the result of some unacceptable action by the male of the Royal household, who carried the DNA and genes of the predatory Romulus, with none of the balancing genetics spirituality that might have been provided by his twin, opposite polarity, brother.

Can you see, Iain? This revived Mother Earth image, recreated to restore balance after the traumatic stress disorder caused by the disturbance factor of Henry VIII; Shakespeare was already preparing the script for Earth Mothers, the leading ladies in this tragedy of Empire, each programmed by the experience of the performance of her predecessors in the role: and the female script, intended to last for seven hundred years, depicted in spirit for Macbeth's three witches, stirring a cauldron of 'bubble, bubble, toil and trouble'

The original 'virgin queen', Elizabeth, who suffered the pain of her father's resentment that she had been born a woman, and the trauma of the impact of her father's fatal abuse of her mother dedicated her life to proving she was as 'good a man' as her father; until this post traumatic stress disorder erupted: and she ordered the execution of her cousin, Mary of Scotland, the queen she might have shared a bi-polar Union of Crowns with, and expansion of Empire, had it not been for her life script. The tragic script demanding that she emulate the example, or act her part in accordance with the behaviour of the influential man who had so dominated her young life. She executed, and killed any possibility of union with this queen.

The cauldron bubbled through three hundred years of turbulence, as the effects of this post traumatic stress disorder, on top of the bi-polar disorder, caused serious disruption of nationality and religious faith and political disagreement throughout the British and Irish Islands. A marriage of convenience, between monarchies, was quickly arranged to contrive unity of nationality. The new Roman empire was struggling to reprise the role that the original Empire had enacted so successfully, in marching, virtually unopposed, from Rome to Hadrian's Wall. Within the next century a form of political unity was forged, which suited the capitalists based at Westminster and a spirit of empire, which the First Roman Empire had fostered so successfully, was engendered through a public floundering through this confusion of leadership. And, while the populace were being rallied to the Imperial cause, the new Roman management established Victoria as the spiritual mother of empire – the new Blessed Virgin of an Earth Mother, to replace the Mother Earth in the minds of the citizenry that Rome was rapidly losing control of.

Victoria was perfect in the role; the success of an expanding Empire inspired the people to give their Empress credit for their prosperity and the Westminster Caesars, with apparent Royal Assent, could initiate Capitalist policies, apparently to the benefit of all. National success, combined with Victoria's happy marriage and frequent royal births and marriages gave the nation much to cheer about. Until Prince Albert, her devoted husband, who managed her life like a caring and protective father, died suddenly at the early age of only forty one. The traumatic stress of this event was compounded by the possibility that, despite Albert already suffering from an unidentified illness, a visit by their son, infected with typhoid, transmitted the fatal germ to his father. Victoria was distraught by this bereavement, having somehow lost the three men in her life; the protective father figure, the loving and dedicated husband and the son who had recklessly killed off the three male loves of a woman's life. The habit of duty instilled in royal families kept her functioning as empress well enough for the Westminster controllers to maintain their policies in pursuit of Empire. But Victoria lived out the remainder of her sixty glorious years in the black mourning garb of the bereaved widow.

Iain, it seems an incredible coincidence to me that, at this time of the Ides of January 2022, the patrician government of this fading empire is holding parties in the seat of government, in spite of its own legislation which obliges the nation, including the head of state, to avoid gatherings and observe social distancing, even at a time of bereavement and mourning. And the photograph of this most powerful women in the land, Queen of a declining empire seeking independence and a disuniting kingdom, mourning alone, unaccompanied or comforted by family members at the funeral of her life's companion, somehow emphasises the indifference and corruption of honesty which pervades this new Roman administration. Even at this moment of bereavement, the Queen appears to be reminded that she is not part of the spiritual influence of the Roman empire, but a captive along with her nation, of the Eton educated pirates who control the capital and keep the Queen and her Plebs pinned to the cross of obedience it seems we all have to bear.

Can you perhaps imagine the parallels, between a Mother Earth, the blessed virgin, abused and dominated by the predatory male instincts of a Roman empire devoid of the gentler, enlightened spirit of Goodness, and Mary, the traumatised mother, of a God crucified by that empire, and abuse of womanhood, generally? Can you see the comparison between the male dominated monarchy, controlled by the spirit of empire, which endeavoured to replace the original virgin Mother Earth with real women, scripted and programmed, as in Dr Eric Berne's theory of female mind games – particularly the three powerful women, conditioned by heredity and duty, to further the cause of empire in the second half of the so-called Christian era, the thousand years of the new Roman era? And, toward the end of the reign of the virgin Queen Elizabeth, Shakespeare visualised the three dimensional mind of women with its tendency to learn from experience and produce a script to prepare future generations of women to cope with life in a male dominated existence.

You know, Iain, I can never get too far from the belief that there must be a God of the Universe, who created the big bang in the first place; perhaps two Gods, a god of Good and a god of Evil to maintain balance in the Universe; because, without that twin polarity there is no friction, no disturbance factor, no dynamism to keep the Earth turning and creating the power to sustain humanity. And I cannot move too far from the realisation that, to create and sustain life, in any form, a fertile Mother Earth must have been there first.

Like the songs blowing in the wind, and the 'sounds like' clues and anagrams I see as a crossword enthusiast, even in this final thousand years of the new Roman era, which is fast disintegrating, the indomitable spirit of women to be heard and respected leaps out at me. Despite the post traumatic stress disorder, or the bi-polar disorder or the determination of a Roman Empire to dominate Mother Earth she manages to shout her name to be recognised.

Elizabeth – the Virgin Queen

Victoria – bereaved wife, disappointed mother and obedient Empress,

Elizabeth II of England – left to grieve alone in Westminster Abbey by family and government.

The three faces of EVE – The Mother Earth who refuses to be dominated by a mankind who created his own God, in his own image, and got above himself by underestimating the Woman called Eve.

And, my old adversary Damian Roth. Maybe he is the third life in the Garden of Eden; like Florence Gray said "Did you see those dead snake eyes?" Maybe Damian is, after all, the Serpent that God has left, just to remind us to beware the negative current, or the Dinosaur of a Pandemic which is waiting to replace us if we don't keep evolving and sustain his Garden of Eden.

Meanwhile, Caledonia is still docked in Aden, at the bottom end of the Arabian Peninsula; we have to move her away from his so called Holy land, to complete the round trip, and bring her back to her home port of Glasgow; The Dear Green Place where, perhaps, Mary Magdalene brought the Navigator, the Captain's Son, to recover from the wounds the Roman Cross inflicted, and be ready for the next voyage of Caledonia.

You know Iain, it is so easy to slip into the 'Fairy story' mode; but I can't help imagining the period following the Crucifixion, when the Legions of Rome occupied Scotland, to search out Christians who had fled persecution in the so-called Holy Land, and come to this Caledonia, as the last outpost of freedom in a world dominated by Rome. The arrogant Empire dismissed the Picti as unrefined Barbarians who daubed themselves with blue paint, which emphasised the primitive backwardness of the people, and their fear of Roman superiority by averting their eyes respectfully, when in Roman presence. It would never occur to the Romans that the Companions of God devised a means of absorbing and protecting those Celtic refugees, by painting everyone blue, and avoiding eye contact with Romans, so that the legionaries could not discriminate indigenous people from darker skinned and brown eyed Christians fleeing Roman persecution. In Caledonia we all appeared as the Bairns of Jock Tamson, the Pict people.

And, Iain, even as I write, the moving finger has edged further and provided a wee miracle for Helen to restore her loyalty to her faith; her nephew has just been released from the fear of liver cancer by reassessment of a debilitating condition which has been corrected. And my Sheila, well she's hanging on to her faith in the World of Now, at the moment; but I can always hope she will hear a song blowing in the wind: perhaps some of the lyrics in 'Midnight Train to Georgia' might strike a wee chord. Hope springs eternal!

I will keep visiting your wee slit trench, but leave the letter writing until we decide to go tilting at a few more windmills, or open another cold case to find the Via to the Veritas of eternal Vita,

Much love

*Ed*

# IAIN MELROSE
## (04/08/1937 – 14/04/2020)

A gentle man, who loved life
And tried to do the right thing!